COOL COMFORT

COOL COMFORT

AMERICA'S ROMANCE WITH AIR-CONDITIONING

MARSHA E. ACKERMANN

SMITHSONIAN INSTITUTION PRESS
Washington and London

A different version of Chapter 6 appeared as "What Should Women (and Men) Want? Advertising Air-Conditioning in the Fifties" in the *Columbia Journal of American Studies* 3 (Summer/Fall 1998).

Editor: Ruth W. Spiegel
Designer: Janice Wheeler

Library of Congress Cataloging-in-Publication Data
Ackermann, Marsha E.
  Cool comfort : America's romance with air-conditioning / Marsha E. Ackermann.
      p.   cm.
  Includes bibliographical references and index.
  ISBN 1-58834-040-6 (alk. paper)
  1. Air-conditioning   I. Title
  TH7687. A25 2002
  697.9′3′0973—dc21   2001049023

British Library Cataloguing-in-Publication Data available

Manufactured in the United States of America
09 08 07 06 05 04 03 02   5 4 3 2 1

∞ The paper used in this publication meets the minimum requirements of the American National Standard for Information Sciences—Permanence of Paper for Printed Library Materials ANSI Z39.48-1984.

Contents

Acknowledgments

I have been a writer all my life but this is my first book. I want to thank the University of Michigan's Program in American Culture, especially Professor David Hollinger, now at the University of California Berkeley, for taking a chance in 1988 on this rather "senior" graduate student. Professors S. Cushing Strout and Joel Silbey inspired me long ago during my undergraduate years at Cornell University; their support, along with that of political scientist Thomas Mann of the Brookings Institution, helped me realize my midlife dream of a Ph.D.

The members of my dissertation committee encouraged my work in ways that belie conventional notions of academia. Chair Martin S. Pernick was consistently available for consultation, imparted his nuanced knowledge of medical history, and entrusted me with library privileges. David M. Scobey shared his lucid insights into the social geography of nineteenth-century New York City. Laurence Goldstein responded swiftly and in detail to both the writing and the content of each emerging chapter. Joel Howell graciously stepped in at a late stage and enriched the final work. Kristin Hass, then a fellow graduate student, materially assisted with her enthusiasm and astute suggestions. At Michigan State University, American Thought & Language chair Douglas Noverr gave me a chance to teach and alerted me to the Syracuse Carrier Dome's odd deficiency.

History is impossible without libraries, archives, and those who make them accessible. During the two extremely hot July weeks I spent with Ellsworth Huntington and Charlie Winslow in Yale University's magnificent Sterling Library, I was grateful not only for the skilled staff but for the phalanx of huge fans that kept the reading room balmy, while the climate-control system, hidden in the nether regions, preserved these irreplaceable records.

Thanks are also due to Cornell University's Division of Rare & Manuscript Collections at the Kroch Library, home to the Carrier Corporation Records. The library's willingness to make most of the collection available on microfilm significantly eased the time and expense of my research. The New York Public Library's New York World's Fair archives and the New-York Historical Society's collection of diaries were also helpful. At New York's East Side Tenement Museum, Vin Lenza let me set up my laptop in the staff lunchroom.

Long before I proposed this book to the Smithsonian Institution Press, the Smithsonian Archives Center at the National Museum of American History had already proved to be invaluable. Special thanks to Jon Zachman, who located pertinent materials while he was still processing the Edward J. Orth Memorial Archives of the World's Fair. Charles F. McGovern and William E. Worthington offered insights into the history of technology.

My research would have been impossible without the spectacularly rich and diverse collection of the University of Michigan library system. As I prowled the stacks of a dozen separate libraries, piecing together the "greatest story never told," I was grateful to have such a wealth of material at hand or just an Interlibrary Loan away.

Many individuals kindly spent time answering my questions in person, by telephone, or e-mail. Joel A. Wasserman of the John B. Pierce Laboratory in New Haven explained its history and ongoing work during our July 1993 meeting there. Douglas Gomery of the University of Maryland's College of Journalism shared his insights into movie theater air conditioning over dinner in Washington, D.C. John M. Anderson of the GE Hall of History, now part of the Schenectady Museum, provided information on General Electric's air-conditioning business. Arlene Mathison at Dayton Hudson's (now Target Corporation) Research Center in Minneapolis located historical information about Detroit's J. L. Hudson department store.

At a publisher's booth in the over-air-conditioned basement of the Washington Hilton, where the Organization of American Historians gathered in 1995, I made a very fortunate "cold call" on Smithsonian Institution Press senior editor Mark G. Hirsch. His enthusiasm, sustained over years, and the astute suggestions and criticisms provided by the two anonymous reviewers he selected, made possible the much-improved version offered herein. Thanks to veteran executive editor Ruth W. Spiegel, a person of unfailing tact, patience, inspiration, and bountiful good sense, the editing process was a wholly gladsome undertaking.

I have not yet met Professor Gail Cooper, but I want to thank her not only for her groundbreaking work on air-conditioning, but also for passing my name along to several editors of relevant reference works. Those exercises in distillation helped this book immensely. An April 1996 Great Lakes American Studies Association symposium on the Cold War gave me a chance to try out some of my ideas on an audience both critical and receptive. My thanks to Professor Russell Reising of the University of Toledo.

Friends and family did not, of course, sit idly by. For clippings both print and electronic, accommodations during research sorties, and much moral and intellectual support, I am grateful to Joan Alexander, Lise Bang-Jensen, Erik Brady and Carol Stevens, Ellen Gardner, Ray and Eleanor Lewis, Susan Metzger, Ruth Metzstein, Saul Metzstein, Tim Murray, Nancy Schwerzler, and especially Charles J. Sennet, photo wrangler.

My dear aunt, Jenny Metzstein, who suffers heat but not fools gladly, has not only welcomed me into her Manhattan apartment before, during, and after research trips, but actually read my dissertation from cover to cover. My husband, Thomas K. Black III, has enhanced my life even more than my Ph.D. did. And he is teaching me how to fish.

Introduction

To a surprising extent," wrote medical ecologist René Dubos in 1965, "modern man has retained unaltered the bodily constitution, physiological responses, and emotional drives which he has inherited from his Paleolithic ancestors. Yet he lives in a mechanized, air-conditioned, and regimented world radically different from the one in which he evolved."[1]

No world is more air-conditioned than the one in which today's American men and women spend their lives. Air-conditioning, defined as mechanical cooling by means of refrigeration, has in just a century transformed the United States. Indoor weather "manufactured" by air-conditioning equipment has—whether we accept the claims of its promoters or the complaints of its detractors—tamed the nation's anarchic seasons and imposed uniformity on a climatically diverse continent. It has helped reshape cities, houses, farms, even our bodies, coming closer than any other technology to producing the "weatherlessness" long envisioned by American utopians who have typically confused technological control with social perfection.

As a child growing up in Buffalo, New York, in the nineteen fifties and sixties, I found air-conditioning ubiquitously seductive. Willie, the Brown & Williamson cartoon penguin, promised "Come In: It's KOOL Inside," as he beckoned from every supermarket and bowling alley entrance, offering menthol cigarettes and air-conditioning simultaneously. It also seemed peculiarly unnecessary. Buffalo is a city far more famous for its

1

blizzards than its heat waves and, in all the years I lived there, the temperature never exceeded 99° and rarely hit 90°. Not until the late seventies did I learn that Buffalo could credibly claim to be the place where air-conditioning was invented. Only in the nineties, when I seriously engaged this topic as my doctoral dissertation in American Culture, did I actually visit the grave of Willis Haviland Carrier, air-conditioning's best-known inventor and promoter. He rests in a family plot in Buffalo's Forest Lawn Cemetery, an especially shady and sylvan example of the nineteenth-century rural cemetery.

By then I had conceived a detestation of air-conditioning, based primarily on childhood experiences and my own tendency, as a woman and a Buffalonian, to prefer feeling warm to feeling cold. When we would visit New York City in the late fifties, a family friend proudly chauffeured us around in his enormous black Lincoln Continental, which was fully air-conditioned, as only the most expensive luxury cars were in those days. Disposed in any case to car sickness, I shivered and suffered in the back seat, made miserable not only by the cold but by the gloomy claustrophobia of heavily tinted windows, tightly closed against any outside air.

As a teenage babysitter, I was supposed to feel fortunate when I was employed at one of the few centrally air-conditioned houses in our suburban neighborhood. Sickened by the faint but pervasive smell of spilt baby milk and soiled diapers, I would futilely wonder what my otherwise kind and generous employers would do if I cracked open a window to dissipate the stale chill.

My rather formless juvenile gripes and discomforts coalesced in 1981 when I was the legislative correspondent in Albany for a Buffalo newspaper. The Speaker of the New York State Assembly had called a press conference in one of the splendid rooms of the New York State Capitol, a dimly lit but grandiose edifice completed in 1899 and subsequently clumsily retrofitted with air-conditioning. Outside it was a warm July day but inside it was frosty. Condensation was trickling down the inside of the windows, making the room look and feel like a pitcher of iced tea. I wrote an opinion piece that blamed my personal discomfort, the rise of the Sun Belt, the decline of Buffalo, and a variety of other social and physical ills on the Syracuse, New York–based, Carrier Corporation.[2] My 1981 tirade was simplistic, but I knew I was on to something. Everybody, I learned as I began to formulate and explain my proposed dissertation, has a story to tell about air-conditioning. My interlocutors' stories were often far more positive and grateful than mine but most admitted that they had rarely before, if ever, actually thought about the thermal environment.

What this book intends is to rescue air-conditioning from both invisibility and inevitability and trace a historical trajectory that helps explain the air-conditioned society of today. To claim that air-conditioning has fundamentally altered this nation where it has been used the most intensively for the longest period of time does not presume that its effects were certain, complete, or unquestioned, or even an inevitable result of the technology itself. Air-conditioning is a particularly pertinent example of the social construction of technology. It has played a key role in a larger story of how the post-Columbian inhabitants of the United States, the "Nature's Nation" in Perry Miller's enduring phrase, have attempted to control both natural volatility and human disorder. Yet air-conditioning, despite its often contentious history, has usually been mischaracterized as simple "common sense."[3]

Only relatively recently has air-conditioning received attention from historians. Raymond Arsenault, a historian of the South, in 1984 wrote an influential essay titled "The End of the Long Hot Summer." Although he was careful not to assert an essential relationship between mechanical cooling and hot climates, Arsenault's southern focus seemed to validate rather than effectively challenge a commonsense linkage of the two.[4] Air-conditioning, especially in its early years, had much less to do with hot weather than it did with prosperity, efficiency, and status, none of which the South could lay claim to during much of the twentieth century.

Gail Cooper's book, *Air-Conditioning America,* in 1998 became the first full-length historically and socially grounded study of air-conditioning's evolution between 1902 and 1955. I am indebted to her pioneering work in part because it makes my own interest in this "invisible" technology seem considerably less idiosyncratic. Cooper's book clearly demonstrates that many aspects of what we now call "air-conditioning" were contested, including its definition, its standards of performance, and the professional credentials required to manufacture, install, sell, and operate it. She also shows how the fledgling industry struggled to differentiate "real" air-conditioning from claims made on behalf of electric fans, ice boxes, mechanical ventilators, and dehumidifiers.[5]

Why did air-conditioning for so long suffer from near-invisibility? As a hybrid of two earlier technological breakthroughs—electricity and refrigeration—air-conditioning has usually been understood as a by-product, just another household appliance plugged into the power grid. The promoters of air-conditioning have been remarkably successful, sometimes too successful, in persuading the American public to take their product for granted. And although air-conditioning machinery is often large and noisy, a properly functioning air-conditioning system makes a "product" that is actually invisible. Engineers from the very beginning have insisted that air-conditioning is a mechanical device or system that produces and maintains specific air temperatures in conjunction with specified levels of humidity. But to the world outside the laboratory, air-conditioning means the promise if not always the delivery of "thermal comfort."

This seemingly simple phrase evokes physiological and mental states and re-lationships so ambiguous that even engineers have acknowledged that their "Comfort Zone," introduced in 1923 and adjusted many times since, cannot sat-isfy all people in all places at all times.

Even if we assume that most members of a group or society can overcome racial, gender, and regional variability and agree on what thermal comfort *is,* who then decides how important it is to be comfortable? Like air-conditioning itself, the idea of thermal comfort proves to be contingent. In our search for excitement, entertainment, or sheer sensation, many of us willingly expose our bodies to extreme heat or cold. Many others among us lack the resources to have or make such choices. Comfort, too, is a human invention rather than a mea-surable and invariable physiological response.[6]

This is not primarily a study of the technological development of air-condi-tioning; Gail Cooper has comprehensively covered that ground. I have chosen rather to emphasize the complicated and by no means linear course by which the idea of cooling captured the popular imagination and became embedded in the social perceptions and expectations of Americans, most obviously the urban middle class. My aim is to connect air-conditioning to larger social processes that produced new standards for how the American middle-class "body"—and eventually how every "body"—was to feel and function. Attitudes towards heat and cold, comfort and discomfort, may begin in our physiology but, like so many other "essentialist" states, have evolved over the course of our nation's history and will continue to do so. Climate control has had the effect of "disci-plining" individuals, in the Foucauldian sense, keeping them indoors with prom-ises of comfort and physically unchallenging uniformity rather than with threats of painful punishment.[7]

This book identifies three periods in the evolving relationship between Americans and air-conditioning and reveals important shifts in the places and ways in which summer cooling was used by middle-class urbanites, shaping their lives at work, at home, and at play. Long before the appearance of "real" air-conditioning, Americans had already developed complicated attitudes to-wards heat and cold and the vagaries of weather and climate in their meteoro-logically extreme nation. Proponents of the new technology of air-conditioning would link these older, even ancient, ideologies of race, climate, civilization, and efficiency to contemporary conditions. Two important champions of both the old ideologies and the new technologies were C.-E. A. Winslow, an es-teemed public health authority and liberal ameliorist, and Ellsworth Hunting-ton, an influential geographer and conservative eugenicist. Their work with one another and with engineers on behalf of the emerging air-conditioning industry significantly helped to develop intellectual justifications and scientific arguments for mechanical cooling.

Although the first mechanical system defined as "real" air-conditioning was used at a Brooklyn printing plant in 1902, air-conditioning's "utopian" possibilities attracted meaningful public attention only after 1920. Initial encounters with cooling took place primarily in contexts of pleasure and consumption, notably movie palaces, department stores, hotels, and transcontinental passenger trains. In each of these settings, subtle differences in air-conditioning practice and promotion would reveal implicit class and gender anxieties. Upper-class Americans traditionally had access to large airy houses, summer retreats, and domestic help, and had an inbred habit of ignoring discomfort. It was the aspiring and perspiring urban middle class that would make air-conditioning a success.

Acclaimed as a modernistic novelty, air-conditioning, like most mechanical wonders, did not always perform as flawlessly as advertised. Still, air-conditioning excited the imaginations of Americans who were exposed to its effects. By the late twenties, this group would include the U.S. Congress, the president, and the Supreme Court. Controversy over air-conditioning the federal city of Washington illuminates the tricky terrain air-conditioning had to negotiate between indulgence and necessity, pleasure and efficiency, to attain broad acceptance.

As capitalism struggled during the coincidentally very hot years of the thirties' Depression, air-conditioning was one of a number of technologies that seemed to offer hope that science and engineering expertise could still solve basic human problems and make the world work better. At the two major world's fairs of the thirties, Chicago's in 1933–1934 and New York's in 1939–1940, air-conditioning was widely used to build "worlds of tomorrow," creating an actual "climate" of hopefulness and assuring fair visitors an ideal experience no matter what the weather.

Recovering along with the nation from the Depression and the subsequent constraints and dislocations of World War II, a cautiously optimistic air-conditioning industry began eyeing sectors that had not previously received much attention, chief among them the single-family American house. The market for residential cooling surged in the fifties. Air-conditioning lost its futuristic novelty and became a consumer commodity integral to a middle-class definition of the American way of life.

During this period of commodification, air-conditioning helped change the meanings of domestic space and family life in the new and predominantly white suburbia. Despite early support for "natural" comfort strategies, packaged mechanical air-conditioning proved almost irresistible to home owners and builders rushing to meet the demand for new housing as cheaply as possible. In this era of status anxiety, home air-conditioning became a useful indicator of middle-class prestige and modernity even—or especially—in regions where mechanical cooling was "necessary" only a few days each summer. Advertising campaigns promised to furnish middle-class suburban families with a domain protected from the sight of streets, weather, and other people. Neglected by national advertisers for a variety of racialist and economic reasons, middle-class black consumers nevertheless participated in the fifties enthusiasm for home cooling.

Air-conditioning helped to shape evolving notions of health and comfort, as well as gender and race appropriateness. Yet the idea eagerly advanced by air-conditioning makers, that their product either guaranteed comfort or was the same as comfort proved to be a persistently contentious one. The final two chapters map some intellectual and sociopolitical dimensions of air-conditioning's "malaise," a period of reappraisal, doubt, even fear, that continues into the present.

Paralleling the expansion of air-conditioning in the fifties, old questions about nature and technology, necessity and luxury, were taken up by new sectors of the American public. Academic and popular critics including Lewis Mumford, John Kenneth Galbraith, and Vance Packard questioned the benefits of an American way of life that fostered waste, extravagance, and new forms of dependency on centralized systems. As an instrument of total climate control and a symbol of bland conformity, air-conditioning was an obvious target of such critiques. The complicated concept of "cool," borrowed in the fifties by white "beatniks" from African American music and urban culture, would also come to suggest a state of mental dominion over one's environment, both social and physical, not the imposition of artificial cooling.

Despite the carping of public intellectuals, racial and cultural outsiders, and politically suspect "cranks," air-conditioning's acceptance grew apace. Between 1960 and roughly 2000, the share of households air-conditioned either centrally or with one or more room units grew from 12.5 to 83 percent. Just 10 percent of automobiles in 1966 came out of the factory with air-conditioning; that figure exceeded 98 percent in 2000. But market success did not necessarily engender enthusiasm or confidence among consumers, as world and local events compelled ordinary Americans to consider air-conditioning's shortcomings and possible negative effects.

The onset in 1973 of an energy crisis severely challenged the deeply held American belief in a future of inexhaustible cheap energy and forced reassessment, although not necessarily transformation, of lifestyles based on that belief. Summer brownouts made the energy gluttony of air-conditioning especially obvious to this newly concerned public. The energy supply crisis in California in 2001 and that year's sudden nationwide surge in gasoline prices, followed briefly by a summer heat wave, demonstrated that the lessons of the seventies had as yet neither been learned nor forgotten.

During the intense heat wave that afflicted America's midsection in 1980, and in subsequent urban heat outbreaks such as Chicago's in 1995, hundreds of deaths were blamed on heat. Such continuing episodes have forced Americans to recognize that air-conditioning, despite its wide availability, is no "magic bullet" for larger social problems afflicting inner-city poor and elderly. Nor can it always protect from "real" weather even those with ready access to cooling and the financial and energy resources to use it. Enthusiasm for air-conditioning, as for many other technological projects of order, control, and system, seems to be, to quote Thomas P. Hughes, "now passing into history."[8]

In our now presumably "weatherless" society, people complain about the weather, watch it, and worry about it more than ever before. The 24-hour Weather Channel has been a cable television staple since 1982. *USA Today*'s full-color, full-page weather map, launched in 1982, has inspired a flock of imitators. The development and mass media diffusion of pseudoscientific calculations like the "wind-chill factor" and "heat index" dramatically exaggerate the presumed discomfort of temperature, wind, and humidity. In a world where terms like "global warming" and "greenhouse effect" are the stuff of daily news reports, air-moving systems might be regarded as indispensable. Instead, like many other technological systems, air-conditioning is popularly believed to be part of the problem, even by those who would not dream of living without it.[9]

1. The Coldward Course of Progress

The Carrier Corporation, America's leading maker of air-conditioning equipment, in 1949 and 1950 ran a series of full-page color advertisements in the *Saturday Evening Post,* then one of the nation's most popular weekly news and feature magazines. "Boomtown—2000 B.C." is the headline under an illustration of a Bedouin surveying a barren desert from the back of a camel. It continues:

Once a thriving city—now deserted ruins! These seven words sum up the history of many a torrid zone metropolis, laid low by the combination of heat itself and conquest by *stronger races from temperate climes.* In ancient days man just had to accept the penalties of equatorial climate (emphasis added).

Another ad in the series shows a dark-skinned man sprawled on the ground, his face covered by a sombrero (figures 1 and 2). "Temperature 102°—Production 0," reads the headline, the ad continuing: "Why have most great inventions and advances in science and industry come from temperate zones? Because for centuries tropical heat has robbed men of energy and ambition. There was no air-conditioning. So they took siestas."

If *Saturday Evening Post* readers imagined such problems only afflicted what would soon be called the Third World, another ad forced the point home. Heat has driven an urban, white-collar, white man in the world's greatest nation to the point of what the ad calls "unconditional surrender:"

8

In Calcutta or Cairo, New York or New Orleans—wherever temperature soars and
humidity is high, men suffer without air-conditioning. They wilt and lose their
drive.[1]

As America's Cold War with the Soviet Union intensified in the aftermath of
World War II, these advertisements strongly suggest that it would be unthink-
able for the "good guys" to surrender to heat.

More than a half-century later, what is likely to strike readers most immediately about these advertisements is their blatant use of racial and ethnic stereo-
typing. In their own time they spoke a language of human achievement and
progress that would have been immediately intelligible to the middle-class,
mass-market audience of the *Saturday Evening Post*. It is a language that even
now is never very far below the surface of popularly accepted explanations of
racial and ethnic attributes. Using simple words and graphic illustrations, these
glossy pages invoked an explanatory formula that had been used from the fif-
teenth century onward to justify European imperialism and celebrate the white
race's apparent success. These advertisements are an especially unapologetic
example of how the air-conditioning industry, during the first half of the twentieth century, appropriated ancient theories about race, heat, and human history,
investing them with the authority of modern science in order to expand the market for cooling technology.

For the air-conditioning industry to succeed it was not enough for most of the
United States to have warm, humid summers. The ascendancy of air-conditioning would require persuasion. A significant portion of the American public
needed to believe that heat was not just an occasional unpleasantness but a serious problem; that this problem could be corrected; and that uniform control
of indoor thermal conditions in all weathers, seasons, and climatic regions was
the birthright of a truly advanced society.

To say that engineers, marketers, and publicists deployed an ancient and by
today's standards offensive ideology to help corporations sell air conditioners
does not imply deception or propose an uncomplicated cause-and-effect relationship between their expertise and the public's generally enthusiastic acceptance of air-conditioning. The earnest sincerity of an emerging cadre of air-
conditioning professionals grew, in part, out of a deep commitment to
progressivist ideals of human betterment and a belief that human invention, expressed through technology, could solve most of society's moral and material
problems. "Ventilation comes next to godliness," Syracuse engineer Edward
P. Bates told the forty-five men who assembled in New York City in 1895 for the
first annual meeting of the American Society of Heating and Ventilating Engineers
(ASHVE), adding, "Our work . . . will not stop with any class; it will benefit all

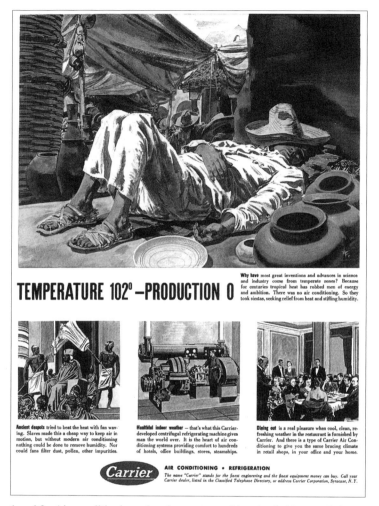

1 and 2. Air-conditioning advertisements evoking the "white man's burden" appeared in the *Saturday Evening Post* in 1949 and 1950.

classes." Steeped in nineteenth-century utopianism and committed to the project of American empire, these engineers found a sense of mission in introducing a new technology to a receptive public raised in the same climate of thought.[2]

Americans had inconsistent and complicated attitudes toward heat long before the development of air-conditioning. Heat and cold had ideological resonance and practical meaning on two closely related levels. Was the United States a vigorous land whose bracing climate made it a cradle of civilization and

progress? Or was it, instead, a nation cursed with tropical conditions that fore-told political and racial decline? At the grass roots, inhabitants of America's wildly variable regions confronted volatile and severe weather conditions that challenged life itself on a daily and seasonal basis. Early transplants from England suffered terribly in the heat, some even finding New England too warm. They feared heat's deadly and demoralizing effects, and eventually de-veloped strategies, including dietary and clothing adjustments, to cope with it.[3]

In most of the continental United States, the climate is extreme in all seasons by western European standards, fiercely cold in winter and scorching or op-pressively humid in summer. Except in the southernmost states, however, winters have tended to be considerably longer than summers. During the early centuries of United States history, cold was a more acute concern than summer's brief, if intense, heat and humidity. American builders borrowed many of Europe's architectural forms but not the heat-conserving materials, such as stone, that made buildings relatively impervious to the weather. The common use of wood and other lightweight and inexpensive materials in America's climatically extreme regions helped the nation expand quickly but also posed a challenge to traditional methods of keeping warm.

By the end of the nineteenth century, steam heat and major improvements in stoves and fireplaces had more or less satisfactorily solved the problem of providing enough heat to keep the majority of the population alive during the winter. The poorest dwellings, especially in rural areas, were no doubt never adequately heated. Yet engineers and craftsmen had by 1900 resolved major technological problems of heat production and distribution.[4]

If anything, efforts to provide sufficient heat were too successful. Foreign visitors and American advocates of public health alike first marveled at and then became worried about the American habit of heating buildings in winter to temperatures more characteristic of tropics or deserts. As early as 1842, touring English novelist Charles Dickens complained of the American penchant for overheating. His Boston hotel, considered one of the nation's finest, was, he wrote a friend, "made so infernally hot (I use the expression advisedly) by means of a furnace with pipes running through the passages, that we can hardly bear it."

Almost thirty years later, Dickens's fulminations still rankled. Admitting in 1869 that "that great American institution, the cast-iron stove, is in disgrace," Lewis W. Leeds nevertheless defended American heating practices in the pages of *The Manufacturer and Builder: A Practical Journal of Industrial Progress,* then in its first year of publication. "Shall [the laboring classes] have stoves, or shall they go without artificial heat altogether?" Leeds asked. "If Charles Dickens were to visit the forty thousand paupers said to dwell in . . . London, he would not, to be sure, find them crowded around . . . the 'infernal red-hot stove,' but, *far worse,* he would find them crowded together in some cold, damp, chilly room" (emphasis in original.)[5]

It is not too surprising that French traveler Paul Blouët would find little changed when he toured the United States in 1888. He attributed American women's pallid complexions to indoor overheating that spoiled the country's otherwise bracing and healthful winter climate:

> I repeat it, the cold is healthy; and the foreigner who visits America
> during the winter only suffers from the suffocating heat of the rooms. . . .

It is not only the houses that are heated night and day to a temperature of nearly 80 degrees, but it is the trains as well.[6]

The dryness of heated air in theaters and concert halls, he added, made it difficult to breathe. Each of these examples of indoor heat was a problem of manufacture, not nature.

The seasonally recurring "natural" heat of American summers, especially in the southern states, was implicated in a more global set of climatic concerns. Prior to the ascendance of Darwinist thought, scientists with both pro- and antislavery positions viewed racial difference as the result of climate and latitude. But they drew importantly different conclusions from this hypothesis. Antislavery doctors and scientists, says William Stanton in his study of pre–Civil War racial science, defined dark skin color and wiry hair as "diseases" caused by excessive heat that might be curable in a temperate climate. This Lamarckian notion was rejected by their proslavery counterparts who had an interest in proving that racial traits were innate rather than environmentally contingent. Black people, the defenders of slavery maintained, were not the product of a specific set of external physical conditions, and so could not be "improved" by relocation to a different environment. God rather had separately created them to endure and labor permanently in hot climates.[7]

As imperial ventures and a new wave of immigration converged in the aftermath of the Civil War, hereditary and environmentally deterministic explanations of human character and behavior also tended to converge. It was commonplace for the United States's northern elites and even some southern historians to attribute the South's "backwardness" and "peculiar" social customs to its high temperature and humidity; the unpleasant traits of Italians and Jews to their "Mediterranean" origins; and the problems of foreign colonization and domestic race relations to tropical climates that debased the black man and depraved the white. As Dane Kennedy points out, imperialists in the early twentieth century simultaneously asserted the power of Western science to transform, indeed "cure," tropical conditions, and expressed acute anxiety about the ability of whites to endure tropical climates and control both the tropics' native inhabitants and themselves. It was commonplace to believe that white people who successfully acclimated to the tropics became permanently unfit for "civilization." This widely held anxiety ironically turns inside out the antislavery theory that hoped climatic moderation would emancipate blacks from the chains of race. As a particular form of racial fear, this theory would decline but not disappear in the late thirties as colonialism faded and sun-tanning was promoted for its assumed therapeutic benefits.[8]

In the United States's "progressive" northeast and Midwest regions, the ill

3. But for some improvements in fire escape design, summertime on New York's Lower East Side changed little in the early twentieth century. A plate from E. Idell Zeisloft's 1899 *The New Metropolis* depicts a teeming "Hot Summer Night on the East Side."

effects of summertime, most notably higher death rates especially among infants in urban slums, were well known and could be devastating. "This is the harvest season for death's reaper," labor leader, minister, and former tenement-dweller Charles Stelzle recollected of a particularly steamy August in New York City. "Restless, wan little children droop on doorsteps and in dark hallways . . . a sticky fog hangs over the city while the sun-baked tenements stifle helpless little children"[9] (figures 3 and 4).

"There were . . . not even fans for people like us," recalled Lily B. Merman, whose father came from Galicia to New York's Lower East Side in 1907. "We would go to the rooftops or the fire escapes for a little relief." On one such "horribly hot summer night," Lily and her siblings awoke when what they thought was rain poured down from the fire escape above. One or more of the nine children asleep on the upper landing had urinated. A five-story tenement building at 97 Orchard Street, built in 1863, had no fire escapes, so sweaty tenants would eat and sleep on the roof. Not until the 1930s, shortly before the structure was

4. Twenty-eight years later, Norfolk Street mother Fannie Kuker put Meyer and Annie to bed outside their tenement during a July heat wave.

declared unfit for human habitation, did the installation of minimal wiring allow the Baldizzi family to use a small electric fan in the tiny front room of their 625-square-foot flat. Josephine Baldizzi, not yet ten, and her brother were more excited to plug in the radio and floor lamp.[10]

Summer outbreaks of such epidemic diseases as cholera and yellow fever, while affecting poor and immigrant neighborhoods more severely, also endangered the solid citizenry of major cities. Heat was dangerous not because humans felt hot and sweaty but because foul miasmas—and later harmful germs—were known to flourish in hot weather amid the deficient sanitary conditions that characterized most urban areas. The rather slow and uneven substitution of bacteriological explanations for miasmic theories of contagion by fetid and poisonous air had relatively little impact on actual methods used to promote urban hygiene. Decaying trash and stagnant pools of wastewater, reeking in the summer heat, were hazards obvious to expert and nonexpert alike, whether or not the danger was understood to emanate from poisonous miasmas or invisible microbes.[11]

Cleaning up worked, even if the reason why was not agreed upon by all involved. When major cities, spurred by an insurgent public health profession in alliance with political and social reformers and scientific experts, built sewers, cleaned streets, sent visiting nurses and doctors into tenements, and eventually forced pasteurization of milk, summer's most fatal effects declined dramatically. Beginning in 1876, for example, the New York City Health Department's "Summer Corps" visited tenements in July and August to examine children, instruct their parents in sanitation, and spot health violations. It was not their mission to help tenement dwellers cool their stifling apartments.[12]

High temperatures and humidity continued to afflict America's cities. Even on the best streets, reported Lady Mary Duffus Hardy, an English novelist who visited Manhattan during the 1880 summer heat wave, "you may glance in at the open windows, and see the elegantly furnished vacant rooms . . . while the inhabitants are taking the air on their doorsteps." She added, "This is an old knickerbocker custom, which still obtains everywhere except on the sacred Fifth Avenue, which confines itself strictly within doors, shrined from the vulgar gaze." In New York's less sacred precincts, she reported, the "death toll is terrible during these hot spells, sometimes amounting from sunstroke alone to twenty in a single day."[13]

Heat-wave-induced class distinctions were not confined to Fifth Avenue. The poor, as Lily Merman and Josephine Baldizzi remind us, had their own ways of dealing with heat. Reformer Charles Stelzle recalled that poor peoples' "snobbishness" meant that ground-floor tenement dwellers, usually native-born and somewhat better off, felt entitled to their buildings' tiny, often garbage-strewn, yards, and looked down (even though it was literally "up") upon the poorer foreign families occupying the higher stories. All this would change, said Stelzle, "during those stifling August nights, when it was simply impossible to sleep in the ordinary dark bedroom, we 'top floorers' slept on the roof. . . . We considered the roof our rightful property . . . and when the first-floor aristocracy came up with their pillows to get a breath of air in the sultry summer nights, we treated them with scorn and contempt. . . . We were the aristocracy of the roof." Stelzle's childhood glee is still evident in the memoir he published some fifty years after his days as a tenement lad who ran with the Lower East Side's "Orchard Street gang."[14]

Traditional strategies for dealing with summer weather—sitting on the stoop, the fire escape, the roof—cold drinks and visits to ice-cream parlors, sleeping in municipal parks, reduced or rescheduled work hours, and vacations for those who could afford them, were pleasanter and more effective in the sanitized city.

In other words, naturally occurring seasonal heat, once disassociated from foul odors, rot, and disease, was not immediately or inevitably conceived as a problem for which a technological solution might be discovered.

After both the electrically powered fan and ice made by mechanical refrigeration became available in the 1880s, some engineers experimentally combined these technologies in a not especially successful effort to cool buildings in the summertime. In St. Louis a beer hall installed banks of refrigeration, renamed itself the "Ice Palace," and lured patrons by decorating its windows with snow scenes. New York's Carnegie Hall connected ice racks to its existing ventilation system but there is no evidence the system was ever used in summertime.[15] In 1902, 26-year-old Buffalo Forge engineer Willis Haviland Carrier installed a system meant to control both air temperature and humidity in Brooklyn's Sackett-Wilhelms printing plant, where the popular humor magazine, *Judge,* was produced. From this modest but important beginning, Carrier went on to "sire" the industry's preeminent company and actively pursue recognition as the "father of air-conditioning" throughout his life. Cotton-mill engineer Stuart Cramer named air-conditioning in a May 1906 speech to the American Cotton Manufacturers Association. The quick and general acceptance of the term "air-conditioning," rather than, say, "air chilling" or "colderizing," or some other more or less fanciful invocation of cold, should remind us that professionals, at least, have always considered this technology's cooling effects merely a by-product. Their ultimate goal was to control both temperature and humidity at *any* desired level.

Even the inventors and practitioners of the new techniques of scientific air-conditioning did not at first construe summer heat as their central challenge. Often, process air-conditioning systems, so called because they facilitated manufacturing processes, would deliberately increase heat and humidity in order to improve the handling qualities of such industrial raw materials as cotton, tobacco, celluloid, chewing gum, and, in the case of Sackett-Wilhelms, ink. Only after World War I did the young air-conditioning industry begin to investigate the market potential of air-conditioning's secondary comfort effects. The redefinition of thermal comfort as coolness and coolness as a necessary condition of daily life required that both winter overheating and summer heat be portrayed as hazardous but curable physical states. It was also essential that comfort be elevated in importance by association not only with health and efficiency, but also with progress and civilization.

In its project of reinterpreting the meaning and effects of heat and cold, the fledgling air-conditioning industry was materially assisted by two authorities who enjoyed international renown in the first half of the twentieth century but whose work is now neglected. Ellsworth Huntington, born in Galesburg, Illi-

5. Geographer Ellsworth Huntington and his wife, Rachel, take the air in this photograph dated some time after 1930.

nois, in 1876, was a politically conservative geographer. Charles-Edward Amory Winslow, born in Boston in 1877, was a progressive public health expert. These men were in many ways typical of the white upper-middle-class social order within which they were raised and spent long and fruitful careers. Their role in this story is much more specific. Although it was for neither man the central focus of his work, throughout their careers both Huntington and Winslow worked closely with the heating, cooling, and ventilating industry to shape popular ideas and normalize standards of climatic desirability and indoor comfort that, they would eventually and authoritatively argue, only air-conditioning could reliably achieve.

Denied a tenured appointment by Yale, where he spent twenty-five years as a poorly paid research associate and was considered an uninspiring teacher and disorganized researcher by his colleagues, Ellsworth Huntington nonetheless became, as the "high priest of climatic determinism," one of the most influential and widely quoted geographers of the first half of the twentieth century (figure 5). Hired by Yale in 1919 at the meager annual salary of two hundred dollars, well below that of an assistant professor, by 1923 Huntington had gained enough professional distinction outside to be elected president of the Association of American Geographers. His modest means and lack of job security spurred him to feats of publishing, speech-making, and mass media punditry that, although unhelpful to his academic prestige, enhanced his standing with the air-conditioning industry and gave his views wide popular currency.

Book royalties and article fees were Huntington's main source of income. "No geographer has had more influence on American thinking about the relationship of the environment to man . . . and few have advocated more strongly the dominance of the physical environment," geographer George F. Martin wrote in 1968. He attributed the depth and breadth of Huntington's pervasive influence to his "numerous, highly readable books," including textbooks used by generations of students. *Civilization and Climate,* the book that first brought Huntington to international attention, was published in 1915. The "authoritative" third edition of 1924 was reprinted five times during the thirties and forties and yet again as recently as 1971.[16]

Huntington's "physiological climatology" was based on ancient ways of understanding human diversity. In the tradition of Hippocrates' *Airs, Waters, Places*, Huntington proposed to explain human behavior and achievement in terms of the climatic factors they experienced, accounting thereby for the rise and demise of great civilizations. Why was it, he asked, that formerly great civilizations had arisen in countries now decadent? Climatic warming, Huntington argued, caused populations to decline in physical vigor and lose mental acuity. With the intellectual certitude so characteristic of his era and Anglo-Saxon heritage, this small, balding, energetic son of a New England minister explicitly set out to explain why "people of European races are able to accomplish the most work and have the best health."[17]

The idea that enduring and even thriving in a cold climate was evidence of racial superiority and masculine vigor was not new. Its most prominent apostle in Huntington's generation was President Theodore Roosevelt who made it part of his cult of strenuous manliness. The future president tramped three miles through New York City's death-dealing blizzard of 1888 to keep an appointment. It was neither the first nor last time he would demonstrate that mere physical comfort was a feminine indulgence and a masculine vice. Roosevelt and other boosters of America's destiny, including William Gilpin of Colorado, readily accepted German geographer Alexander von Humboldt's theory that true civilization was only possible in regions where the average annual temperature was about 50 degrees.[18]

Boosters and promoters also enthusiastically adopted Bishop George Berkeley's 1752 effusion "westward the course of empire takes its way," converting it from a celebration of British imperial expansion to a prophesy of eventual world dominion by the United States, or at least those parts of it blessed with a salubrious climate. As William Cronon points out in his discussion of Chicago's "booster dreams," promoters rushed to endow their chosen urban sites with an array of God's blessings and natural advantages. One such advantage, often flagrantly misrepresented, was "global climatic forces which had historically created great urban civilizations elsewhere . . . and which now, supposedly, were starting to operate in North America."[19]

What Huntington brought to this stew of climatological and folkloric theory was empirical research. He investigated human efficiency under varying seasonal conditions, compiling 15,000 records on workers and students at the U.S. Naval Academy and West Point, cities in Pennsylvania, Virginia, and Florida, and three factories in Connecticut. He used statistical methods to link death rates in several cities to weather events. Huntington used copious tables and graphs, inserting forty-eight of them into the 1924 edition of *Civilization and Climate* to imbue his conclusions with the scientific objectivity and modernity to which he aspired. Certainly in the teens of the twentieth century, few disputed Huntington's underlying assumptions about the meaning and manifestations of "civilization." Not until 1928 did Russian-born sociologist Pitirim Sorokin, then teaching at the University of Minnesota, attack Huntington at length. In a survey of contemporary sociology that was both magisterial and opinionated, Sorokin spent most of a chapter taking particular issue with Huntington's efforts to connect climate, health, efficiency, and achievement.

Sorokin started by calling Huntington's work "some of the best in this field," but then proceeded to dismantle the "geographical school" of sociology that Huntington epitomized. Sorokin questioned the validity of Huntington's data and picked apart his manipulation of statistics. "It is rather fallacious to try to find a uniform influence of temperature or of seasons upon all workers, of all ages, of both sexes, and so on, as is done by Huntington," Sorokin wrote. Sorokin concluded his admittedly "severe" treatment of Huntington and his disciples by saying, "We are grateful . . . for [the Geographical School's] valuable contributions. This, however, does not oblige us to accept its fallacious theories, its fictitious correlations, or finally, its overestimation of the role of geographical environment."[20]

By the fifties, Huntington's ethnocentric superiority was widely "decried, ridiculed, and dismissed." Yet the explanatory power of climate, although no longer respected by scholars, still finds a place in the popular imagination. In his 1997 bestseller, *Guns, Germs, and Steel,* biologist Jared Diamond notes that

Europeans and North Americans have found and continue to find many ways to make climatological explanations seem to prove their superiority. Diamond's own book does not completely discount climatic factors, but manages to wring out most of their tautological racist content.[21]

On the basis of his experimental data, Huntington concluded that physical activity is most effectively accomplished when the daily average temperature falls between 60° and 65° Fahrenheit, and mental work flourishes when the average temperature, presumably outdoors, is just 38 degrees. But temperature alone could not assure a civilization's survival and progress. A "deadening monotony" in the weather, Huntington said, was especially detrimental, as were excessive indoor dryness and overheating. Huntington followed his own prescriptions. According to a biographer, "both at midmorning and midafternoon, regardless of the weather outside, he opened the windows wide, and left them open long enough to bring a complete change of air into the office." Each evening Huntington walked three miles from his Yale office to his home in the New Haven suburbs.[22] Because he believed storminess and changeability to be as important as moderate temperatures to creativity and productivity, Huntington declared American weather the world's most conducive to progress. His definition of an ideal yearly mean temperature range—between 38° and 64°— hardly described normal weather anywhere in the United States.

In 1920, 31-year-old sociologist S. Colum GilFillan, inspired by Huntington's *Civilization and Climate,* explicitly linked cold climates and human achievement. His article, "The Coldward Course of Progress," artfully conjoined Bishop Berkeley's and Alexander von Humboldt's prognoses, as filtered through Huntington's empiricism. GilFillan's was a blunt explication of an ideology of race and power implicit in the past fifty or more years of European imperialism and American adventurism at home and overseas.[23] Like Huntington, who became both a disciple and a mentor, helping the younger man find a teaching position at Grinnell College in 1925 and maintaining a lifelong correspondence, GilFillan believed in the determinacy of climate. Civilization may have begun in hot countries where a long growing season assured agricultural success, but did not significantly improve or expand until it moved northward. Like Huntington, GilFillan mustered the trappings of scientific methodology in support of his thesis. A graph titled "The Path of Supremacy" in his article tracks civilization northward through ever colder national capitals. When, late in the essay, GilFillan discloses that his purported data are almost entirely conjectural, he nevertheless asserts "the logical inference is that each grade of civilization has an appropriate temperature in which it will especially flourish." He added, "[warmth's] harmful effects upon health and mind cause the scene of maximum efficiency in civilization . . . to withdraw ever farther from the tropics" (pages 393–94).

GilFillan was less sanguine than Huntington about the assured supremacy of the United States. By situating the modern domain of civilization north of the 50° isotherm, he intentionally excluded such important United States cities as New York and Chicago, where he spent much of his career. By the year 2000, GilFillan predicted, civilization would be centered in such cities as Detroit, Moscow, and Montreal. The southern hemisphere, he noted, is "climatically hopeless for leadership in civilization, so we have ignored it herein . . ." (page 403n). Oddly enough, GilFillan fancied himself a sun-worshiper, once writing to Huntington on the occasion of a summer solstice, "I'm happy to greet you, on this Day of the Sun . . . Nature's natural holiday. It's the only holiday I believe in."[24]

Both Huntington and GilFillan lent the language and evidentiary tools of science to already hoary theories of tropical life and its impact on the white race. *Civilization and Climate* contains an entire chapter on "The White Man in the Tropics." Huntington blamed equally the tropics' "dull unprogressive population" and its climate for a decline in the energy and achievement of white settlers. A trip to tropical northern Australia in the mid-nineteen-twenties did not reassure Huntington. In an undated, unpublished article prepared during this period he complained that white men's ways of staying cool there included nakedness and laziness. Using the racialist discourse of his times, GilFillan blamed the tropics and hot weather generally for obstreperousness, crime, suicide, assaults, insanity, and revolutions. For both men, despite their apparent inconsistency, the chief culprit was temperature and the potential tragic degeneration of the white race was the only important problem.[25]

Huntington's embrace of GilFillan's "coldward" thesis, upon which GilFillan elaborated in many subsequent writings and maintained to the end of his long life, does not make the Yale geographer a clear choice for air-conditioning industry spokesman. Many aspects of Huntington's thought and his personal habits suggested that the use of technology to homogenize climatic conditions to a state of perfect consistency would be detrimental to true progress. In the concluding chapter of the 1924 edition of *Civilization and Climate,* by which time he was well acquainted with the air-conditioning industry, Huntington proposed that factories adopt more natural standards of productivity by adjusting output seasonally. He even argued that workers should change location with the seasons, despite the obvious impracticality of the idea. He was ambivalent about indoor cooling. "In equatorial regions there is as much reason for equipping the houses with coolness as there is in temperate regions for equipping them with heaters," he wrote near the end of *Civilization and Climate*. He went on, "in both cases uniformity of temperature is apparently a mistake, for moderate changes from day to day appear to be favorable" (page 409).

Yet it was obvious to engineers and manufacturers of various air washers, blowers, coolers, and purifiers that a theory that connected weather and climate with the most centrally important aspects of human life—health, work, intelligence, power—could not help being beneficial to their interests. After 1915, Huntington was regularly approached with endorsement requests for various air devices and systems. In 1918, for instance, a solicitation from the Air Moistener Company of Chicago got this response from the geographer: "The only chance of making your moisteners a commercial success lies in convincing people that the value of their use is a scientifically proved fact." In response, the firm bragged that its device could frost windows and produce icicles outside the sash. This was not the kind of proof Huntington was seeking. Despite his constant financial struggle, Huntington appears to have insisted that the makers prove the efficacy of their products. In later years, Huntington's fame sometimes interfered with his ability fully to control the use of his name. An October 17, 1938, advertisement touting the English tourist resort Claxton-on-Sea said "Dr. Ellingsworth Huntingdon" had called it "the Best Climate in the world for human health."[26]

Huntington's rapprochement with the burgeoning cooling industry was furthered in 1922 when the National Research Council agreed to fund a Committee on the Atmosphere and Man at the geographer's suggestion and named him its chair. The committee, composed of academics and physicians, had no overt commercial purpose, but the six-year-old NRC, the federal government's primary agency for coordinating scientific, business, and national defense initiatives, was already launched on a mission of making science a more "popular" and vital component of American culture.[27]

In February 1922, the panel issued a three-page statement in support of its request for an initial appropriation of $11,000. From the outset, there was special concern with the effects of high temperatures. "Formerly it was man's boast that he could go everywhere and live anywhere regardless of climate," the statement said in language clearly borrowed from GilFillan's 1920 article. "By means of clothing, houses, and artificial warmth he protects himself against low temperature, but millions of people every year are sick or die because man has not yet learned to protect himself against high temperature." Notwithstanding Huntington's earlier enthusiasm for the American climate, the mission statement gloomily asserted that even in the northern United States, "ideal conditions" could be found only in May or late September. During the rest of the year, bad climatic conditions "seem to be the cause of a vast amount of poor and inefficient work, bad temper, misunderstandings, and many other evils," including "moral weakness" and poor health due to "unfit" conditions of the air.[28]

Huntington proposed to launch three simultaneous projects, all of which meshed neatly with his own geographic research. He planned to study correlations between mortality and weather in New York City; expand his work-site efficiency studies of factory operatives; and conduct lab experiments to test the effects of temperature on infants and young animals on the assumption that babies are routinely kept too warm. Huntington even dared dream of a tropical laboratory, should sufficient funds become available. The committee's work would be *Civilization and Climate,* then undergoing revision, brought to concrete and practical life. Huntington spent months trying to entice corporate support for his proposed investigations. The response was lackluster at best. A number of industries spurned the committee on the grounds that its studies would just upset workers without providing any useful application to actual factory conditions. In May 1922 a new round of solicitations elicited a flat refusal from John B. Berryman of the Crane Company. "It is well known that on a hot and humid day production falls off but as we are unable to control atmospheric conditions, an investigation designed to establish this fact seems futile," said Berryman. Yet by summer Huntington and the committee had somehow assembled enough participants to launch the study in December. This start-date suggests that Huntington and his colleagues were still more concerned about winter overheating indoors than they were about hot summer weather outdoors.[29]

Huntington's difficulty in gaining the cooperation of bosses such as Berryman—twenty years after Carrier's first factory installation in Brooklyn—would become a recurring theme in air-conditioning's industrial history. Air-conditioning's acceptance by factory owners and managers would lag for decades. A professional journal reported in 1956 that less than one percent of the nation's factories were air-conditioned. Even in the South, where air-conditioning was christened in 1906, the technology made little headway. Working in the nineteen-fifties and sixties as a cotton spinner in the aptly named Amazon Mill in Thomasville, North Carolina, Clara Thrift recollected dripping with sweat and choking on lint particles that filled the humid air. "The department I worked in was not air-conditioned at all," she said. As late as 1965, Thrift added, "we left the doors open at night hoping some night air would come through."[30]

In the first quarter of the twentieth century, the notion that machinery could cool and control air moisture might have been expected to appeal to the new breed of scientific management engineers who singlemindedly pursued labor efficiency and industrial productivity. Yet the transatlantic circle of scientists, engineers, and reformers who "invented" the idea of human fatigue seem to have taken almost no notice of issues of seasonality and workplace thermal conditions. Fatigue specialists' main goal was to extract maximum productivity from the individual human "motor" and the workforce "mechanism." Their methods generally included better wages and shorter hours to encourage more efficient work, or imposed tighter supervision and more streamlined procedures to compel it. That there might be specific and manageable workplace conditions of heat and humidity that impeded worker efficiency was not a central concern.[31]

Frederick Winslow Taylor, America's best-known advocate of scientific management, focused his efforts on the "factory system," a masculine realm within which men fabricated such mighty products as steel and engines. Frank Gilbreth, Taylor's most prominent disciple until he and his psychologist wife Lillian Moller Gilbreth fell out with Taylor in the teens, was a bricklayer by training. Even though Taylor was a cousin of labor and consumer crusader Florence Kelley, neither he nor the Gilbreths showed any special interest in the evocatively named "sweating system." In the nineteenth and early twentieth century, the sweatshop came to define a form of labor exploitation that preceded the advent of air-conditioning and has persisted since. In these sweatshops, concentrated on New York's Lower East Side, a primarily immigrant and female workforce produced soft goods in basements, lofts, and other makeshift workrooms, and were usually paid by the piece. "I used to work in a shop that didn't even have a window—a real sweatshop," garment worker Mabel Frazier of Harlem, a 1963 retiree, told a reporter in 1975.

The Gilbreths advised plant managers to consider indoor climate, but only as a minor factor affecting worker output. Although they favored an "oversupply" of fresh air "unless the work itself demands peculiar temperature or humidity conditions," the possibility of mechanical air-conditioning was not specified. Meanwhile, the nascent International Ladies Garment Workers Union concentrated on wages and hours and on the hazards of tuberculosis and fire in the crowded sweatshops.[32]

Even though its factory studies moved slowly, Huntington's Atmosphere and Man panel could boast some results at the end of its first year. In February 1923, Metropolitan Life Insurance of New York, whose medical director Dr. Louis I. Dublin was a committee member, published a preliminary version of "Temperature and Mortality in New York City" in its regular *Statistical Bulletin*. The study used vital statistics from the years 1883 through 1888, the most recent available, to show how death rates vary with temperature. It also tried to determine what portion of this variation might be preventable. The study forthrightly proposed to revive a climatic or atmospheric theory of human health that the researchers felt had been slighted by Pasteurian germ theory and by modern ideas that attached greater significance to nutrition.

Death rates, the study showed, were lowest on days when the twenty-four-hour average temperature was between 60 and 75 degrees. Although the death rate increased rapidly at temperatures above 75°, low temperatures had seven times the ill effect, simply because there were seven days below 60° for each day above 75 degrees. Fewer than 10 percent of the days during the six years studied had averages above 75 degrees. What makes these results interesting is how the committee chose to interpret them. Cold temperatures were not blamed for high death rates on cold days. Rather, such factors as air contamination, bad ventilation, incorrect humidity, high indoor temperatures, and inadequate clothing were found to be at fault. Said the study: "It is not improbable that the benefit to be derived from the stimulus of going into the cold outdoor air in winter is greater than the harm due to chills" (page 6).[33]

High temperatures were not similarly exonerated, but were directly linked to higher death rates. This seemed to lend substance to GilFillan's argument that physical and mental progress were possible only in cool climates "since man has gradually learned to protect himself against the cold days of winter but hardly against the hot ones of summer." Years later, the *Washington Evening Star* would proclaim that Huntington and his committee had discovered and defined the "White Man's Ideal Day."[34]

2. No Calcutta

harles-Edward Amory Winslow, who reigned as America's foremost public health expert in what would be the golden age of American public health, had meanwhile launched his own investigations into the effects of temperature and air movement. Ellsworth Huntington's magisterial examination of climate and civilization only perfunctorily considered the efforts human technology had made to accommodate climate to human purposes. But Winslow began his own inquiry at the level of human physiology, focusing on such specific environments as factories, places of public assembly, and classrooms. His researches, undertaken in pursuit of specific public health objectives, aimed to connect the physical and chemical properties of air to respiratory health and disease prevention.

Unlike Huntington, Winslow not only was a popular success but also was highly regarded in academe. He was born in Boston in 1877 to Erving Winslow, a merchant who traced his ancestry to John Winslow, a founder of the Massachusetts Plymouth colony, and Catherine Reignolds, an English actress who introduced America to the plays of Ibsen. Charles taught at his alma mater, the Massachuetts Institute of Technology, and was curator of public health at New York's American Museum of Natural History from 1910 to 1922. Winslow in 1915 joined the faculty of Yale's Medical School where he was the Anna M. E. Lauder Professor of Public Health for thirty years.[1]

As he established himself between 1908 and 1913 as an expert on the practical consequences of ventilation, Winslow came out forcefully against lingering theories of miasmic "bad air" still widely current in this post-Pasteurian era. Physical conditions of heat and humidity, not invisible poisons, created discomfort and inefficiency; they also impaired or even destroyed health, Winslow would argue. Throughout his career, Winslow's touchstone for the worst that heat could inflict upon hapless humans was the Black Hole of Calcutta. This was the infamous—and possibly fictional—1756 incident in which an Indian ruler, Siraj-ud-daulah, the Nawab of Bengal, imprisoned 146 Englishmen in a tiny, airless dungeon cell superheated by the hot sun, killing all but twenty-three of them. This extreme illustration of the effects of heat on human survival was widely familiar and readily invoked during the late Victorian era of Winslow's youth. Whatever its truthfulness, it remains an easily grasped racial parable of wretchedly maladapted Europeans confronting malevolent tropical despots who summoned climate as their weapon.

Winslow's first published ventilation article, "The Cash Value of Factory Ventilation," while stressing tuberculosis prevention, also offered some interesting insights, of the kind missing in the work of efficiency experts, into the relationship between heat and working conditions. Sixty female employees at the New England Telephone and Telegraph Company of Cambridge, Massachusetts, served as his experimental subjects. In 1907 a seventy-five-dollar ventilating system, intended for winter amelioration and consisting of forty-three feet of perforated iron ductwork and two sixteen-inch electric fans, was installed along the ceiling of the workroom. In summer, Winslow reported, "no direct effect could be expected . . . since in warm weather, with windows open, natural ventilation of the room could scarcely be improved upon." But during the winter months, absences due to illness dropped significantly, he found, and the favorable effect carried over into an unusually hot summer in 1908. Perhaps, he speculated, the "good air" provided by the fan-duct system in winter made the workers "better able to stand the general strain of hot weather conditions. . . . The employees are women, and therefore more susceptible to unfavorable influences than men would be."[2]

Throughout his long career, Winslow would attack what he called the "vicious national habit" of winter overheating, saying that high indoor temperatures were the single most pressing problem of factory air. His insistence on the efficacy of open windows, a view he shared with antituberculosis activists and other fresh air advocates, gained him—in the teens and twenties—a reputation as a fresh air "nut," and was soon to catapult him into serious conflict with promoters of mechanical ventilating systems. As early as 1912, though, Winslow was attracted to the idea of artificial summer cooling. In an article he published in both medical and engineering journals, his advocacy of fresh-air ventilation was tempered by the obvious appeal of man-made systems. After expressing general agreement with a "strong movement today in many quarters to cast aside entirely ventilation by fans and to rely on open windows alone," Winslow wrote admiringly of a New York bank in which air temperature was maintained at 10° below outdoors. In hot weather, said Winslow, there was "just one serious trouble. . . . People who come in can never be persuaded to leave." He went on:

> It is somewhat strange that we freely pour out money to heat and even overheat our buildings in winter and seldom think of cooling them in summer. . . . If we should cease to accept summer heat as a dispensation of Providence . . . this procedure might be used to an extent now undreamed of.[3]

Years would pass and much controversy ensue before Winslow would again express such a positive view of mechanical air-conditioning, although when he did it would give his endorsement enormous credibility both inside and outside the industry.

Governor William Sulzer in June 1913 appointed Winslow as chairman of the New York State Commission on Ventilation. Sulzer would not survive his first year in elected office. In a political test of wills pitting Democratic Party factions, he was impeached in September and removed by the state legislature in October of that year. The six unpaid members of the Winslow panel nevertheless soldiered on until 1917, although their final report was delayed by World War I and was not issued until 1924. The comission was inescapably allied with a particular ideology of American urban improvement. Established by New York State, as its stationery announced, "at the request of the New York Association for Improving the Condition of the Poor," it owed its $189,000 budget to Elizabeth Milbank Anderson. A major benefactor of Barnard College, Mrs. Anderson donated more than nine million dollars to settlement houses, social work agencies, and health research between 1905 and her death in 1921, at which point the Milbank Memorial Fund continued—and still continues to this day—its work of improving the "physical, mental, and moral condition of humanity."

In the teens, Mrs. Anderson became seriously concerned that stuffy air in schoolrooms was impeding student performance. She had come to recognize, Winslow said at the Milbank Fund's twenty-fifth anniversary dinner, held in April 1930 at New York's Park Lane Hotel, "that sickness is a major factor in poverty and that an unwholesome environment is, in turn, a fertile cause of sickness." He called his speech "The Living Hand: Elizabeth Milbank Anderson," distinguishing his benefactor from adherents of what Winslow had for years called "the dead hand" of overheating and poor ventilation.[4]

Her attention, said Winslow, "was called to conditions in the Lower East Side of New York where she saw crowded tenements and unsanitary streets swarming with dirty children." Her foundation and the commission it funded shared a set of assumptions that looked to the schools as the key institution capable of turning a wretched immigrant population into productive Americans through the provision of pure food, water, milk, and, in this case, air. The right kind of influences on the young—later labeled "positive environmentalism"—would promote a more progressive society and a higher form of civilization. Bad influences, including bad air, were a reason for social despair and moral panic.

Correspondence between Winslow and Ellsworth Huntington began in 1913, months before the commission on ventilation was formally announced, when Huntington wrote Winslow to thank him for information on the new investigative body and to ask about Winslow's research plan. In keeping with his own changeability thesis, Huntington was especially curious to know if hot weather might be shown first to stimulate but later enervate workers and students. The geographer recommended that schoolrooms be kept at 60° with 75 percent relative humidity, showing again his "coldward" proclivities and basic affinity with the fresh-air position. Winslow's commission ultimately recommended an indoor temperature of 66°–68° Fahrenheit with 50 percent relative humidity. Like his Yale colleague, Winslow practiced what he preached (figure 6). In 1944, when he was 67 years old, Winslow complained that Yale's lecture halls were overheated to 80°, telling his "Principles of Public Health" class that he kept his own home at 50° and his laboratory at 60° during the winter. It was common knowledge that Winslow daily walked the two miles to and from his office.[5]

By 1916 Huntington had published *Civilization and Climate* and the two men had become colleagues at Yale. "I have 'Civ. and Climate' with me this summer and admire it more than ever. It is one of the few books that mark an epoch!" Winslow wrote Huntington in July. He had already publicly praised the book, calling it "stimulating and original," although he mildly chastised Huntington for work more "popular" than rigorous. Winslow went on to link the geographer's ideas to the practical problem of salutary and sanitary air:

> If the conclusions drawn by Prof. Ellsworth Huntington in his striking book are confirmed by future study, countries whose natural climates do not conform to the ideal he has worked out may find it possible to produce and maintain on an extensive scale those artificial conditions of coolness and changeableness which he finds necessary to stimulate the highest human efficiency.[6]

By the early twenties the two men were freely and enthusiastically quoting one another. Huntington found in Winslow's work the physiological evidence that

6. Although he was not an air-conditioning engineer, public-health physician C.-E. A. Winslow, shown in his Yale Medical School office in 1939, played a central role in its success by affirming the safety and desirability of mechanical cooling.

gave a more profound scientific dimension to his speculations. For Winslow, Huntington's brand of geography provided a grand theoretical framework that lent a universal significance to Winslow's sanitary and health concerns. Not just a roomful of immigrant school children but America's world position was at stake.

While Huntington chaired his Committee on the Atmosphere and Man, Winslow was active as a paid consultant. At the Fisk Rubber Company in Chicopee Falls, Massachusetts; at Ellis Island in New York harbor; and, in the winter of 1924–1925, at Manhattan's 4,000-seat Metropolitan Opera House, Winslow conducted ventilation studies. He focused on artificial overheating almost exclusively, virtually ignoring summer heat issues. As Winslow explained in the Fisk report, "we dress lightly in summer and keep our windows open to secure the beneficent cooling effect of a breeze. . . . The human body becomes gradually acclimated to the increasing heat of the summer season."[7]

Huntington wrote in August 1924 to tell Winslow that he planned to mention the just-published New York State Ventilation Commission report in his new edition of *Civilization and Climate*. So he did, adopting Winslow's recommendation that "every effort should be made to keep the temperature of the schoolroom, the workroom, and the living room at 68°F or below." In his 1926 popularized version of the Ventilation Commission report, Winslow in turn cited

Huntington extensively. Huntington, Winslow wrote, had put the idea of the influence of climatic conditions "upon a sound statistical basis." "It will be obvious," he added, "that these zones of ideal climate correspond exactly to the centers of culture which dominate the world today."[8]

Winslow's chairmanship of the Ventilation Commission placed him at the very center of the long-running battle between advocates of fresh—and cold—air and those who believed that mechanical systems of air distribution were needed to insure healthy indoor conditions. Public health historian John Duffy has noted that the "replacement of the miasmatic theory of disease by the germ theory merely changed the rationale for justifying fresh air." In New York City in 1902, five schools built open-air rooftop playgrounds (oddly analogous to the rooftops where tenement families fled summer heat) to foster their young charges' vigor in all seasons. Yet, just four years later, the city began installing mechanical ventilation in all its schools.[9]

Governor Sulzer's appointment of Winslow, an expert whose endorsement of fresh air was already on the public record, made it fairly obvious what kind of conclusions the Ventilation Commission would draw. Most people agreed it was a good idea to keep air moving indoors; arguments erupted over whether the air should be "natural" or "artificial" in its origin and method of distribution. Both sides used the health of public schoolchildren as their raison d'être and state and municipal legislatures as their battleground, with engineering interests often the victors.

The decisive showdown took place in Buffalo on January 28, 1926, during the thirty-first annual convention of the American Society of Heating and Ventilating Engineers (ASHVE). Almost three years earlier, the engineers had named their own experts to assess the Winslow commission's report, taking care to pick members "in no way interested commercially" in the outcome of the debate.[10] This ultimate encounter between Winslow's seemingly dogmatic fresh air position and the engineers' equally self-righteous endorsement of air-moving machinery would focus on ventilation, not air-conditioning properly defined. But by that day's end, the *idea* of air-conditioning emerged considerably elevated in prestige and importance, and with a very important new ally and advocate—ASHVE's erstwhile bogeyman, Charlie Winslow.

Along with greater knowledge of air chemistry had come new explanations for "bad air" and competing proposals for its alleviation. Did the air in a building seem stuffy? Perhaps it was low in oxygen and high in potentially enervating carbon dioxide. Or maybe it was just too still or too warm. Did human breathing and sweating produce toxic substances that lingered in air exhaled too many times? The very idea of "bad air," as opposed to air that was simply uncomfortable or unpleasant, gives some notion of the strong passions aroused by these debates. Highly regarded and well-organized, engineers were well placed to persuade local governments to invest in new "scientific" approaches to old problems of building performance. They would have been joined in their blandishments by sheet metal fabricators and fan manufacturers. Local officials very likely would be more interested in spending public money (some of which might remain in their own pockets) on sophisticated mechanical ventilation systems than adopting cheap, "natural" methods like open windows that enriched no one. Besides, as Gail Cooper points out, only the most zealous fresh-air advocates were prepared to argue that there was anything "fresh or natural about the fouled air of modern cities."[11]

At least half the states and dozens of municipalities by the late teens had legislated ventilation standards for public schools that could only be implemented with mechanical equipment. Yet, as Winslow's panel was to conclude, schoolrooms were routinely overheated in winter as janitors stoked furnaces to counteract the drafty effects of mechanical systems designed to blow air around at a rate of thirty cubic feet per person per minute. In a June 1925 article titled "The Dead Hand in School Ventilation," Winslow repeated his by now ritual invocation of the Black Hole of Calcutta as he called the thirty-cubic-foot regulation a costly "fetich" that actually damaged student health. It was an uphill battle. Of 700 school buildings built in the United States since 1918, Winslow acknowledged, 513 were equipped with mechanical ventilation.[12]

Winslow mounted a well-publicized and broad-based national "open window" campaign in 1924 and 1925, enlisting antituberculosis groups, fifteen thousand school superintendents, and the American Public Health Association, whose president he was in 1925–1926. That influential national body resolved unanimously that systems of mechanical ventilation wasted thousands of dollars and were "positively harmful to the health of school children."[13]

Just a few weeks before Winslow's confrontation with the engineers in Buffalo, Perry West, former chief engineer for the Newark Board of Education and a member of the ASHVE panel assessing the commission's findings, had written to Winslow's friend and colleague, Ellsworth Huntington, imploring him to help ASHVE rebut Winslow's recommendations. West's letter was rancorous:

> While natural ventilation may suffice in many cases, if anything more than the uncertain hap hazzard vagrancies [sic] of ordinary weather are desired, mechanical ventilation must be employed. . . . [The Winslow recommendations compare with] the overthrow of the Russian government and the temporary reign of Bolshevism.[14]

Huntington responded quickly, although he ignored West's invective and avoided any direct criticism of Winslow. Tentative results from his own experiments at Westinghouse, said Huntington, showed that uniform indoor conditions would produce the best work in all seasons. "If the records from other factories substantiate this," the geographer wrote, seeming to abandon his former advocacy of climatic changeability, "it means that air-conditioning has a much greater importance than almost anyone except a few enthusiasts has ever realized." Huntington declined to attend the upcoming showdown but was invited in February to join an advisory board charged with revising the annual ASHVE *Guide*, bible of the industry. He accepted, commencing a formal association with the engineering group that would endure for more than a decade.[15]

Winslow began his January 28 address deferentially. He praised the engineering "art" and assured his audience that biologists and engineers "are all engaged in one common task, the promotion of the health and well-being of mankind" (page 119).[16] But he soon plunged into those fundamental criticisms of heating and ventilating practice that he had already broadcast widely in his "dead hand" articles and speeches. He told the skeptical engineers that a "large thermometer with 68 degrees Fahrenheit clearly indicated as a danger point should be displayed in a prominent position on the teacher's desk" (page 124).

The assembled engineers relished the chance to talk back to their nemesis. In a comparatively restrained statement, Perry West bemoaned this "chaotic and hysterical period" for mechanical ventilation, a period to which he had contributed his own hysteria. Winslow's solutions, he said, were seductively simple but unworkable. He cited, without direct attribution, Huntington's finding that "men do their best work at about 70 degrees and 40 percent humidity and women at 78 degrees" (page 133). If engineers were to be prohibited from modifying schoolroom conditions, as Winslow seemed to suggest, they would be "allowing the school-children to stew in their own juice at the mercies of the vagrancies of window ventilation" (page 136).

The afternoon's strongest attack was delivered by F. Paul Anderson, who, as engineering dean at the University of Kentucky and second director of the ASHVE research lab, was one of the association's most distinguished members. Delivering what he called a "manifesto for progress against primitivism," Anderson labeled Winslow a "fundamentalist," comparing him to William Jennings Bryan, who had become the laughingstock of the scientific community during the recent Scopes Monkey Trial. The Yale expert, said Anderson, was out of his scientific depth. The engineer, declared Anderson, could and would develop and provide "perfect" ventilation:

> He is making God's forces and materials do his work systematically and positively. This suggestion that we go back to the open-window ventilation is out of harmony with all the progress man is making. . . . The ventilating engineer resents a suggestion so primitive and so unprogressive (page 156).

When it was all over at six that Thursday evening, Winslow was unbowed, despite having been assailed by West as a communist and scorned by Anderson as a fundamentalist within the space of a month. He called the three-and-a-half hour session "delightful" and "stimulating," characterized by "frankness" and "good sportsmanship." Obviously charmed, the assembled engineers adjourned the intense and argumentative session with a "rising vote of thanks."

In the ensuing weeks, rapprochement between Winslow and the industry proceeded swiftly. This new era of good feeling was facilitated by the ascendancy of air-conditioning, as the engineer-practitioners of mechanical cooling began to claim a central role in ASHVE. While engineers, physicians, and social reformers had been debating the fine points of fan speed and window size and position, air-conditioning was fundamentally changing the meaning of ventilation. Winslow had seen real promise in air-conditioning as early as 1912 when it was a fledgling technology used primarily in a few factories. By 1926, air-conditioning could be found in movie theaters, stores, and other places of public assembly. If it could fulfill its advocates' promises of clean air, cooled and dehumidified—or heated and humidified—to a level consistent with the season and human comfort, then air-conditioning might provide what mechanical ventilation alone never could: an improved, less drafty, and consistent indoor climate, complete with air that if not actually fresh might certainly seem fresh.

Winslow seems to have met with Willis Carrier and other ASHVE leaders in May 1926 for a friendly exchange of views. The New York Commission on Ventilation was reconstituted in 1928 without state sponsorship but with a renewed grant from the Milbank Fund and, it appears, its chairman's pledge to take a fresh look at a variety of school ventilation issues. Re-formed, the commission invited ASHVE to appoint three of its members to help run school-room tests and even backed away from Winslow's crusade to repeal state laws requiring certain standards of air movement and mechanical ventilation. In its 1931 report, the revamped Winslow commission would endorse fan ventilation, with the recommendation that air volume and speed be halved.

Another indication of air-conditioning's growing clout within the realm of thermal engineering was the creation in 1929 of a new journal named *Heating, Piping & Air-Conditioning*. Willis Carrier, in the inaugural issue's lead article, predicted an air-conditioned brave new world. Perry West asked Winslow in April 1931 to join Ellsworth Huntington on a panel charged with revising the 1929 ASHVE *Guide*. Apparently West had by then absolved him of the charge of Bolshevism.[17]

Winslow became an ASHVE member a year later and was chosen by John B. Pierce, president of American Radiator and Sanitary Standard Corporation—an important heating and air-conditioning manufacturer—to head a new laboratory of hygiene that Pierce had endowed in New Haven. The John B. Pierce Foundation Laboratory continues to this day to research air conditions as they relate to physiology and comfort. More recently, the laboratory has investigated environmental quality, institutionalizing the kinds of early studies undertaken by Winslow and Huntington. Huntington was on the guest list for the November 4, 1933, public reception at the newly completed laboratory on Congress Street and was a regular and welcome visitor. Geoffrey Martin writes that "experimental work at the laboratory seemed to confirm the validity of Huntington's earlier work on climatic optima."[18]

Winslow served as ASHVE's president in 1945 and was named a life member in 1948. In 1950 he accepted the professional association's highest honor, the F. Paul Anderson Medal "for meritorious service." This gold-colored medallion, about one and a half inches in diameter, bears a high relief bust of Anderson on one side and on the other, alongside the recipient's name, two stylized female nudes, one working a bellows while the other hovers above a dish engulfed in flame. Willis Carrier had been the medal's first recipient in 1932. The medal memorialized the engineering dean who had likened C.-E. A. Winslow to William Jennings Bryan twenty-four years earlier.[19]

Their long association and mutual expressions of admiration notwithstanding, Winslow and Huntington were evolving differing and at times contradictory perspectives on the potential role and social impact of air-conditioning. The air-conditioning industry would have no trouble turning both men's visions to the proximate purpose of promoting its products. Although they shared a Eurocentric notion of civilization that equated cold climate to societal "virility," Winslow was a Democrat who supported women's suffrage well before 1920, played an instrumental role in creating public housing, and advocated national health insurance in the nineteen thirties and forties. Huntington, a Republican, turned his major energies in the 1930s to the work of the American Eugenics Society. Although the two men would serve, separately and together, on a variety of ASHVE committees, study groups, and technical advisory panels, in 1941—by this time he was being addressed as "Dear Charlie"—Winslow declined Huntington's invitation to participate in a eugenics conference.[20]

Winslow, the ameliorist, believed that an environment that included technological improvements could overcome human shortcomings resulting from both environmental conditions and biological factors. Huntington, the determinist, clearly viewed many ethnic and racial groups as less capable of leadership, holding out little hope—for black Americans in particular— that modern technology could overcome inherent genetic deficiencies bred by millennia spent in the humid heat of Africa and in the southern states.

Although Huntington's essentialist racial views colored all his endeavors, they were most overtly stated in his 1938 book, *Season of Birth*. Inspired by his sociologist friend S. Colum GilFillan's assertion that a disproportionate number of the world's greatest men were born between December and April, Huntington set out to prove it with his customary mix of scientized data and cultural certitude. Huntington scholar John E. Chappell Jr. summarized the *Season of Birth* argument this way: In backward nations, most babies are born in spring, giving them better access to food and the greatest chance of survival. In culturally advanced nations like the United States most births occur in late summer and early fall. Despite this shift, related in an ill-defined way to technological progress and the creation of artificial environments, the most energetic, talented, and long-lived people are still born according to the original seasonal plan.

Huntington was maddeningly vague about the importance of differentiating between conception and birth. In a letter to GilFillan in September 1936, Huntington wrote, "I find that the month of birth, or rather, of conception, is a very important matter." In a 1938 essay for the *Good Housekeeping Marriage Book*—to which Eleanor Roosevelt was one of eleven cocontributors—Huntington was somewhat more explicit. June, he declared, was the ideal month for conception; midwinter months were worst:

> A study of season of birth in many countries indicates that children who are conceived when optimum weather [daily average of 63°] . . . arrives in the spring have stronger constitutions and greater powers of application than do those conceived at any other season.

Huntington concluded that in any case a significant number of the famous men he picked from standard reference works were born in February and March. This birth timetable would require the mothers of these "great men" to endure pregnancy during the hottest summer months. Winslow was among Huntington's friends who teased that, just as the geographer had discovered the world's ideal climate in Connecticut, he was now trying to prove himself born at the ideal time. But Huntington readily admitted that his birth month of September was only middling in desirability. The skeptical Winslow was born in February.[21]

The popular press bestowed extensive and respectful comment on Huntington's book, responding to what would, to most of their readers, sound like a renowned expert's validation of common sense.[22] Not all were persuaded. The *Chicago Tribune* of December 31, 1937, printed a letter from L. O. Sweeney of De Paul University who cribbed from sociologist Pitirim Sorokin's 1928 analysis to attack Huntington, GilFillan, and all the "fallacious theories and fictitious correlations of the geographical school of sociology." These, said Sweeney, were better suited to astrology than to science. The space and prominence the *Tribune* had accorded Huntington's birth-season theorizing, Sweeney added, meant, that the "eugenists' worries are over. Air-conditioning business should skyrocket during July for those who overlooked the magic mean 63 degrees Fahrenheit of June."[23] Sweeney's sarcasm was lost on the air-conditioning industry. Huntington's season-of-birth theory could be and was used by the industry to enhance its argument that cooling was not just a suspect indulgence in personal comfort but a matter of national necessity and civic well-being.

If the industry could find promotional opportunities in Huntington's work, it was even easier to "sell" the idea of air-conditioning by reference to experts who believed it could fundamentally change the exigencies of human existence. Exponents of geographical explanations of human advancement, including Winslow, did not discard GilFillan and Huntington's "coldward" thesis, but incorporated the potential of artificial cooling into their prognoses for civilization. A good example was Englishman Sydney F. Markham whose *Climate and the Energy of Nations* appeared in 1942 in the United States and, despite wartime publishing constraints, was reprinted in an enlarged and revised edition in 1944. Focusing heavily on the climatic destiny of the United States, the book bore the imprimatur of the ASHVE hierarchy and was enthusiastically received in air-conditioning industry circles.

At Markham's invitation, Ellsworth Huntington proofread the 1944 edition and the author thanked Cyril Tasker, director of research at ASHVE's Cleveland laboratory, for helpful suggestions. Tasker later wrote a favorable review. Although objecting mildly to Markham's assertion that climatic problems in the United States might impede national progress, Tasker was satisfied that the author "agrees, however, that the United States is solving this problem in another way, namely, by a great expansion in environmental control by the use of air-conditioning."[24]

Markham did not view the effects of climate on the human species as innate or unalterable. Rather than moving inexorably north, Markham posited that "civilization follows man's control of his own environment" (page 213). He also situated the frontier of human progress at a mean annual temperature of 70°, not GilFillan's 50° isotherm (figure 7). Markham wrote "I am convinced that one of the basic reasons for the rise of a nation in modern times is its control over climatic conditions: that the nation which . . . will lead the world is that nation which lives in a climate, *indoor and outdoor,* nearest to the ideal" (page 20, emphasis added).

No country has a naturally ideal climate, wrote Markham, and in the United States forty million people, especially those of the "humid South," continued to

20°C isotherm (c. 70°F)

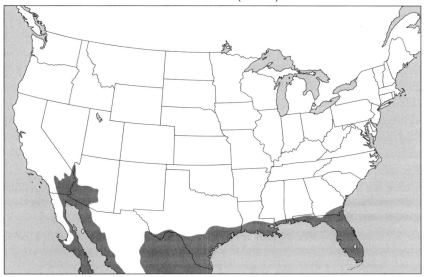

10°C isotherm (50°F)

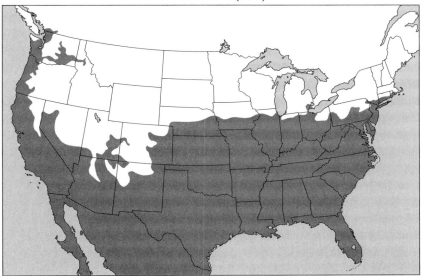

7. By choosing the 70° isotherm (~20°C) to mark the borderline of civilization, British writer Sydney Markham in 1942 included almost twice as much of the United States as S. Colum GilFillan had twenty-two years earlier when he held out hope only for those parts of the continental United States where the mean annual temperature was 50° (10°C) or less.

labor under major climatic handicaps. He used this proposition to explain, among other things, the northern states' "energy" and the South's loss of the Civil War. Because almost half of the forty-eight states, wrote Markham, suffer between one and five months annually of weather that hinders efficient work habits, immigrants from colder European countries are in danger of losing their native vitality. Even domestic animals in the southern states are not exempt from heat's perils, but require air-conditioned stables to retain their "virility unimpaired." Markham predicted that rural areas of the United States would lag until air-conditioned tractors and jeeps could be provided to farmers (pages 168, 215).

There was air-conditioning, fortunately, to mitigate climatic stress and cure the United States' obvious climatic defects, although Markham was mindful that artificial cooling was neither inexpensive nor universally available:

> At present, methods of cooling and dehumidifying a house to any extent are beyond the means of most workers in any country. Air-conditioning, fans, and dehumidifiers are . . . becoming more and more common a feature of the houses of the well-to-do in the United States and Canada, but even this is not sufficient to justify us in considering the control of high temperatures . . . as within the power of the masses of any country (page 103).

But, he said, air-conditioning would be America's great hope for physical, mental, and moral progress. Markham excluded no race or regional group from his prescriptive vision:

> The Mason-Dixon line, instead of being the boundary between initiative and conservatism, may become the axis of culture. . . . The greatest contribution to civilization in this century may well be air-conditioning—and America leads the way. . . . The Negro may yet reach heights of intellectual attainment undreamt of by Booker T. Washington . . . may, by climate control, leap forward again into the van of scientific progress (pages 205, 213).

It was a message well chosen to promote wartime confidence and set forth a future that could be embraced by those, like Winslow, who were receptive to racial differences and found in eugenics too narrow a view of human potentialities. In his annual climate lecture at Yale in 1944, Winslow suggested that the effects of high temperatures might differ depending "on what people are used to." Alluding to a graph, he said, "That is the colored race and the colored race like it a little hotter . . . somewhere around 66° instead of 64 degrees." Like Markham, Winslow did not believe the "darker" races were somehow doomed to tropical conditions.[25]

A generation after he had antagonized an entire industry with his misgivings about tampering with indoor air, C.-E. A. Winslow in 1949 summed up his career at the Pierce Laboratory in a way that unambiguously advocated the use of man-made methods to produce thermal comfort. In *Temperature and Human Life,* Winslow shifted his attention from air movement, or ventilation, to air temperature, devoting two full chapters to the objectives and methods of air-conditioning, based on the two lectures on air-conditioning he had delivered at Yale in 1944.[26] The purposes of his laboratory's research, Winslow said, had been to devise a thermal environment within which the human body is kept always at the optimally efficient temperature for doing its work, and to lay the "basis for a sound solution of the problems in the field of air-conditioning" (page viii).

Organized around Winslow's customary invocation of the Black Hole of Calcutta, the chapters on air-conditioning did not claim that the Pierce Lab, or anyone else, had resolved these problems. For one thing, a clear definition of thermal comfort was proving both elusive and extraordinarily subjective. Winslow and coauthor L. P. Herrington mentioned a 1947 study of ideal summer indoor office temperatures which showed that, at 74°, 15 percent felt too cold and 15 percent too warm. Winslow also conceded that the Pierce Lab had collected almost no experimental data on how women and older people reacted to temperature, humidity, and air movement. He urged more study. "After all," he wrote to University of Illinois engineering professor M. K. Fahnestock, "air-conditioning is not solely designed for the comfort of young men."[27] The effect on the body of passing between outdoor heat and indoor coolness and back again—the infamous air-conditioning "shock"—was described in *Temperature and Human Life* as "unpleasant and dangerous." Winslow also suggested it would be unrealistic for any but the "very elaborate house" to be equipped with year-round residential air-conditioning. He proposed alternative methods of promoting desirable indoor temperatures, such as house orientation, construction materials, and window placement.

There was very little left of what an engineering journal had once called Winslow's "window complex."[28] In his concluding chapter Winslow asserted the superiority of controlled indoor air to the variable outdoor product, saying "we must look to the creation of artificial climates by the air-conditioning of houses and schools and work places" (page 255). He accepted Huntington's connection between civilization and cool climates but endorsed the 70° isotherm as propounded by Markham. Air-conditioning, he predicted—now on the brink of its greatest growth—could be a tool that would allow all humanity to progress beyond the accidents of climate:

> Today we can cool in summer as well as we can heat in winter. The powerful and efficient nations of the past century have been those . . . where mean monthly summer temperatures of over 75° are rare. . . . May not vast areas in the subtropics become the seat of mighty civilizations as summer air-conditioning meets human physiological needs with similar efficiency (page 256)?

The coldward course of progress would not, after all, require the physical migration of vast populations, as envisioned by GilFillan and sanctified by Huntington's biologically deterministic version of human history. It would come instead at the hands of men like engineer-industrialist Willis Carrier who were bringing beneficent cold to people in places once written off the rolls of civilization. The Carrier Corporation's *Saturday Evening Post* ads of 1949 and 1950 would be the logical culmination of centuries of interpreting and reconfiguring the relationship between climate, heat, and human progress in America.

3. Pleasures and Palaces

*T*he Great Gatsby reaches its cruel climax on the day when Tom Buchanan learns of his wife Daisy's past affair with Jay Gatsby, and a hit-and-run driver mows down Tom's mistress, Myrtle. It happens to be, according to narrator Nick Carraway, the "certainly warmest" day of the summer of 1922 in which F. Scott Fitzgerald's novel takes place. At the Buchanans' Georgian Colonial house on Long Island Sound, awnings darken the French windows of the spacious salon. There, Daisy and her golfer friend, Jordan Baker, lie motionless on an enormous couch, wearing white dresses that billow in the "singing breeze of the fans."

After a hot, dusty automobile ride into Manhattan, this party of five fuels its underlying emotional turmoil with liquor in a stifling room at the Plaza Hotel where open windows admit only gusts of hot wind. Daisy, whom Nick later describes as "gleaming like silver, safe and proud above the hot struggles of the poor," tells Gatsby "you always look so cool." Only then does Tom Buchanan, a habitual adulterer with a taste for working-class women, suddenly understand that his wife has a connection with a man whose social position is ambiguous, to say the least. In 1922, coolness—here the ability to transcend hot weather—was the prerogative if not the outright birthright of the ruling classes.[1]

The 1920 U.S. Census had shown, for the first time, that the number of Americans living in urban areas exceeded the nation's rural population.[2]

Although "urban" was rather generously defined as a place with a population greater than 2,500, it was already obvious that patterns of seasonal behavior in America's most important cities were only superficially analogous to rural cycles of planting, growing, and harvest. Extreme weather events such as blizzards, thunderstorms, and heat waves might slow or delay the business of the largest cities but were almost never permitted to dictate the content or pace of city work and leisure.[3]

The opportunity to mark the seasons, as opposed to simply enduring them, was explicitly related to class. Wealthy city dwellers "summered" at the shore or in the mountains even though their spacious houses in town — or the Buchanans' suburban mansion — well before air-conditioning, were far pleasanter than the sweltering tenements of the poor. The exclusive shops and cultural institutions that catered to this clientele would close in summertime as well. In *Gatsby,* Jordan Baker, sensing the pending crisis of that "certainly warmest" day, urges a cooler alternative to drinking at the Plaza. "Those big movies around Fiftieth Street are cool," suggested Jordan. "I love New York on summer afternoons when every one's away." Her rather déclassé suggestion is ignored, and tragedy ensues.[4]

Before 1920, air-conditioning was used almost entirely in factories where its role was to produce not human comfort but manufacturing consistency. Under the controlled conditions of temperature and humidity that were made possible by this new apparatus, every bolt of cloth, stick of chewing gum, or machine-rolled cigarette was supposed to look and perform alike, no matter what time of day or season of year it was made. As air-conditioning expanded into new realms of urban pleasure and consumption, it would likewise be expected to produce consistency of results by smoothing seasonal fluctuations in the business cycle and "delivering" customers throughout the year. Factory air-conditioning was sold with promises of worker efficiency and product uniformity. The new "comfort" air-conditioning pledged an ideal day repeated over and over again, always the same and always dependable. Promising, as Carrier Engineering did in 1919, that "every day" would be "a *good* day," the air-conditioning industry set out to make nineteenth-century poet James Russell Lowell's "rare" day in June absolutely routine.[5]

In the factory or office, expectations of comfort necessarily took second place to the promise of a paycheck or the threat of its denial. But it took persuasion, not power, to mobilize and manage a growing urban middle class's desires for leisure and enjoyment. In splendid movie palaces and lavishly appointed and stocked department stores, the use of indoor climate control helped blur the boundary between the perquisites of the wealthy and the aspirations of the middle class.

Air-conditioning installed in opulent club cars and Pullman sleepers helped distinguish the rail experience from the primitive amenities of buses and automobiles, then interstate railways' chief transportation rivals. Air-conditioning would eventually help the grander hotels assert their claims to offer the most innovative comfort technology available. From 1829 onward, hotels in the United States fought to outdo one another in size and innovation, offering conveniences, gadgets, and comforts that even their wealthiest patrons could not yet buy for their own homes.[6] By mastering the capriciousness of heat, wind, dirt, and noise, these providers of consumer services expected to benefit from an expanding and reliable commerce in urban pleasure.

Air-conditioning's huge machinery and enormous expense, both heavily publicized, lent prestige and glamour to the establishments capable of installing it. A man or woman's encounter with air-conditioning was embedded in ideology even before it was experienced physiologically. It *felt* modern. The "shock" of exposure to refrigerated air on a scorching summer day, although criticized by engineers and disliked by some members of the public, was nonetheless an intrinsic part of the air-conditioning experience. It was a way to render the invisible "visible" to its new audiences.

Neither region nor climate can explain the distribution pattern of early comfort installations. Air-conditioning appeared first and expanded the fastest in the nation's most important—not its hottest—cities. Movie air-conditioning was pioneered in Chicago, New York, and Los Angeles. Although the fanciest movie palaces in places like Houston also added cooling, southern installations for many years constituted only a tiny segment of the total market. Air-conditioning expressed a city's influence and affluence, its aspirations to modernity and ability to control its domain. Not until the end of World War II did air-conditioning help turn population concentrations in the nation's hottest regions into fully urbanized areas. Nor was air-conditioning uniformly distributed within its largest markets. In hotels and on trains, air-conditioning was used first to cool dining areas and public rooms, rather than private guest rooms or passenger compartments. In department stores, basements were cooled long before plush upper-floor salons.

Implicit class and gender expectations shaped the decision to install air-conditioning, the choice of where and how to use it, and the manner in which it was advertised. Older institutions catering to the rich were slower to embrace the air-conditioned future. They also made more limited use of the apparatus and were more restrained in claims for its benefits. Where the new movie palaces used painted icicles and blazing marquees to proclaim the coldness within, not until 1935 did a "legitimate" Manhattan theater, the Henry Miller Theater, become the first traditional playhouse to install air-conditioning.

When air-conditioning was urged on a predominantly male clientele, it was depicted as an interlude of comfort to reward past achievements and as an impetus to greater business success. Air-conditioning in female-dominated venues, by comparison, stressed health, purity, and personal fastidiousness. Engineers who tried to enforce reasonable standards of air-conditioning use and performance were often horrified by customer practices and public attitudes that highlighted and exaggerated air-conditioning's power to make summer into winter.

"We can never explain demand by looking only at the physical properties of goods," anthropologists Mary Douglas and Baron Isherwood write in *The World of Goods*. Nor, they argue, can the emergence and success of various goods and technologies be adequately accounted for by simply looking at human physical needs. It may be true that there is a physiologically fixed and universally experienced minimal necessity for food or shelter but it is minimally explanatory. Goods are the visible markers of a continual process through which social relations are revealed, social values redefined, and social choices made. This process transforms oddities or novelties into luxuries, luxuries into necessities, and makes desirable goods seem indispensable. In the two decades before World War II, air-conditioning evolved from a ballyhooed novelty into a standard expectation among middle-class users of public facilities.[7]

In the early twentieth century, there were few places where an investment in human thermal comfort could return profits large enough to make the outlay worthwhile. Huge halls in which multitudes assembled for entertainment were an exception. Leisured throngs expected comfort, or at least the absence of discomfort, to be part of their interlude of paid enjoyment.[8] Mary Duffus Hardy, the English novelist who visited New York during the hot summer of 1880, marveled at the coolness in a theater crowded for a performance by Edwin Booth on a 100° day. "By some simple contrivance," she wrote, "the outer air, circulating through and among tons of ice, is forced to find its way through a thousand frozen cracks and . . . renders an afternoon in Madison Square Theater a luxury during the hottest of dog-days." But seventeen years later, engineer B. F. Stangland was less enthusiastic about the efficacy of theater cooling efforts. All newly built theaters in New York "will hang out their gorgeous posters saying: 'this theater is cooled by ice,'" he told his colleagues, but added that attempts to lower indoor temperatures just four to six degrees usually failed.[9]

Early in the new century, the ascendant public health profession pushed many local governments to legislate ventilation standards to protect theater patrons against such respiratory perils as tuberculosis. Although public health authority C.-E. A. Winslow and ventilating engineers disagreed about the air exchange needs of schoolchildren, the installation of vast mechanical systems in large

halls proceeded with little opposition and was assisted by the persistent if dis-
credited belief in the dangers of "bad air."[10]

When the promoters of motion pictures began relocating their spectacles from
neighborhood nickelodeons to deluxe downtown movie palaces accommodat-
ing thousands, air-conditioning would become not only financially feasible but
also an attraction in its own right.[11] As virtually the first public leisure spaces
equipped with effective air-conditioning, the movies easily differentiated themselves from most other urban entertainment choices. By promising to do more
for comfort and health than simply move air around, air-conditioning reinforced
the novelty, modernity, and luxury of the movie-going experience.

Chicago movie entrepreneurs Balaban & Katz hired a meatpacking refrigeration company to install cooling in their Central Park Theater in 1917. By
1921, they had cooled two more theaters, the Tivoli and the Chicago. Chicago's
Health Commissioner urged pregnant women and people with weak lungs to
frequent these movie houses, calling their air "purer than Pike's Peak." Almost
as heavily promoted as the films themselves, air-conditioning enabled movie
magnates to stem seasonal fluctuations and made their venues, unlike earlier
vaudeville and the legitimate theater, consistent year-round "manufacturers" of
reliable popular entertainment.[12]

The picture palace, which reached full flower in the nineteen twenties and
thirties, was a lower-middle-class fantasy of upper-class opulence with its gilded
balustrades and moldings, sumptuous restrooms, massive chandeliers, plush
seats, pipe organs, full orchestras, and deferential uniformed ushers. The sen-
sory environment that helped make movies wildly popular included not just
moving images and, later, sound, but a cool darkness that allowed the rapt
viewer to forget the time of day or the season of the year. Relatively low ticket
prices and convenient locations meant that this escape was affordable and accessible to moviegoers only slightly "classier" than those who had patronized
the less pretentious nickelodeons, provided they were willing to behave in keeping with the magnificence that surrounded them.

It also helped to be white. According to film scholar Douglas Gomery, until
the nineteen sixties overt policies and local custom made movie palaces, especially but not exclusively in the South, far less accessible to black audiences.
Methods included steering black patrons to inconvenient and less comfortable
seats, setting different viewing times for black and white audiences, and opening smaller, plainer movie houses in predominantly black urban neighborhoods.
Movie theaters in ethnically or racially segregated neighborhoods generally
lacked the palatial appurtenances, including air-conditioning, of the big downtown movie houses.[13]

There is little doubt that the expensive new technology thrilled patrons entering on a sweltering day. It is not as clear how much moviegoers, especially women who were already known to be more susceptible to chills, actually enjoyed the air-conditioned experience. Early patrons of air-conditioned movies would wrap their legs in newspapers to thwart cold drafts emitted by floor-level ventilators. Carrier Corporation cofounder and executive L. Logan Lewis admitted years later that this early refrigeration had "merely substituted one discomfort for another." The problem was partially corrected by engineer Lewis's invention of a new "upside-down" bypass system that cooled a smaller volume of air twice as much and redistributed it through ceiling outlets rather than floor vents.

On May 30, 1925, New York City's Rivoli theater just north of Times Square became the first movie palace equipped with bypasses. A brilliantly lit marquee announced "The Rivoli Cooled By Refrigeration Always 69 Degrees." The $100,000 cost of the installation at a time when the top ticket price was 75 cents was recouped—so Lewis would later claim—in just three months of summer operation. The "really cool" Rivoli boasted in its ads of "refrigerated mountain ozone," and advised patrons that "great refrigerating machines are at work all summer purifying and reducing the temperature . . . to just the desired degree."[14]

Air-conditioning did not so much change the way in which theater owners promoted the moviegoing experience as it altered the climate patrons actually encountered inside. As ventilating engineer Stangland had noted in 1897, the practice of advertising with icicles, pasteboard cutouts of snowy pines, and boasts of "20 degrees cooler inside" preceded any actual ability to provide specified temperatures within. Theater managers, Lewis recollected in 1963, had long used such images to lure customers into establishments that lacked the physical capacity to fulfill their promises. When Carrier installed a massive new system in Newark's Branford Theater in 1927, the manager insisted on keeping the temperature as low as possible. Letters from patrons complaining they had frozen or caught cold were so numerous that the manager featured them in a full-page newspaper ad, apparently reasoning that negative publicity was bet- ⋅ ter than none. The manager told Carrier that, "He had used the '20 degree cooler' sign for so many years that he had proven himself a liar and had to go to extreme measures to prove that he was now telling the truth."[15]

The engineering profession regularly protested the picture palaces' flamboyant promotion of their expensive new cooling systems, fearing that misuse of the technology would discredit air-conditioning among the very consumers the industry was working to impress. In 1929 Esten Bolling, a Carrier publicity engineer, attacked signs on "the ornate facades of sundry movie theaters that it is '20 degrees cooler inside.'" This, said Bolling, fools fewer each day as the public learns "that a mere sign, despite its dangling painted icicles, and a great rush of air through the entrance doors, do not connote air-conditioning, with its attendant comfort and health."[16]

Such warnings appeared to have little effect. As an irate E. Roger Hewitt wrote in the September 1932 issue of *Heating, Piping & Air-Conditioning:* "The public complains about the frigid temperatures of many theaters and auditoriums, and is gradually rebelling against the ice-box coldness. . . . It is the topic of cartoons, slap-stick comedy, and general comment." The indoor temperature, he advised, should never be set more than 12° below outdoors.

Physician and pioneering industrial hygienist Carey Pratt McCord tried in the late thirties to mobilize doctors against what he saw as air-conditioning abuse. Writing in December 1936 to the Pullman Company's house physician, McCord said he had heard many complaints "condemning air-conditioning" and anticipated "clinical disturbances resulting from exposure to unsuited air conditions in theaters, on Pullman cars, etc." By and large, he griped later, "too much is expected of air-conditioning."[17]

Hewitt's rebellion and McCord's "clinical disturbances" never really came to pass. In 1939 theater owners were still being exhorted to promote and use air-conditioning more scientifically. Icicles, snowdrifts, and igloos were ballyhoo that encouraged some patrons to avoid theaters on account of their coldness. "Never, never, never refer to air-conditioning in the terms of refrigeration and coldness," an article in *Better Management* asserted. Adherence to the "comfort zone" devised in 1923 by professional engineers would satisfy 97 to 98 percent of the audience, the article added.[18]

At the very same time as urban movie houses were offering patrons arctic conditions, drive-in movies emerged to challenge the idea that moviegoers more than anything wanted to escape summer heat. The first drive-in opened in June 1933 in Camden, New Jersey. Generally located on cheap vacant land on the urban fringe, drive-ins carved out a niche among families seeking a cheap outing and teenagers in search of privacy, achieving their greatest success in the fifties; by this time movie-house air-conditioning was commonplace.[19]

Movie theaters' apparent refusal to renounce their right to make patrons' teeth chatter could indicate that patronage was meeting their expectations or might reveal a fear that more moderate temperatures would disappoint patrons' expectations. The chill of the over-cooled movie palace demonstrated both its pleasurable novelty and conspicuous modernity. Movies were supposed to provide patrons an escape from ordinary life by making them feel different inside the movie palace than they did outside. Air-conditioning was part of the total entertainment experience. The sensations cooling produced, even if perceived

8. In 1940, air-conditioning was still a reason for celebratory promotion, as the arctic décor of this Chicago movie theater shows.

as discomfort, felt very different from the unpleasant and involuntary constraints of the stifling urban tenement or stuffy office (figure 8).

Moviegoer revolt was not apparent at the box office. Attendance at the 1800-seat Texan Theater in Houston soared over year-earlier levels after owner Will Horwitz Jr. installed an air-conditioning plant in 1926. It was one of the earliest movie air-conditioning installations in the South. Unlike most operators, Horwitz adjusted the auditorium temperature in consultation with actual customers. When patrons said the original setting of 72° was too cool, engineers raised the temperature a degree each week, finally settling on 76° with 55 percent relative humidity.

"With practically the same character of features, it was apparent that many patrons attended to get relief from the oppressive heat," the A. C. Nielsen Company reported in a June 1926 survey apparently commissioned by the Carrier Corporation. Before air-conditioning, "it was general practice for the producers to make the cheapest kind of a picture they could make for summer rentals," Logan Lewis recalled some thirty years later.[20] The Houston experience suggests that producers could continue to distribute "cheap" summertime pictures, now confident that theater cooling would draw huge crowds to see them. In any case, summer grosses in most cities were soon exceeding proceeds from what had formerly been the peak winter season. The air-conditioning industry set a 1936 sales record because its product seemed to be the single technological improvement that could boost movie-house business, or at least blunt Depression-era losses. By 1937, the Carrier Corporation alone had installed systems in 461 movie houses, more than half of them in the major cities of New York, California, Illinois, Ohio, and Pennsylvania.[21]

If the air-conditioned movie palace was a cheap form of mass entertainment laying claim to luxury and prestige, air-conditioning played a subtly different role in the venerable domain of consumption known as the department store. Its arrival came at a time when the grand urban emporium, beset by chain retailing, was beginning to decline in dominance and prestige. This signaled a shift from upper-class exclusivity to mass satisfaction; from a realm of expensive objects of desire protected by showcases and haughty saleswomen to tables loaded with bargains and self-service shopping.[22]

Like the movie palace, writes Rosalind Williams, the department store was spectacular in the most expansive sense: a theater of *things* in which potential consumers were the audience, permitted to gaze at objects they might never buy.[23] Like the movie-going experience, the department store experience offered visually seductive images and objects in a setting of cocoonlike comfort. As William Leach notes in his discussion of the American department store, such innovations as electric lighting, plate glass, and dazzling new modes of presentation turned department stores into quotidian world's fairs that offered a magical escape from the ordinary constraints of class, season, and geographic location. In the fairyland of the department store, as at the movies, respectable workingmen's wives and middle-class ladies could enjoy, perhaps even purchase a reasonable facsimile of the pleasures of the rich. John Wanamaker in 1906 actually called his grand Philadelphia department store "land of desire." It was a place dedicated to pleasure, security, comfort, and material well-being.

During its early golden age in the 1890s, the big city department store's main goal was to reinforce and exploit the customer's sense of her class position and personal attractiveness, staging a "drama of persuasion" that included lavish appointments, deferential service, and comforts that only the wealthiest customers would encounter in their own homes. Less daunting than such other palatial urban structures as the private mansion, public library, or marble-columned museum, the department store welcomed shoppers who dressed and behaved properly.

Detroit's first J. L. Hudson store opened in the ornate former Detroit Opera House in 1881. Nationally prominent architect Daniel H. Burnham designed William Filene's Sons new Boston store in 1912. These and similar palaces of commerce in major cities were gracious public spaces within which respectable women could see and be seen without reproach. Customers were valued not only for their disposable income but for the leisure they had to spend it impulsively. Shopping for such women was, like the picture show for a broader segment of the public, not a chore but an entertainment event or outing.[24]

Unlike the motion-picture palace, the department store could not charge its customers simply for walking into the building and looking. If patrons never bought anything, it would not ultimately matter how much they admired the store's elegance and comforts. Prior to the nineteen-twenties, department stores, while striving to maintain their status as palaces of consumption by providing lavish service and genteel surroundings, already faced a business need to appeal to the consuming masses and make the execution of each sale more efficient. The department store needed to become what Boston merchant and New Dealer Edward A. Filene would call in 1937 "a machine for selling." As scholar Susan Porter Benson points out, the very idea of trying to make every square foot of a "palace" produce revenue is a built-in contradiction.

One result of this evolution in retailing was the bargain basement. Filene's original basement store opened in 1900. When Chicago's magnificent twelve-story Marshall Field store opened amid civic fanfare in 1902 it, too, consigned bargains to the basement. By 1910, basements were commonly being used to sell unglamorous lower-priced goods, groceries, and housewares. This practice transformed "spartan" and previously wasted space into a revenue-producing zone and allowed stores quite consciously to segregate, by price, amenity, and decoration, their "salon" and "basement" customers. In Detroit, Hudson's, responding to a working-class population growing in size and affluence, opened a 25,000-square-foot basement store in March 1915. In its first year, sales were one million dollars; in 1916, the basement store posted a profit of almost 33 percent.[25]

The principal department stores were cautious users of new technologies. Air-conditioning was one of only three major developments in department store engineering between 1890 and 1940. The others were escalators and floor-through-construction that added selling space by eliminating the stores' traditional open-court or rotunda configuration, thereby creating enclosed spaces within which it was possible to calibrate temperature and humidity effectively.[26]

As early as the 1880s, Macy's, Wanamaker's, and Marshall Field had all experimented with air-moving systems. The first system capable of controlling both temperature and humidity was installed in 1924–1925 in the basement of Detroit's twenty-one-story Hudson's, the nation's tallest and third-largest department store in what was then the country's fourth-largest city. It cost Hudson's $250,000 to air-condition its basement, the equivalent of about two million today. Filene's added air-conditioning in 1926, but its four upper floors, each higher floor plusher than the one below it, remained unairconditioned until the mid-thirties.

Manhattan's Macy's, befitting its rank as the nation's largest emporium, installed retailing's largest air-refrigeration system in its 1.5 million-square-foot Herald Square store in 1929. Rich's of Atlanta opened its "great white store" on Whitehall Street in 1907 but did not until 1937 install air-conditioning in any department, including its twenty-acre basement store. No department store was fully air-conditioned before World War II. Heating and cooling improved in the "big commercial palaces," Leach notes, although not enough "to overcome completely the summer heat or winter cold that afflicted stores in what merchants called the 'dull season.'"[27]

In every case, air-conditioning was installed and operated in the lowly basement and heavily trafficked main floor years, even decades, before its extension to the department store's exclusive upper reaches and staff offices. At Hudson's, air-conditioning was extended to most public sales areas between 1935 and 1946, but it was 1953 before the entire store, including staff offices and work areas, was included.

Basement space in a large building is undoubtedly difficult to ventilate or cool in any nonmechanical way, yet bargain basements had clearly become popular sales spaces a decade or more before they were air-conditioned. Nor did department stores use air-conditioning as a reason to abandon traditional summer hours and seasonal promotional events. Like legitimate theaters, and unlike the movies, they expected their select patrons to be out of town in summer and their sales personnel to take time off. Department stores hesitated to sacrifice their reputation for luxury to their equally crucial efforts to make more intensive use of floor space and personnel. While more genteel and experienced women staffed the stuffy, opulent salons upstairs stocked with the finest and most expensive goods, it was standard practice to assign young, immigrant saleswomen to the basement. As one poetic basement saleswoman at Boston's elegant Jordan Marsh versified:

> Of course we admire the vast upstairs
> With its velvet carpets and easy chairs,

But it's nice to be serving the human throng
Down in the basement all day long.[28]

Heat was a problem for all ranks of department store saleswomen primarily because it severely affected customer traffic and compromised the merchandise. Pay packets, based largely on sales commissions, would plummet in July and August. In the summers of 1926 and 1927, Frances Donovan, a high school teacher by profession, worked "undercover" as a sales girl in several New York City department stores, producing a richly textured sociological study published in 1929. In the high-class department store she called "McElroy's," summer was when saleswomen's feet swelled, customers stayed away, and the perspiration of the few who shopped turned stylish crepe and georgette dresses into "drab, crushed" markdowns. Donovan remarked "not even the flowered chiffons can wave with any spirit in the suffocating breezes made by the electric fans." The "looker," a most undesirable sort of customer, was most likely the only kind of customer to show up on an oppressively hot day. Donovan's colleague enlightened her, saying "they can't afford to go to movies or theater . . . so they hang around department stores trying on dresses they can't afford to buy."[29]

On the evening of July 29, 1926, during a major heat wave that she called the hottest "known in New York for years," Donovan took part in "McElroy's" dreaded summer inventory, held after normal business hours. Attendance was mandatory; the store laid on a splendid but heavy supper, but the night porters had, as usual, closed all the windows, rendering the electric fans utterly ineffective. "My throat was choked with dust; my spectacles steamed with perspiration," said Donovan, who, by prearrangement and without revealing her real occupation, left the next day after five weeks on the job. She had earned $10 a week and $23.57 in commissions overall, despite the severe heat wave and a brief subway strike. It was a good job for a woman, Donovan would conclude in her study.[30]

The slow acceptance of storewide air-conditioning reflected not only its high cost but also a common belief that gentlewomen, and the type of women fit to serve them, were by nature and culture less bothered by heat. As a well-known proverb of rather obscure origin has it, horses might sweat and gentlemen perspire, but "ladies merely glow." The hope that modern grooming preparations could help ordinary strivers acquire the bodily mastery that supposedly came naturally to the upper classes fueled much of the "social anxiety" advertising that dominated the twenties and thirties.[31] Those few ladies who ventured into the department store basement supposedly did not require its coolness to maintain their daintiness or their bodily comfort. Rather, the chillier air and perhaps the breeze from a blower would assure them that both their persons and the goods on display were protected from the potentially unhealthful proximity of the sweaty "human throng."

So while movie houses equated air-conditioning with cold and cold with modern comfort, publicity for bargain basement air-conditioning instead emphasized purity and fastidiousness. Leach draws an apt contrast between the open-air markets of the poor and rural and the palatial urban store's plate-glass display windows where a profusion of goods was seductively accessible to the eye but not to the hand.[32] Like showcases that protected goods from weather, dirt, and the manipulations of the unworthy, air-conditioning—especially in the basement—shielded elite customers from the bodily exhalations of the unwashed. At a time when Filene's "automatic bargain basement" was thronged daily with "rich, poor, and average," demonstrating that even women of means craved bargains, ladies could shop there confident that both the merchandise and their own persons would remain pristine. If the "rich, poor, and average" also spent more in a cool environment, that was also a plus. The economics of the department store required the basement to contribute 15 percent of overall sales volume.[33]

Hudson's first air-conditioned summer in 1926, the same summer Frances Donovan was passing as a salesgirl in New York, started out uncommonly cool. A full-page ad for the basement store appeared in the *Detroit News* nearly every day. Amid the drawings of summer frocks, cheap shoes, domestic goods, and undergarments, boxed text promoted the basement's new climate in a style quite different from that used by the movies. There were no icicles. The term "air-conditioning" was not used. Instead the ads described an "improved" or "modern" ventilating system in terms of air movement and employed such key words as "fresh," "pure," and "healthful."

SHOP IN COMFORT the headlines proclaimed. PURE FRESH COOL AIR MAKES SHOPPING IN THE BASEMENT STORE A PLEASURE. IT'S COOL AND COMFORTABLE IN THE BASEMENT STORE. When the unusually cool summer gave way to the record-setting heat wave of July 1926, the size of these announcements swelled but not the rhetoric. ON WARM DAYS IT'S 8 TO 12 DEGREES COOLER IN THE BASEMENT STORE THAN STREET TEMPERATURE said one ad, although some others claimed a 15° temperature differential. On July 21, one of the hottest days, the store ad failed to mention basement cooling at all. This promotional restraint was at odds with the glee some Hudson's executives exhibited privately. Asked about the system's performance during the heat wave, Hudson's building superintendent on July 28, 1926, told Carrier the store was *"fifteen to twenty-five degrees* cooler than outside. . . . We have received many compliments from our customers on the air condition in our store" (emphasis added).[34]

By 1930 Hudson's considered its air-conditioning costs to be part of its ad-

There's a bargain in the basement

This is the J. L. Hudson Company department store in Detroit. And there's a bargain in the basement . . . a bargain that has been there for over 25 years.

For Hudson's was the first department store to provide air conditioning for the comfort of customers. And in the basement three Carrier Centrifugal Refrigerating Machines

—among the first built—are still providing refrigeration for Hudson's air conditioning.

These Carrier machines have company now, of course. Today Hudson's has 11 Carrier Centrifugal Refrigerating Machines . . . is completely air conditioned.

J. L. Hudson Company originally selected the then new Carrier Cen-

trifugal for these reasons: it used a safe refrigerant; it saved space; it could be automatically controlled. They tell us now that Carrier machines are efficient, vibrationless and remarkably low in maintenance cost. Clearly, they believe that Carrier is their best investment. And that's something for you to remember. Carrier Corporation, Syracuse, N. Y.

Carrier **AIR CONDITIONING**
REFRIGERATION
INDUSTRIAL HEATING

9. As late as 1950, Carrier still advertised its role in making Detroit's J. L. Hudson's the nation's first air-conditioned department store. Known as "The Grand Old Lady of Woodward Avenue," this downtown landmark closed in 1983 and was demolished on October 24, 1998.

vertising budget. In the wake of a "recent countrywide hot spell" in July 1934, Carrier's advertising department wired its department store clients to solicit testimonials. Filene's and Hudson's both telegraphed on July 18. "Our air-conditioning system is now so much a part of our basement that we would not consider for a moment operating without the comfort and shopping ease it produces," Filene's declared, adding "quite frequently the basement is an oasis for hot tired shoppers." Hudson's response was similarly enthusiastic:

10. The space-saving centrifugal compressor that made projects like Hudson's feasible was invented in 1922 by Willis H. Carrier. This unit was donated in 1960 to the Smithsonian Institution's permanent collection after thirty-eight years cooling Onondaga Pottery in Syracuse, New York.

> AS THE FIRST LARGE USERS OF AIR-CONDITIONING WE HAVE NEVER REGRETTED INSTALLATION [STOP] EFFECT ON BUSINESS HAS BEEN GOOD BEYOND QUESTION [STOP] DURING HOTTEST DAYS HAVE BEEN MAINTAINING INSIDE TEMPERATURES FROM SEVENTY TO EIGHTY DEGREES AS DESIRED [STOP] IF BUILDING AGAIN WOULD UNDOUBTEDLY AIR CONDITION WHOLE STORE [STOP][35]

Little wonder, then, that in 1950 Carrier was still using J. L. Hudson's 1926 installation in its advertising (figures 9 and 10).

Although department stores and movie theaters dealt differently with issues of class and comfort, both offered their palatial attractions primarily to women and their families. The promotional efforts of railroads and deluxe hotels, by comparison, focused on business travelers, who were almost all certainly male. These men of affairs, it was believed, would transform luxurious mobile accommodations and deluxe hotel sojourns into business effectiveness, helping the nation's economy by indulging themselves. Both long-distance trains and grand hotels were readily persuaded by air-conditioning manufacturers that they should be prepared to offer businessmen a seamlessly uniform experience of the United States's diverse regions and climates.

The newly air-conditioned dining car of the Atchison, Topeka & Santa Fe was introduced in August 1930 to a "select" group of businessmen. As the train rolled across the 118° Mojave Desert toward Needles, California, the inside temperature was kept at 68° and the smoke of the men's cigars "disappeared as if by magic." "This," warned an otherwise laudatory article, "was merely a demonstration, and not the temperature which experts believe proper for travelers in hot weather," adding, "ordinarily 75 or 78 will be maintained to avoid unpleasant possibilities due to sudden changes of temperature from diner to coach—for the air-cooling machinery is not yet applied to other cars."[36]

In August 1931, after its engineers felt they had worked out "bugs" in the pioneering cooling apparatus in the Baltimore & Ohio's Martha Washington dining car, Carrier invited two hundred "top brass" to a demonstration of an improved system. Logan Lewis proudly recalled the event years later:

> Small groups were led into a hot, humid, dusty enclosure. Then, when they had developed a good sweat, they were led into the cool, clean car. The contrast was simply unforgettable. . . . Whereas the theater had introduced air-conditioning to the masses, Pullman diners and sleepers introduced it to the man in a position to buy it to attract the masses.[37]

Train air-conditioning offered multiple engineering challenges. The equipment was extremely heavy and space-consuming, especially before the introduction in the thirties of the refrigerant Freon and the more compact machinery it used.

Maintaining a consistent level of cooling as a train constantly stopped and started, speeded up and slowed, was a major problem, as it would prove to be for buses and automobiles. Not the least of the difficulties was the promotional challenge of winning over a traveling public "vigorously opposed to the idea of having car windows fastened down."[38] Air-conditioned cars not only felt different, but looked different. Instead of screen doors they had "substantial wood and glass doors." Window "ventilators" that could be manipulated to admit outside air to cars were kept closed under the supervision of train personnel. Ceiling fans vanished. Passenger demands for fresh air, or at least a sense of individual control, evidently continued. The Santa Fe Railroad in 1935 installed grilles that allowed passengers in air-conditioned sleeping cars to admit between 25 and 100 percent air from outside.

Even Carrier's Lewis felt the need to put train air-conditioning to a personal test. "I am completely sold on air-conditioning for passenger trains," he wrote his Aunt Lizzie on June 10, 1932. "I was comfortable at all times and felt just as clean when ready to leave the train as when I entered it in Lexington, Kentucky."[39] Railroads collected and publicized glowing passenger reviews. The "distinctive" dining-car service on the Missouri-Kansas-Texas Railroad—affectionately known as "Katy"—was a smashing success, employees learned in a November 1932 in-house publication. "Katy air-conditioned diners still are

11. At Chicago's Century of Progress Exposition, a 1934 Frigidaire Comfort Zone brochure summed up a roaring decade of pleasure cooling installations.

the wonder of the Southwest," it reported. Patrons, some needing reassurance they were breathing "real" if treated air, not some "synthetic product," were astonished that a "railroad would go to such lengths to add to the comfort of its passengers." Wrote Dallas patron P. V. Keating, "Every member of our party visited your air-conditioned diner and found awaiting them, in an enjoyable atmosphere, one of the finest and most pleasing dinners imaginable (figure 11)."[40]

At first limited to such public spaces as dining cars where cooling might enhance discretionary spending, air-conditioning became common in the thirties on important routes. The "firsts" came thick and fast: the B&O's New York–Washington Columbian, the first entirely air-conditioned train, entered service in May 1931. In April 1932 the New York–St. Louis National Limited weighed in as the first air-conditioned long-distance sleeping-car train. And that May the New York–Chicago Capitol Limited claimed to be the first all-air-conditioned, all-Pullman train. There were 10,325 passenger cars by December 1937 owned either by Pullman or by individual railroads that were air-conditioned. Of these, 46 percent plied routes in the West; 38 percent were in use on eastern lines; and just 16 percent were in service in the South.[41]

As in the case of the department store, the actual impact of cooling on passenger traffic was unclear and bottom-line results difficult to quantify. Speaking at a 1931 meeting of the Western Railway Club, E. W. Test, an assistant to Pullman's president, said air-conditioning was absolutely essential to passenger rail competitiveness. "I have some friends who during the hot weather last summer took an airplane to St. Louis, Grand Rapids, and other places rather than endure the heat of a railroad train," he told the gathering. But, he continued, it would not be easy for the railroads to pay for this competitiveness. One possibility would be to charge increased fares for the privilege of riding in air-conditioned cars, or the lines might begin using lighter weight, more plainly decorated cars. Apparently even Pullman, the company whose name was a synonym for luxury in rail travel, would have to decide "what is the greatest 'drawing card' or inducement: air-conditioned cars which are simple and somewhat plainer in their appointments or more elaborate cars without air-conditioning." It might not be possible for the "pleasure" and the "palace" to coexist.[42]

In August 1932, *Railway Age* published a pair of articles about the growth of air-conditioning. "Appeal of restful quietness and cool, even-temperatured cleanliness on such trains has become a most potent sales argument of traffic representatives," the trade journal declared. Was the argument working? In the depths of the Depression, and after years of sagging ridership, it was hard to tell. One traffic officer told *Railway Age* that the air-conditioning trend was a "step in the right direction to retain and to recapture passenger traffic, but we have no authentic statistics indicating any definite increase in business." Still, optimism ran high. Air-conditioning would bridge "seasonal valleys" in the business cycle and a "prediction may be ventured that long-distance railroad travel will soon stand out in the mind of a fastidious public as one of the most comfortable experiences offered by our modern civilization."[43]

Not everyone would be satisfied with sporadic summer relief. Once it became widely known that engineers had found a way to master heat in the movie theater or train dining car, surely they could also make other aspects of summertime more comfortable, or at least more consistent. If machines could control indoor climate, although they did not always work exactly as promised, the seasons—and summer in particular—need no longer be accepted as inevitable. The "problem" of summertime only awaited the ultimate solution offered by air-conditioning. In Washington, the nation's capital, implementation of an air-conditioned answer to the twin woes of economic depression and debilitating summer heat was already well underway.

4. Cooling the Body Politic

 date the end of the old republic and the birth of the empire to the invention of air-conditioning. Before air-conditioning, Washington was deserted from mid-June to September," the politically well-connected writer Gore Vidal, who grew up in the nation's capital, wrote nostalgically in 1982. "The president—always Franklin Roosevelt—headed up the Hudson and all of Congress went home. . . . But since air-conditioning and the Second World War arrived, more or less at the same time, Congress sits and sits while the presidents and their staff never stop making mischief."[1]

Although the cooling of official Washington actually began more than a decade earlier, just three year after Vidal's birth in 1925, his explanation of its effects on the political scene is still popularly accepted, if not especially accurate. Toward the end of the 1920s, installation of air-conditioning in the United States Capitol and White House would endow these national edifices with the appearance of modernity informed by science. During the ensuing Depression and the onset of World War II, much of official Washington was similarly cooled. Advocates of this new technology promoted the idea that air-conditioning would enable political leaders and government workers to put in longer hours and perform consistently on behalf of their constituents, doing a better job of guiding the nation's destiny in hard, hot, and dangerous times.

Congress's quirky schedule was historically more sensitive to members' electioneering needs than to Washington's weather. The Sixty-ninth

Congress adjourned at 3 P.M. on July 3, 1926, its members rushing home for Independence Day rites just days ahead of a serious Washington heat wave. Soon air-conditioning would effect a partial transformation of the malarial marsh, once classified as a "tropical" posting by the British Foreign Office, where the founders had situated America's capital city. Cooling official Washington proved to be a massive and costly undertaking, beset with political and ideological complications. It took the authoritative blessing of C.-E. A. Winslow—himself a recent convert to the efficacy and usefulness of air-conditioning—to realize the first important project: the air-conditioning of the United States Capitol.

The condition, composition, temperature, and safety of the air in the nation's most prestigious and hallowed meeting place had been issues of deep if intermittent concern since the Capitol underwent a major expansion in the decade before the Civil War. Congressional complaints about the atmosphere in the windowless House and Senate chambers led to studies in 1852 and 1876. A seven-member House Standing Committee on Ventilation and Acoustics, created in 1893, presided over the construction six years later of a system of towers and tunnels on the Capitol grounds that drew outside air into the building.

Although this committee was abolished in 1911 by a reformist Congress, the ventilation system it spawned was still in use when the Architect of the Capitol ordered a study that prepared the way for the consideration of "real" air-conditioning. Undertaken in February 1924, that study found the air in the House Chamber wholesome, even on the day when the hall of the House was filled to capacity for a memorial to President Warren G. Harding. But the report did conclude that conditions in the chamber were almost always more desert-like than tropical, with the temperature too high and the humidity too low.

As the proceedings of a House Appropriations subcommittee hearing held in February 1928 reveal, it was not easy to persuade members of Congress that modern mechanical air-conditioning was the politically or medically correct response to their concerns. Congressmen wary of air-conditioning's comfort effects urged reluctant experts to declare that "bad air" was impairing congressional performance and causing premature deaths in House and Senate ranks. It would not do for Congress to become or, worse yet, to be perceived as the moral and material equivalent of a picture palace or railway club car. "In the new theaters throughout the country are they installing plants of this kind?," Representative Edward T. Taylor of Colorado asked suspiciously. The answer, of course, was yes.[2]

The subcommittee's hearing was more than a formality. The previous year a proposal to air-condition the Senate chamber had been defeated owing both to House jealousy and to high cost. Subcommittee Chairman Frank Murphy, an

Ohio Republican, and the other members pressed again and again for proof of the extreme danger of existing conditions and for promises of health and vitality commensurate with the air-conditioning project's $323,000 price tag. "There have for several years been some complaints about the condition of the air in the chamber," said Murphy. "Many of our members have died recently." Perhaps, responded William P. Holaday of Illinois "their deaths were caused by hard work rather than the air in the chamber." Added John N. Sandlin of Louisiana, "I imagine an analysis of the air would show whether the air is poisonous or detrimental to health" (page 136).

Taylor, the member from Colorado, said he had a better solution. He proposed extending the House chamber to the outer wall of the Capitol to allow sunlight and air to enter directly (page 136). Taylor worried that the downward air diffusion system suggested by engineers would force members to breathe air exhaled from the public galleries. Bad air could work both ways. "Women complain that when they go and sit in the galleries, when the Hall of the House is filled by Members, that the air is bad," Taylor fretted (page 139).

Although by April 13 Taylor was convinced enough of the wisdom of air-conditioning to serve as the measure's floor manager, it was comments like his, recurring throughout the hearing, that put hearing witness and sanitary engineer Leonard Greenburg in a delicate position. As an engineer trained in modern ideas of air chemistry and physics, he could jeopardize his professional standing by appearing to endorse the congressmen's "miasmic" notions. Yet he was understandably reluctant to denounce the congressmen's views, preferring to let them use their mistaken ideas to shore up political justification of the proposed expenditure.

Struggling to justify the air-conditioning plan, Greenburg turned for help to L. R. Thompson, his boss at the Public Health Service. Dr. Thompson's testimony before the House committee wove a fine line between disrespect and obsequiousness:

> Most of us have reached the age where we should not be subjected to constant extra strains put upon us. . . . We felt that you were entitled to a system which would be equal to what they have in theaters and places of that kind for maintaining the comfort and health of their people (pages 138–39).

Pressed again later, Greenburg also framed a tactful answer:

> I hesitated very much to say that the existing system was actually detrimental to health. On the other hand, we must not minimize the feeling of discomfort because when you are uncomfortable it is definite evidence that conditions are wrong. If this continues long enough, it seems very fair to assume that it will harm the body (pages 157–58).

Greenburg suggested that members of Congress, like the schoolchildren studied by Winslow, might suffer fewer colds and "feel more active and alert" with a proper air treatment system. But he doughtily refused to concede poisonous elements or menacing exhalations in the air of the House of Representatives.

Representative Holaday was not worried about bad air but he also remained unconvinced of the urgency of air-conditioning. "Personally, I have not noticed anything wrong with the air in the Hall of the House," he said (page 136), later adding:

> As I understand the testimony it is to the effect that the present air conditions are not unhealthy, and about the only thing that this proposed system will do will be to perhaps make it a little more comfortable. It was said that the members, at the end of a day's session, feel a little bit depressed. That can be said whenever a man leaves his office after being in it all day (page 157).

Without an obvious medical justification to prevent constituents from drawing unflattering comparisons between the halls of Congress and luxurious New York movie theaters, the congressmen gratefully acquiesced to the prestige of the scientific-engineering establishment. C.-E. A. Winslow was, after all, the man who had proposed open windows for schoolchildren. Now he and his committee of experts had, after "mature deliberations," enthusiastically endorsed the latest— and most expensive— in mechanical air-conditioning for the nation's elected leaders.[3] Chairman Murphy was certainly impressed by the expertise of the "number of eminent men" (page 128) who had recommended action, saying:

> Science has developed a ventilating system which is far superior to that which we now have and that being the fact, I think that the Capitol of the Nation should have the very best system obtainable . . . following the great business interests of the country in acting in a humane way for the preservation of life (page 143).

He later asserted, "I do not believe there is any place in the country where there would be any fault found with action of this kind" (page 157).

When the full House debated the legislative appropriation bill that included money for air-conditioning the House and Senate chambers and cloakrooms, almost three pages of the April 13, 1928, *Congressional Record* were used to tabulate the 290 representatives and senators who had died while in office between 1893 and 1928. With their own mortality so firmly in view, the representatives readily endorsed the project. "Then for humanity's sake, let us go ahead and do it," one member cried. Members applauded as the bill was debated and passed. The bill that air-conditioned the United States Capitol became law on May 16, 1928.[4]

By the time the Seventieth Congress returned to Washington for a lame-duck session in December 1928, Carrier Engineering Company, the high bidder, had completed the installation. Chairman Murphy rose in the House on December 4 to advise his colleagues of their new work environment. He described the system with emphasis on the "group of scientific men," headed by Winslow, who had prepared the bidding specifications, and he defended the propriety of awarding the job to high-bidder Carrier. The new system, said Murphy, was designed "for maximum comfort and for health." He even hinted that the April 27 death during the previous session of Appropriations Chairman Martin B. Madden made him the last of a long roll of congressional martyrs to bad House air. The size of the new system befit the grandeur of the Capitol. In the summer, Murphy bragged, cooling in the chamber would be the equivalent of melting nine tons of ice every hour. A "ton" of air-conditioning is cooling power equivalent to melting 2,000 pounds of ice over a 24-hour period. This now quaint terminology (although hardly more quaint than "horsepower") would have been far more meaningful and impressive to twenties politicians, or their wives, accustomed to using iceboxes back home (figure 12)[5].

The first official complaint was logged when Representative John E. Rankin, a Tupelo, Mississippi, Democrat, rose shortly after noon on May 28, 1929, to make a parliamentary inquiry. This interchange ensued:

> *Rankin:* It is more in the way of calling attention to the fact that the atmosphere is too cool in this room. On yesterday it was 75 by the thermometer . . . and 91 on the outside. Fifteen or twenty degrees difference is too much. I do not know who has charge of this, but I suggest that whoever is conducting this ventilation is making a mistake in pumping too much cooled air into this room when it is so warm on the outside.
>
> *La Guardia* [R-New York]: It is well to have some cool air here during this discussion.
>
> *Rankin:* This is regular Republican atmosphere, and it is enough to kill anybody if it continues. [Applause.][6]

Perhaps no one better illustrates congressional ambivalence towards the new air-conditioning system than Senator Royal S. Copeland, a New York Democrat who, for most of his fifteen-year tenure, was the only physician serving in Congress. Born in Michigan where he served a term as a Republican mayor of Ann Arbor, Dr. Copeland moved to New York City to run the homeopathic Flower Hospital and became, controversially, New York City's health commissioner during the influenza epidemic of 1918–1919. By 1920, he was writing a popular syndicated newspaper health column, "Your Health," and soon extended his celebrity in the new medium of radio and health films. Copeland's surprise Senate candidacy in 1922 resulted from a political tug-of-war between Governor Al Smith and publisher William Randolph Hearst. Copeland was re-elected easily in 1928 and 1934.[7]

The beautifully designed and installed Supply Ducts and Diffusers in the Attic above the glass-Panelled Ceiling of the House. This is one of the most remarkable Installations ever made. Some of the famous cast iron Truss Members, designed by Captain Meigs, are shown clearly.

12. Ducts supplying conditioned air to the U.S. House of Representatives were concealed in the attic above the chamber's glass-paneled ceiling. This photograph appeared in a 1929 Carrier Engineering promotional brochure. The panels were ripped out during a 1949 renovation.

Like his contemporary C.-E. A. Winslow, and many other health experts of an era whose world view was shaped by the perils of tuberculosis, Copeland was a fresh-air man, who built a roof garden for his child patients at Flower Hospital. Unlike Winslow, he never really moved beyond his faith in fresh air and sunlight, becoming an enthusiastic promoter of sun-tanning and of outdoor strolls in all seasons. His concern for the health of Senate colleagues was famous, and often the butt of good-natured mockery. As plans for air-conditioning the House and Senate chambers proceeded, Copeland clung to his proposal to install large windows at the north end of the Senate chamber. In a "Your Health" column drafted on Senate stationery in March 1928—it appeared in print that September—he wrote "there are other methods of ventilation, but I have little faith in a single one of them as the sole means of sustaining life and energy."[8]

As the Senate debated the House's legislative appropriations bill on April 24, the doctor from New York was still promoting open windows. "Since I have been a member of this body I have been sorry I am a doctor," Copeland declared. "It saddens me now when I look into the faces of men here to see how health is melting from them." Disappointed in the legislative outcome, he reported in his July 10, 1929, column: "For years I have battled to make the Senate chamber a liveable place. Now it is a Thermos bottle, cut off from outside light and air." Copeland that year would successfully insist that Dr. George W. Calver—a U.S. Navy Medical Corps commander who since December 1928 had been assigned to the House of Representatives—likewise be designated as the Senate's in-house health overseer.

Calver would view Congress as a laboratory where, he wrote in 1930, a well-defined age group, medically well-supervised and engaged in known pursuits under relatively constant conditions, could be observed and its health tracked. The new air-conditioning was drafty, he said, and, although air bacteria counts were lower than they had been in 1925, nine different molds were found in the system's spray wash-water. Calver ordered the water changed after every hundred hours of operation. It was hard to please members, he suggested, because most were over fifty and "hence have the lessened powers of resistance common to the group." Calver also offered regional and operational explanations:

> They also come from many climates, and the Member from the South or Southwest does not stand too great a rate of change, especially in the summer when the cool dry air in motion rapidly evaporates the moisture in the skin and clothing. A drop of only 7° with a humidity of approximately 50 percent has been the cause of complaint, yet frequently in motion-picture houses differences of 20° to 30° are maintained and are advertised as a drawing attraction.

On the other hand, Calver reported, attendance at House sessions seemed to be up and quorum calls needed to herd members into the chamber had declined. "Numerous favorable comments have been received from the members, and one might be quoted who said, 'It's the best thing that's ever happened to the House,'" Calver declared.[9]

Congressmen remained mortal. On July 14, 1937, just two days after Dr. Copeland had warned him against the strain of a summer session, Majority Leader Joseph Robinson of Arkansas died suddenly. A year later, in the waning hours of another extremely busy session, it was Dr. Copeland's turn. Attended by Dr. Calver, the Senator from New York died at his Washington apartment while awaiting the president's signature on his crowning achievement, the Food, Drug, and Cosmetic Act of 1938. Said the *Washington Herald:* "The veteran Senator, 69, died just as he had predicted dramatically a year ago . . . from exhaustion in the heat of Washington, and the sudden changes from the comfortable, air-conditioned chambers of Congress to the heat and humidity of the city outside." The medical explanation for Copeland's death was kidney disease, aggravated by overwork.[10]

Still Capitol air-conditioning was adjudged a huge success by the industry, making the head of the national heating and ventilating engineers' association wonder why the U.S. Public Health Service continued to insist upon open-window ventilation in public schools "while at the same time the government is spending millions to condition the Halls of Congress for the congressmen." The Carrier Corporation, for whom the high-profile Capitol project was the "most significant acknowledgment ever accorded to the far advanced though relatively young science of air-conditioning" predicted in a promotional broadside:

Inside the historic walls of Congress it will always be comfortable, not only but also healthful, invigorating, inspiring. . . . Congress may voluntarily remain in session throughout the summer, in order that our congressmen may be protected from the intolerable discomforts and dangers of the ordinary outdoor weather.[11]

Echoing Carrier and anticipating Gore Vidal, Genevieve Forbes Herrick, society page columnist for the *Chicago Tribune,* in 1933 held Capitol cooling responsible for Congress's reluctance to adjourn:

Here's the theory. The air cooling system operative in the Senate and the House is so efficacious that the boys don't even know it's sweltering outside. Hence, they can orate all through the night and never wipe a perspiring forehead. Their linen suits never get wrinkled.[12]

Until 1935 the rest of the Capitol complex still lacked air-conditioning. Legislators who had removed coats, vests, collars, and ties learned to don them hurriedly when called from their warm offices to the House or Senate chambers for a debate or vote.

As President James Garfield lay in the White House dying from an assassin's bullet during the summer of 1881, inventors rushed forward with devices they hoped would aid the president's recovery, or at least ease his discomfort. The most promising of these used an early electric-powered blower, a large box filled with ice to absorb excess humidity produced in the cooling process, and a network of tin pipes to distribute the cooled air. This noisy contraption so distressed the patient that Navy engineers hurriedly substituted canvas ducts. Although in need of constant tinkering, the muffled system cooled Garfield's sickroom quite effectively. Ultimately, a half-million pounds of ice were delivered to the White House. "Our operations at the Executive Mansion have proved that it is possible to place the relative humidity of definite quantities of air, at any desired point," the engineers declared. Garfield, who had been shot on July 2, nonetheless died in September.

Prior to workable air-conditioning, many White House rooms would be closed off in summer and their furniture and fixtures swathed in white linen, giving at least the impression of coolness. The next attempt mechanically to cool the White House was made during construction of the Oval Office and the Executive Office Building during the William Howard Taft Administration of 1909–1913. Writes White House historian William Seale, "electric fans blew over great bins of ice in the attic, cooling air which was then forced into the air ducts of the heating system. This never worked and was soon abandoned."[13]

As much of the East Coast and Midwest sweltered in July 1926, *Detroit Free Press* readers learned that the White House in Washington was "entirely comfortable" and "well equipped with all modern luxuries, such as awnings, screens, and electric fans."[14] The "people's house" was clearly neither as modern nor as luxurious as Detroit's largest movie theaters or its leading department store. Only when Herbert Hoover had the West Wing and Executive Office Building completely remodeled in 1929 was a thirty-ton Carrier centrifugal air-conditioning system installed. Significantly, it provided cooling only to public and work spaces, not the White House's family quarters. But the new cooling system proved itself during the record-setting summer of 1930 when a series of 100° days in July killed sixteen people and forced thousands to sleep in city parks under the watchful eyes of city police. Air-conditioning "similar to that in movie palaces, kept the temperature of the Executive Mansion 20 degrees cooler than the street all day," the *Washington Post* reported.[15]

Carrier executives circulated a congratulatory memo among themselves when *Time* reported on May 2, 1932, that the "temperature rose to 78 degrees in Washington one day last week. The air-conditioning machine was turned on at the White House." Other observers were less impressed. The installation of air-conditioning at the White House, editorialized the *Chicago Tribune* on July 10, 1933, "reminds us that Washington is climatically and geographically unsuited to be the capital of the nation." Harking back to nineteenth-century boosterism, the newspaper recommended relocating federal functions to Benton Harbor or New Buffalo on Lake Michigan's shore, where they "would be centrally located in the best climate on this continent and stimulated to energetic work by proximity to Chicago."[16]

Franklin Delano Roosevelt's New Deal administration would preside over a huge expansion of air-conditioning in official Washington. The new Supreme Court Building, begun in 1932 and completed in 1935, was outfitted with air-conditioning, bringing climate control equity to all three branches of government. Carrier replaced its 1929 White House installation with a unit more than twice as large when West Wing executive office space was expanded in August 1934.

The patrician Roosevelt's personal attitude toward all this air-conditioning was a complex mixture of social class and upbringing, politics and practicality. Carrier's Logan Lewis recalled much later that Hoover was "well satisfied" with the White House installation, but FDR "had a strong dislike of air-conditioning of any kind and never hesitated to say so. The outspoken comments that he frequently made to the press gave the installation some pretty bad publicity."[17] Seale offers a rather different perspective of the FDR White House:

> As a group, they liked their comforts. When they got their first taste of the Washington heat, [FDR confidante and permanent White House resident] Louis Howe ordered air-conditioning for six rooms on the second floor— those of Roosevelt, Mrs. Roosevelt, Lorena Hickok, and himself—and for the bedroom of Missy LeHand's

suite on the third floor. Westinghouse made the installation in May 1933, placing the units in the fireplaces (pages 926–27).

As members of the nearest class the United States had to an aristocracy, "racially" endowed with the physical and moral traits that analysts like S. Colum GilFillan and Ellsworth Huntington attributed to "coldward" lineage, the Roosevelts partook of upper-class disdain for the exigencies of bodily comfort. Hardly willing to concede his crippling polio, FDR was even less likely ever to admit, at least in public, that he suffered from the temperature.

Roosevelt actually seemed to find air-conditioning more uncomfortable than heat. In a 1952 memoir, brain truster and FDR speechwriter Samuel I. Rosenman said he sometimes had to flee the president's stifling study for an air-cooled White House room to get any work done during hot spells:

> The President did not like air-conditioning. It seemed to affect his sinuses. He did not even use an electric fan . . . ; he never seemed to mind the heat. He would take off his coat and tie, unbutton his collar, and roll up his sleeves. He perspired freely, and constantly mopped his brow. But he seemed to enjoy it—at least he seldom had the air-conditioning turned on.[18]

The Roosevelts' housekeeper Henrietta Nesbitt marveled at the family's seeming disregard of the heat during the especially oppressive summers of 1933, 1935, and 1939.[19] "But this was the sort of summer when people go around gasping for air, and the air-conditioning we had put into the White House wasn't working and had to be taken out," she wrote in her 1948 memoir. FDR did not oppose an array of other conveniences and comforts. The mansion's kitchen was completely remodeled in 1935 and outfitted with such electric appliances as an exhaust fan, ranges and ovens, refrigerators, dumb waiters, a meat grinder, mixers, warming ovens, dishwashers, waffle irons, a soup kettle, deep fryer, griddle, and a cart designed to deliver hot and cold foods to offices and private quarters. Nesbitt said the White House spent a thousand dollars a month on electricity.

FDR's refusal to acknowledge heat interestingly resembled the British royal family's response to the Washington summer of 1939. When King George VI and Queen Elizabeth visited the White House that June, temperatures were in the 90s, Nesbitt reported. Still the royal couple insisted on winter-weight bedding and their customary hot water bottles and hot milk nightcaps during their White House stay.

After the White House was again remodeled in 1952, Seale writes, "Deep in the new sub-basement engineers turned on the electrical systems, heat and air-conditioning sufficient to serve a skyscraper."[20] Some thirty years after FDR, the decidedly nonpatrician president, Richard M. Nixon, reputedly would turn the White House air-conditioning to maximum cool so that he could enjoy roaring fires during the summer months. The diaries of White House chief of staff H. R. Haldeman reveal that Nixon certainly insisted on building fires in all seasons, be it at the White House, Camp David, or the western White House at San Clemente in southern California. Haldeman's August 1, 1971, diary entry describes how Nixon and his valet, Manolo Sanchez, struggled on a "boiling hot" day to nurse a smoky fire in the president's study at Camp David. "Kind of incongruous in August in Washington," Haldeman commented dryly.[21]

By launching a massive expansion of air-conditioning throughout official Washington's vast marble halls, the Roosevelt administration — at least on the official level — shifted the rationale for air-conditioning from comfort, or even health, to efficiency and productivity. The federal government justified air-conditioning with arguments more closely aligned with the technology's early use in factories and manufacturing processes than with the appeals to middle-class comfort advanced by movies, department stores, hotels, and trains. If government buildings were the factories of democracy where bureaucrats worked long days and hours to rescue America from the Depression, then air-conditioning was not a palatial comfort but a stimulus to greater achievement. For the executive branch, as for Congress, comfort alone was a politically suspect indulgence.

"Department of Justice Air-Conditions its new building FOR OFFICE EFFICIENCY" proclaimed the August 1934 issue of *Heating, Piping & Air-Conditioning*.[22] Congress approved a deficiency appropriation of $2,255,000 in 1935 mainly to provide air-conditioning for the remainder of the Capitol and the Senate and House office buildings nearby. The York Ice Machinery Corporation got a million-dollar contract to install a thousand tons of air-conditioning in the Interior Department Building. Advocates of these massive installations suggested that they would enable government employees to work longer hours and permit Congress to work through the summer on New Deal programs.[23]

Perhaps because they were designed to extract longer hours of harder work, these projects provoked worker complaints. The gripes in turn elicited annoyance and scorn from engineers. "Of the complaints received from occupants of conditioned rooms, a few are purely imaginary, some are justified, and others are just a question of personal opinion," *HPAC* said in its discussion of the Department of Justice job. "The engineer has to be a man of wondrous understanding to separate wheat from the chaff" (page 334). As examples of folly among those who should count themselves lucky to work in air-conditioned buildings, the journal mentioned two men, one claiming to be too hot and the other too cold, although they worked but four feet apart, and twelve switchboard "girls," one of whom complained of a draft no matter where she was moved.

Charles A. Peters of the National Park Service Buildings Management told fellow refrigerating engineers in 1939 what it was like "Operating the World's

13. When this photograph was taken in July 1942, the federal war effort made even a Washington, D.C., commissary a front line in the national defense. The original caption read, "Engineer Graham is . . . on call at all hours of the day and night. He is responsible for air-conditioning and keeping the storerooms and cold room at the right temperature."

Largest Conditioning System."[24] His office maintained and operated 12,000 tons of refrigeration, wrote Peters, possibly the largest concentration of mechanical air-conditioning in the country. Since 1934, he said, new government buildings had been planned for air-conditioning, adding, "there are many other buildings in Washington, some of which were erected just prior to the general acceptance of air-conditioning and which, we believe, should be air-conditioned" (figure 13).

All this air-conditioning capacity was not without its problems, Peters conceded, showing more sympathy than the HVAC industry had five years earlier. The miraculous new refrigerant Freon was expensive and leakage was common and costly. Centrifugal compressors were prone to emit an objectionable high-pitched noise. Cooling water was scarce in summer, when the temperature of Washington's muddy Tidal Basin, a water source, reached 87 degrees. Cooling towers, an alternative way to provide adequate water circulation, were expensive to operate and likely to cause corrosion and marine growths.

Finally, Peters said, workers subjected to uneven temperatures, drafts, and noise were apt to denounce their new air-conditioning systems. These kinds of

14. Residents of the nation's capital found cooling opportunities where they could. In September 1938, children swam in a marble fountain in front of Union Station.

complaints, he suggested, were behind the House Appropriations Committee's recent refusal to approve a five-year, twelve-million-dollar Interior Department plan to air-condition eight more government buildings. High operating costs were also a factor. Peters included a chart showing the annual cost of running air-conditioning in just one building: the new post office at 12th and Pennsylvania Avenue NW. Electric bills for June through September were $17,154 compared to $4,573 for the other eight months of the year. But, he argued, the issue was larger than cost, narrowly defined:

> At first glance, these figures may appear rather high, but when you consider that the summer in Washington is so uncomfortable that it is often necessary to excuse the government clerks on hot afternoons, you will realize that the clean, quiet, comfortable atmosphere of a fully air-conditioned building is worth considerable.

Not until the nineties did federal administrators abolish the Misery Index that had long allowed federal workers to stay home if temperature readings in their Washington offices hit 95° with 55 percent humidity, a rare event after the advent of air-conditioning. Official Washington was so massively air-conditioned that the local electric utility began recording summer usage peaks in 1942, some twenty-one years before most utilities did so.[25]

Only a tiny segment of the nation's white-collar workforce toiled in Wash-

15. When black and white Civil Rights marchers massed on the Mall on August 28, 1963, for Martin Luther King Jr.'s "I Have a Dream Speech," the Reflecting Pool provided some relief from temperatures in the 80s, although two thousand were treated for heat and fatigue.

ington's marble-clad "factories." For most Americans in the twenties, thirties, and beyond, air-conditioning remained an indulgence associated with entertainment and consumption. When summer heat became too oppressive, a chilly movie house or a cool hotel restaurant provided temporary relief. These were escapes, not ways of life. Yet even such modest comforts were often not available to black Americans in segregated communities, such as Washington was.

For journalist Carl Bernstein, growing up in Washington in the early fifties, air-conditioning was still something that happened at the movies, not at home or in an ordinary workplace. He wrote, "The Trans-Lux had air-conditioning. Next to the ticket window a big sign announced in shimmering blue-tinsel-icicle lettering, 'It's Kool Inside.' Some evenings my mother and I would go to a movie to cool off." Bernstein was recalling the summers of 1951–1952, when he was seven and eight and, with his mother Sylvia, would flee to the Trans-Lux after sticky days spent sitting-in with black Washingtonians at whites-only lunch counters. These were mainly located in F Street dime stores cooled only by "big rotating floor fans" (figures 14 and 15).[26]

Even for Lucian K. Truscott IV, son and grandson of distinguished military men, memories of Washington would center on stormy summer nights in 1953, when he was six and would sleep almost outdoors. In the "fetid darkness" Lucian and his little brother Frank "spent every summer sleeping on a screen porch when air-conditioning was an exclusive feature of the movie theater downtown, nowhere in evidence in our home or the homes of anyone we knew," he wrote in June 2000. He vowed to recreate the sleeping porch experience for his six-year-old daughter in his 1921-vintage California house.[27]

Gore Vidal's recollections of the capital city's pre-air-conditioning days were rather more romantic than those of Carl Bernstein and his left-wing activist parents and less rustic than Lucian Truscott's childhood experiences. "But here and there in the city one still comes across so many relics of lost time — when men wore white straw hats and suits in summer and one dined at Harvey's Restaurant, where the slow-turning ceiling-fans made the hottest summer day seem cool." Vidal rhapsodized about the former sleepy village on the Potomac that, within his own lifetime, and under the direction of a president who personally disliked air-conditioning, had traded its languid southern charms for efficiency and power.

5. Always Fair Weather

*U*topianism is a way to imagine a future that seems to redress the defects of an intolerable present. During the nineteen thirties, a period of economic distress and widespread suffering, major corporations in the United States—and the scientists, technicians, engineers, and publicists who worked for them—took the lead in constructing utopian scenarios of abundance, efficiency, and social harmony. Corporate visions of an achievable future permeated contemporary advertising and were the stuff of movies, newspaper editorials, and hopeful forecasts of business magazines. But the depictions of the future that most obviously captivated the American public were offered at two of the largest and most successful world's fairs in the nation's history: Chicago's Century of Progress Exposition (CPE) in 1933–1934 and the New York World's Fair of 1939–1940.

These fairs were stages upon which corporate America proclaimed its ability to build a future that would work better than the present. They were colorful and awe-inspiring "theaters of power" that used spectacular although temporary architecture and technological magic to persuade the American public that the tomorrow that seemed to have slipped away was still within their grasp. In both Chicago and New York, organizers created marvelous and dramatic settings within whose carefully drawn boundaries they could exercise the perfect control so obviously missing elsewhere.

Already associated with modernist spectacle, through its wide use in movie houses and other popular palaces of pleasure and consumption, air-conditioning was literally and figuratively used at the thirties' fairs to create a climate of hopefulness. Fair visitors would be assured an ideal experience no matter what the weather—and return home convinced they had seen and felt the future of all America.[1] At Chicago's fair, and even more extensively in New York six years later, air-conditioning would play two complementary roles. Air-conditioning was presented as a powerful agent of the future, a marvel both scientific and magical. Its use promised to transform an uncomfortable today into a wondrous tomorrow and to restore individuals and society as a whole to physical and economic health. At the same time, fair exhibitors cast air-conditioning in the more subservient role of a silent servant that functioned automatically to make other aspects of the future possible: windowless skyscrapers, weatherless cities, a world freed from geographic and climatic necessity.

To the extent that these fairs represented themselves as utopias, their use of air-conditioning demonstrates how entwined this relatively new technology had become with the idea that climate control was necessary to the full realization of a perfected America.[2] Studies of utopian thought have tended to emphasize its many blunders and rare successes in predicting the technology of the future, or have revealed the authoritarian tendencies of its highly structured social arrangements. Less often examined is the extent to which mastery of weather is implicit in most utopian speculations. In Edward Bellamy's 1887 vision of Boston in the year 2000, continuous waterproof sidewalk coverings create a giant communal umbrella protecting every citizen from the annoyance of rain. It would be, Bellamy wrote, "an extraordinary imbecility to permit the weather to have any effect on the social movements of the people." Outlining a composite vision of the ideal world imagined by the American tradition of technological utopianism, Howard Segal writes:

> Utopia's climate would be pleasant and nearly uniform—another achievement of technology. . . . How? By the use of vaguely described, enormously powerful tools and machines. "We have absolute control of the weather," declares one utopian.[3]

Central to the utopian project is a belief, Segal argues, not just that nature can be controlled by human inventions but that the very tools we use to dominate nature, such as electricity, can themselves be domesticated and reliably harnessed to human purposes. The engineers' role in early-twentieth-century America, Cecelia Tichi notes, was to cause machine-made regularity, efficiency, and stability to seem more truly "natural" than nature's "aberrations." Bellamy and his readers, she argues, "mistook the attainment of comfort for the achievement of happiness."[4]

By the thirties, utopian ideas were finding expression in the newer but closely related genre of science fiction. H. G. Wells's 1933 novel of technological prediction and political pessimism, *The Shape of Things to Come,* drew a large American readership and was made into a popular and well-regarded 1936 film, *Things to Come.* In Wells's world of 2054 (changed in the film to 2036, exactly a century later), windows and weather are symbols of backwardness. They are sentimental impediments in a society within which work goes on ceaselessly under constant conditions and where the frontiers of geography, day and night, summer and winter, have been technologically erased.

Although Wells's vision of the future is war-torn and by no means celebratory, weatherlessness is its foremost achievement. While the people of his Everytown live in pristine white multitiered underground "skyscrapers" that prefigure shopping malls and the Portman-designed Hyatt hotels of the seventies, the "new order" has put its vast machinery to work outside leveling hillsides and otherwise mining nature for its resources. "Old" New York is described as "all sticking up and full of windows," and an old man tells his disbelieving great-granddaughter of a world in which "they'd no properly mixed and conditioned air."[5]

Unsurprisingly, air-conditioning engineers and manufacturers found a great deal of appeal in this description of the future. The October 1935 issue of the *Aerologist,* a journal for air-conditioning engineers, praised Wells's prediction that "within a century air-conditioning will have progressed to the point where every residence and office will be equipped for manufactured climate and artificial sunlight." The journal oddly highlighted an excerpt in which Wells's heroes, the scientists Passworthy and Cabal, self-consciously take a break from their controlled subterranean environment. "I'll confess," says Cabal, "I like the varying breezes and the shadows and the clouds — now and then."[6]

Wells would be an honored guest at both the Chicago and New York world's fairs. The weatherless future he and other science-fiction seers envisioned was gratifying, but the air-conditioning industry had already shown itself quite capable of advancing its own predictions. Writing in the May 1929 inaugural issue of *Heating, Piping & Air-Conditioning,* Willis Carrier had been confident about air-conditioning's present and expressed buoyant optimism regarding its future. He imagined windowless office skyscrapers free of noise and dust and predicted air-conditioned comfort in the homes of average Americans as well as the wealthy. The air-conditioning industry could take credit, said Carrier, for the "present-day prosperity of the people of these United States." Its growth, he predicted, would be geometric.[7]

The Depression had so severely affected the Carrier Corporation by 1932 that the company did not participate in Chicago's Century of Progress. But Willis Carrier, as befit his strenuously cultivated image as air-conditioning's Thomas

Edison, expanded and intensified his prophecies in the thirties. As Americans suffered not only economic distress but also a series of scorching heat waves, Carrier and his associates spoke to the general public via radio, mass-magazine interviews, even Rotary Club publications, sharing a Wells-tinged vision of perfect weather: perfect weatherlessness. In an interview with Robert D. Potter in a 1940 issue of *The American Weekly,* the Hearst newspapers' Sunday supplement, Carrier even asserted that available technology would soon surpass H. G. Wells's fantasies of glass-domed cities.[8]

In an August 27, 1936, interview on WABC radio, a fawning announcer elicited a characteristic prediction from Willis Carrier. "The air-conditioned life of the future will be something like this," said Carrier, himself an avid golfer, hunter, and sportsman,

> ... at any time of the year: The average business man will rise, pleasantly refreshed, having slept in an air-conditioned room, he will travel in an air-conditioned train, and toil in an air-conditioned office, store, or factory—and dine in an air-conditioned restaurant. In fact, the only time he will know anything about heat waves or arctic blasts will be when he exposes himself to the natural discomforts of out-of-doors.[9]

Both the Chicago and New York fairs attempted to make this fantasy real for their visitors. Their efforts revealed limitations both physical and social that inevitably compromised the overarching vision of perfect weatherlessness. The fairs of the thirties certainly found ways to represent utopia but, as it turned out, could never be Utopia.

The Century of Progress Exposition, conceived and named before the October 1929 stock crash, opened after the Depression had become the central fact of American life. Still it was enormously successful. Unlike most world fairs, the CPE returned money to its backers. Thirty-nine million paid admissions made it the best-attended American fair up to that time. Seven hundred fifty tons of refrigeration provided cooling to all or parts of many of its 140 structures. In the prevalent terminology, a "ton" of air-conditioning provided cooling equivalent to melting 2,000 pounds of ice over a 24-hour period. The 1939–1940 New York World's Fair would boast seven times as much cooling tonnage.

With its "architecture of science fiction," the CPE was at once more backward-looking and more futurist than the New York World's Fair would be a half-dozen years later.[10] Paradoxically, the CPE had to be, and could be, more boldly futurist because it was taking place in a present that was economically much bleaker than the makers of the 1939 fair would encounter. The "century" on display was Chicago's just past, not the one yet to arrive, and the fair glorified "progress" already achieved. But, as Robert Rydell points out, the CPE was also an "empire of science," a showcase for the presumed benefits of a positive fusion of American business and the nation's top scientific minds, working together to turn the fair's fantastic skyscrapers into urban fact. The CPE's epigraph was the authoritarian "Science Finds—Industry Applies—Man Conforms."[11] One of the ways to impose this conformity and control of the bodily experience of fairgoers was by using air-conditioning in vast public spaces.

The CPE's chief claim to architectural modernity was its calculated absence of windows. In an official guidebook, the predominance of windowless exhibition structures was explained this way: "Windowless these buildings assure that on no day of the Fair, no matter how dark and gloomy, can visitors be deprived of the full measure of beauty." Windowless design allowed more efficient use of interior space and "healthful, controlled, filtered ventilation." Architect and critic Albert Kahn was not persuaded. "As for the windowless buildings," he wrote, "no substitute will ever serve for sunshine and daylight, and attempts to do without them, even with air-conditioning, will prove failures." He was not alone in his disapproval. In the same special CPE issue of *The Architectural Forum,* architect Frank Lloyd Wright called the fair "petty, strident, and base." Futurist inventor R. Buckminster Fuller, rather rudely, considering his own significant presence at the CPE, called it "pseudoscientific" and "garish."[12]

Windowlessness made possible a streamlined architecture, emancipated from the forms of the past by new lighting and ventilating technologies. As Jeffrey Meikle explains, streamlining, acclaimed by the thirties public as "modernistic," was the visual representation of "frictionlessness," the achievement of social and physical control sought by leading designers and industrialists with a Depression-driven sense of urgency. "Streamlined" was shorthand for unimpeded progress and smooth forward movement. It connoted control of air movement in the same way that air-conditioning signified control of air temperature. Both air-conditioning and streamlining obligated the very atmosphere to conform to a human plan.

Six months after *Popular Science Monthly* heralded the New York City test run of the "First Air-Conditioned Auto," Buckminster Fuller's egg-shaped and air-conditioned Dymaxion car was a major attraction in the CPE's 1934 season. Visiting the fair, H. G. Wells himself posed for a photo with Fuller's vehicle. Also drawing huge crowds were the extravagantly streamlined new passenger trains, including the cocoon-shaped Twentieth Century Limited. The hermetically sealed perfection of these trains' climate control echoed their aerodynamic shape and was central to their appeal. Despite a spate of such innovations, the railroads, already in trouble in the twenties, were still losing market share to interstate buses and the automobile. Fuller's Dymaxion car aside, reliable air-conditioning systems for these conveyances were far in the future. The best that Ford Motors, biggest exhibitor at the CPE, could claim was that front wind-shields on some of its cars opened so that "in hot weather you can have all the air you want."[13]

As the Century of Progress Exposition opened on May 27, 1933, an article in the *Chicago Tribune* hailed the windowlessness of five major exhibition buildings as evidence that indoor lighting "is entirely under man's control." The manufactured coolness that went along with it also received favorable press attention. American Radiator's indoor-outdoor Garden of Comfort, a Michigan state exhibition, kept the temperature at 64° and temperature control in General Electric's House of Magic all became part of the larger story of the fair's embrace of a scientized future.

Perhaps the most unexpected instance of air-conditioning at the fair was the cooling of the *Christian Science Monitor*'s pavilion by two Trane unit coolers that maintained a constant temperature of 80 degrees. *Science and Health,* the authoritative text of the Church of Christ Scientist, published in 1875 by Christian Science's founder, Mary Baker Eddy, specifically declares that "temperature is mental," stating elsewhere: "We say man suffers from the effects of cold, heat, fatigue. This is human belief, not the truth of being, for matter cannot suffer." Yet in practice, Mrs. Eddy was an enthusiastic user of technology. She eagerly adopted the vacuum cleaner and was one of Concord, New Hampshire's, first motor car owners in 1902, although she declined to ride in the car herself. She also owned but would not speak on a telephone.[14]

Christian Science had a long tradition by 1933 of welcoming non-Scientists, most visibly through the provision in major cities of comfortable rooms stocked with Christian Science literature, including the *Monitor,* a respected daily newspaper started in 1908 when Mrs. Eddy was eighty-seven. Christian Science was conspicuously present at almost every world's fair in the United States of the twentieth century. The circular Christian Science building at the New York World's Fair would be located in sight of the Perisphere, and would feature two free air-conditioned reading rooms.

The Chicago fair and American scientists took each other quite seriously. The American Association for the Advancement of Science held its 1933 annual meeting in Chicago, lending legitimacy and an important audience to the fair's scientific aspirations. A week later, in the midst of a record-setting heat wave, eighteen engineering societies likewise assembled in Chicago. Yet the difficulties of conveying scientific ideas to a mass audience, and the clashing demands of commercial appeal, would produce at the Century of Progress displays that promiscuously mingled religious awe and the "astounding" types of contemporary science fiction. Westinghouse advertised its exhibition as a "Hall of

16. Audacious nude dancer Sally Rand put down her feather fans, put on her clothes, and put up her hair to advertise a General Electric home air-conditioning unit in 1933 at Chicago's Century of Progress Exhibition.

Miracles," while General Electric's "House of Magic" proposed to dazzle visitors with advances in the "electrical art" and the "wonders" of modern science and engineering. As a technology that was noticed least when it was working best, air-conditioning was an unseen dimension of this wonderment.

To meet the challenge of making air-conditioning visible, General Electric, for one, went beyond scientific magic-making. GE air-conditioning publicity photos featured the famously audacious fan dancer, Sally Rand, in sedate attire (figure 16). By temporarily setting aside the ostrich-feather fans that she deployed as a star in the CPE's "naughty" Streets of Paris midway show, Rand was presumably exhibiting with her body the superior efficacy of General Electric's air-conditioning equipment. What need was there for fans, or nudity, when an air-conditioner was available?[15]

Before the fair even opened, the *Tribune* noted that workers at the American Radiator exhibition were "laughing" at other construction crews because the "recently perfected steam refrigerated air-conditioning plant . . . is now in working order and provides a constant temperature of 60 degrees in the building." In the wake of June 1933 heat waves during which temperatures more than once exceeded 100°, the July *Heating, Piping & Air-Conditioning* declared "Chicago World's Fair Proves Air-Conditioning Attracts the Public," and has shown itself "an irresistible lure to the public on a hot day." The *Tribune* was certainly convinced; in July Chicago's major newspaper announced plans to air-condition totally its downtown Tower, aligning itself with the CPE as a vanguard of Chicago's modernity. "There is no doubt that the public wants artificial cooling in summer," the editors wrote, saying they had received "a flood of letters and inquiries" about the project.[16]

Scholars of world's fairs have tended to depict them as sites of control from which nature has been rigorously excluded or allowed only under strict constraints. Burton Benedict, for example, declares, "At world's fairs man is totally in control and synthetic nature is preferred to the real thing."[17] This may have been the plan, but there is ample evidence that the promise of controlled weather had less effect than did actual weather on how the fair was experienced. The CPE was certainly a carefully designed and engineered realm studded with windowless, climate-controlled buildings, but its opening and closing dates and the location on Lake Michigan's shore identified it as a summer resort, an open-air entertainment with strictly seasonal appeal—not a movie palace or department store. On May 27, the Exposition's opening day, an article in the *Tribune*'s women's pages suggested Chicago's air-cooled movie houses as a break from the heat sure to prevail at the fair.

The fair's success in attracting large crowds and persuading them to "buy" the future was highly sensitive to the weather. People stayed away when it was too hot or too cold, too rainy or windy. A 218-foot tall, three-sided thermometer was installed at a main CPE entrance. Visitors were clearly supposed to think about the temperature, and they did. During heat waves, CPE attendance slowed. When the temperature on June 7 reached a record 100°, five visitors were treated for heat prostration. When the heat abated, the *Tribune* attributed an attendance rise to the cooler weather. Those who braved the heat may well have sought out the most comfortable exhibits. The June 12 *Tribune* reported that the heat had "forced most of yesterday's visitors to remain inside the exhibition buildings." But there was no indication people went to the fair because it was air-conditioned, even though Chicago temperatures exceeded 100° several times during June 1933.[18]

The quickly constructed and frankly temporary fair buildings were especially susceptible to power failures that could render control systems in windowless buildings inoperative, even dangerous. A June 4 thunderstorm temporarily broke the heat but its seventy-mile-an-hour winds did $8,000 damage and injured fifteen at the fair. Late in the season, an October 17 transformer short circuit cut all fair power for thirty minutes. "The failure of current emphasizes the dependence of the Fair upon electricity," the *Tribune* reported. "The exhibition buildings, dependent upon artificial light, went dark, and guides were sent among the crowds to urge them to go outdoors." Midway rides, water pumps, and an electric tally system also failed.[19]

As the CPE's first season ended, its success nonetheless assuring a second season in 1934, *Heating, Piping & Air-Conditioning* was ebullient. "Millions Have Experienced Air-conditioning at the Chicago Fair," declared the November 1933 issue, "some of whom have experienced perhaps for the first time the advantages of air-conditioning for comfort." On its face, this claim seems improbable. Americans who could afford to visit a world's fair in the worst years of the Depression were precisely those best able to patronize better hotels or department stores, or at least go to the movies whenever they liked. The CPE seems not to have astonished its public with air-conditioning in the way that the 1939 fair would dazzle with television. What the fair experience did was naturalize indoor climate control as an essential aspect of modernity and key to an overall vision of the future.

The term "air-conditioning" itself, although not as evocatively modernistic as "streamlining," was attached to a whole variety of "cool" products and conjured up a desirable state of being. But awareness of the technology and the desire for comfort did not necessarily or naturally translate into a desire to purchase air-conditioning, which was seen as grandiose, costly, and luxurious. At a time when less than a third of American households were equipped with gas or electric-powered refrigerators, still considered "semi-luxuries," selling cooling for humans was a somewhat quixotic project. During the June 1933 heat waves, the *Tribune* set up its customary charity ice fund for poor Chicagoans. Everyone understood that the ice money would be used to keep baby's milk fresh, rather than cool the family's sweltering apartment.[20]

The thirteen single-family model houses displayed along the lakeshore at the CPE occupied an anomalous "middle landscape" between the fair's futurist aesthetic and the actuality of life in thirties' Chicago, between immediate prospects for comfort and modernity and the reality of dreams deferred.[21] The Chicago fair's housing vision was neatly summarized in a June 1933 newspaper headline: "HOUSE OF TOMORROW AT CENTURY OF PROGRESS / TWELVE SIDED DWELLING IS NEWEST IDEA / NO WINDOWS TO OPEN; AIR-CONDITIONING MACHINE DOES ALL THE WORK." Designed by modernist architect George Fred

Keck of Chicago, the duodecagonal House of Tomorrow was all-glass, but had no operable windows. It was also all-electric, from the "eyes" that opened the doors of its garage and "standard" airplane hangar, to its dishwasher, garbage disposal, push-button Murphy beds, and, of course, 24-hour, year-round air-conditioning. Its flat roofs on three levels served as outdoor recreational space. This house, Keck's Americanized interpretation of Le Corbusier's "Machine for Living," was assembled in 48 man-hours and finished in two months. It was the only one of the thirteen models to charge an extra dime admission.[22]

Although she said the house "turns topsy-turvy most of our established ideas of what a house should be," *Tribune* reviewer Louise Bargelt did not find Keck's ideas or techniques offensive:

> The designers of this home are frank in their admission that this house is an attempt to introduce drastic changes in home construction and home planning. We may not reach the point . . . where we contemplate building just such a home for ourselves. But [we wonder] if it may not be nearer than we dream to the houses which our children, some score of years from now, will be building.

The CPE houses attracted thousands of fairgoers who seemed both fascinated and repelled by the extremity of some of the designs. "Some of these model homes are too much like prisons," an Oak Park, Illinois, housewife told *Architectural Forum.* A Danish-born carpenter from Brooklyn was dubious about the ubiquitous flat roofs. "You must figure on storms in winter and a flat roof isn't so good" he remarked astutely. But others called the houses "lovely" and "the last word." The House of Tomorrow, said an advertising man from Chicago, was "very fine" and "looked so very comfortable."[23]

Bargelt did not list a price for the Keck house because, she wrote, it was "built purely and simply for the public to look at." Although clearly too expensive for most fair visitors, it was well positioned to demonstrate the possibilities of a more streamlined and prosperous future. It was a future built around air-conditioning. A promotional brochure available at the CPE had this to say about the Keck house:

> The house is designed around an air-conditioning system. [Such] a system works most efficiently when operated within a closed space, when its balance of air output and intake is not disturbed, as by open windows and doors.

The air-conditioning system in fact worked so poorly that the House of Tomorrow's invariably overheated master bedroom had to be closed to visitors.[24]

A three-story Crystal House erected for the CPE's 1934 season was a further attempt by Keck "to solve problems of housing through technology." It was in front of this structure that Buckminster Fuller exhibited his air-conditioned

17. The State of Florida–sponsored Tropical House was the only Century of Progress model built without air-conditioning. Now located in Beverly Shores, Indiana, the pink stucco house, seen here in winter, is slated for renovations that are likely to include central air.

Dymaxion car. Built on a concrete slab at a personal cost to Keck of $15,000, the Crystal House was all plate glass, airily supported by structural steel. No interior partitions disrupted the flow of light, or conditioned air, from room to room. Both Keck houses were spectacular constructions that highlighted imagination, not "homes" that directly promoted products.[25]

Somewhat more mainstream, but still futurist in feeling, was a *Good House-keeping*–sponsored model built for the Century of Progress by Stran Steel Corporation of Detroit. This $8,000 Town House featured a steel frame to which other building components could be attached. With its flat roof, an exterior of lightweight concrete faced with baked enamel, two fireplaces, a second-story outdoor terrace, and full air-conditioning, it was overtly modernist. Said a Stran Steel brochure, "Modernism means air-conditioning. . . . How refreshing to step into your home and know in advance that the temperature and humidity will be just right."[26]

After the CPE ended, developer Robert Bartlett moved the House of Tomorrow and five of the other twelve prototypes to Beverly Shores, Indiana, to attract attention to his new resort, now part of the 15,000-acre Indiana Dunes National Lake Shore on Lake Michigan. A later private owner replaced the House of Tomorrow's immovable expanses of plate glass with smaller, operable sash windows. In 1986, the structure was listed in the National Register of Historic Places. In 2000, Indiana's Historic Landmarks Foundation devised a plan to allow the House of Tomorrow and four other surviving CPE houses to be "born again" in the twenty-first century by encouraging preservationists to spend up to $600,000 apiece remodeling them in return for long-term, minimal-cost leases. The foundation's plans included restoring the House of Tomorrow's original fixed-window design, using a high-velocity forced air system to—finally—keep the house cool.

Hammond, Indiana, manufacturer William Beatty in 2000 took on the task of restoring Florida's prototype house, the only CPE model sponsored by a state. This concrete-roofed, pink stucco Art Deco "Tropical Home" featured a fireplace and two rooftop sun decks, but no air-conditioning. Accompanying literature claimed that its seventy-four windows were oriented to take full advantage of the "constant trade winds of southern Florida." That those "winds" might sometimes be hurricanes was not mentioned. Built without insulation or weather stripping, the Florida House, said Beatty, had not weathered very well during its years in Indiana. Despite the house's plentiful cross-ventilation and considerations of historic authenticity, said Beatty, "If I plan to live in it, it will have air-conditioning" (figure 17).[27]

Thirties' architects might have been willing to look toward a distant future, but air-conditioning manufacturers like American Radiator of New York City and General Motors' Frigidaire division strove to turn the world's fair display of their products into present-day consumption. These promotional materials mobilized appeals to health, efficiency, and modernity, at times defining comfort as scientifically measurable while at others, as a psychological necessity.

A brochure for American Radiator's Campbell Room Unit Air Conditioner is an especially good example. "You cannot depend on Nature: Science is the Dependable Weather Man," the brochure warned. Scientific-looking bar graphs showed "excess" summer heat in a "typical American city." Air unprocessed by technology was described as "imperfect," "destructive," "literally poisoned," loaded with dangerous dirt, bacteria, and pollen. Campbell-produced air, by comparison, was praised as "vital."

The noise of an open office window or pitifully ineffectual fan might bring on a nervous breakdown, or at least the pathetic sight of a shirt-sleeved executive with an "unpresentable" wilted collar. And it was all so unnecessary. "No need for envying the wife and children, enjoying the matinee in an air-cooled theater. No need for looking forward to the noontime relief in the modern air-conditioned club or restaurant." Air-conditioning was portrayed as a marvel comparable to aviation, "undreamed of by our grandfathers" but actually available now, at least to the kind of modern white-collar executive who might attend the fair.

A 1933 Frigidaire booklet contrasted "old" ways of avoiding heat—the cold drink, the electric fan, the time-consuming vacation—with modern air-conditioned efficiency. A 1934 brochure addressed the insecure businessman:

> Today, as you walk along any city street in summer time, you notice signs . . . which read like this: "It's Cool Inside," "This Store Is Air-Conditioned," or "Dine in Comfort." You see similar signs upon trains. In a few years these signs will disappear . . . because of this significant fact: conditioned air will be universal and taken for granted.[28]

Looking forward in 1938 to the potential of the New York World's Fair, air-conditioning manufacturers noted with satisfaction that the Chicago exposition "did more to familiarize the general public with the comforts of air-conditioning than any other single event in the history of the industry."[29] Facing a perception that their technology was becoming ordinary and was in danger of being banished from utopia to the commonplace, air-conditioning exhibitors at the New York fair would struggle to endow their product with new magic.

In 1939–1940, as war loomed over a fragile economic recovery, the New York World's Fair, alternately identified as the "World of Tomorrow" and "Dawn of a New Day," arose in a former garbage dump in Queens. It epitomized modernity for a generation, prefiguring theme parks like Epcot Center and shopping malls. The fair's fantastic architectural forms manipulated outdoor and indoor environments in ways that made visitors who were also customers feel they had entered a perfected present or wondrous future.

Impressed by the recent success of the film *Things to Come,* officials of the New York fair actively sought H. G. Wells's imprimatur on their representations of the future even though they did not ultimately share his fantastic yet fundamentally pessimistic futurism. The 1939 fair was described more than once by its publicists as the realization of the "shape of things to come" and the film's set design and special effects strongly influenced the fair's architecture, especially the Trylon and Perisphere. The novelist was treated to lunch and a special tour of the Queens construction site in November 1937 and, for a press release, declared himself duly impressed with its builders' "real attempt to concentrate here all that is new, all that is being invented." Not all fair creators were enthusiastic about Wells's influence. Said designer Walter Dorwin Teague, the "danger of being fantastic in a Wellsian sense, and of being too definitely prophetic, must be avoided."[30]

At this fair, more than at Chicago's, the future presented to the public was not a distant speculation but very close at hand, almost literally "tomorrow." The corporations that underwrote this world wanted people to understand that they were seeing not a dream of the future but an achievable goal. As Jeffrey Meikle puts it, "commercial exhibitors implicitly stated that the future was already here if people would only realize it."[31]

The fair's furthest look into the future was also its most popular and costly exhibition, attracting an estimated twenty-five million visitors over two seasons. The Norman Bel Geddes–designed General Motors Futurama depicted a "frictionless" city of 1960, just twenty-one years away and well within the imaginative purview of most fairgoers, rather than a distant "shape of things to come" a century or more hence. It was, said the *New York Times,* what tomorrow would look like. A city of towers separated by highways carrying sleek air-conditioned automobiles at 100 miles per hour, it was described as sunny, bright, and airy, yet was displayed in a darkened, cooled, windowless space: a movie theater in which the seats moved. Futurama envisioned a metropolis so perfectly organized that no one need ever go outside one's "air-conditioned" tower or "raindrop" automobile.[32]

The Fair Corporation's own "official" city of the future was Democracity, designed by Henry Dreyfuss and housed in the iconic Perisphere. Although publicized as Everyman's Fair, Democracity nonetheless charged an extra 25-cent admission fee, one possible reason why Futurama was a greater draw. Promotional materials describing Democracity were careful to situate it just thirty or forty miles and a half-hour away from the present, telling visitors "see where you will live . . . tomorrow morning."[33]

This was a suburbanized vision reminiscent of the one conjured up by H. G. Wells in his keynote "World of Tomorrow" essay in the *New York Times*'s special world's fair section of March 5, 1939. There, Wells had endorsed the decentralizing potential of technology, in effect saying that crowded New York City ("all sticking up and full of windows," as his film had put it) and its fair's urbanized representations of the future were already obsolete. Democracity was not a towering metropolis but a dispersed community, spreading 1.5 million residents over 11,000 square miles. A series of Democracities would dot America, each adapted to the land and weather of its particular location. "Democracity hasn't managed to manage the weather . . . but it can cope with it. . . . In your own home, air-conditioning and automatic heat control will help," a fair brochure asserted. On the streets, arcaded sidewalks (à la Bellamy) would provide shade and shelter from sudden storms. Inside the Perisphere exhibition space itself, the "treatment for sound and air-conditioning have been so worked out as to give you, as you move around the vast hemisphere, exactly the sensation of floating high in the air . . . the air is purified; nothing that smells of the earth remains to destroy your illusion of flight."

Democracity, the literature emphasized, would not be a dictated utopia, "but an entirely practical city." "You can start to build this city tomorrow morning. There are no trick materials, no imaginary machines." Unlike Futurama, which overtly exhorted government to build the national and regional highways central to General Motors' vision of 1960, Democracity more clearly expressed the individualist and consumerist ideology of the fair. Millions of Americans, if they would just eagerly buy the products and services American industry was already capable of selling them, could—by the accumulation of individual acts of consumption—bring a better world into being "tomorrow."

As details of these two exhibits suggest, air-conditioning was an intrinsic part of the New York World's Fair, used everywhere to create "tomorrow's" ideal climate. More prevalent than in Chicago, mechanical cooling was also less remarkable and less "visible," noted primarily by the profession. According to a May 1939 fair cover story in *Heating & Ventilating,* seventy-two fair buildings and exhibits would use at least 5,400 tons of air-conditioning—seven times the Chicago fair's cooling capacity apportioned among about half as many structures. The ubiquity of cooling apparatus, said a trade journal, shows "what great strides have been made in the public acceptance of air-conditioning during the past few years." Margaret Ingels, a Carrier engineer and publicist, reviewed the fair for the July 1939 World's Fair number of *Refrigerating Engineering.* The refrigerating engineer, she wrote, "may be proud to view the 'World of Tomorrow' and realize that he, too, is one of its builders."[34]

While the desired message of the fair may have been frictionless technological perfection, the implementation of fair air-conditioning reveals that, as always, technology was compromised in its application. Depicted as the epitome of fantastical modernism, in reality air-conditioning at the fair was subject to limits imposed by design specifications, construction costs, electrical power capacities, and restrictive city water use regulations.

The illusion of Outer Space in the windowless Perisphere, as an example, had to be achieved with an air temperature just 10° cooler than the outdoors. At a time when movie theaters routinely promised and frequently delivered "20 degrees cooler inside" and embellished their summertime newspaper ads with icicles, chief fair engineer John Hogan was somewhat defensive about the fair's more modest air-conditioning strategies. He assured his audiences that the "more elaborate industrial exhibits effect much greater reductions and can maintain indoor comfort at most any condition of outside air." Sanford Apt, the fair's chief mechanical engineer, admitted there had been severe criticism from all-day building occupants but, he added, visitors commented favorably on the absence of temperature shock when entering and exiting fair buildings. In an internal memo on air-conditioning maintenance, Hogan seemed prepared for gripes:

> My experience with air-conditioning would indicate that from 5 to 10 percent of the people do not like it and that something under 5 percent are unfavorably affected by it. There are many more complaints received when the air-conditioning fails sometimes than there are from those who are adversely affected.[35]

As this memo suggests, the desires of fair visitors—for cold or heat—did not always correspond to the controlling agendas of fair planners. In his article, "Refrigeration's 'Greatest Story Ever Told,'" which led off the special fair edition of *Refrigerating Engineering,* editor David L. Fiske explained why the fair would be a boon for the air-conditioning industry. "Millions of people in a receptive, holiday mood, in weather generally hot, find coolness available at every hand, and they love it." But elsewhere in the magazine, the "greatest story" revealed some ambiguities. A roundup of fair miscellany noted that the "Ford air-conditioning job is remarkable but the Ford gardens, with real if hot sunlight keep the crowd moving outside for a sojourn." Hugely popular outdoor dining areas were "no boon to refrigeration" because customers preferred them to adjacent air-conditioned indoor seating.[36]

In New York, as in Chicago, a fair was a seasonal event subject to the vagaries of weather no matter how perfectly controlled it was. In 1939–1940, as in 1933–1934, newspaper articles routinely linked fair attendance to weather conditions. "With clearing weather and cool breezes replacing the overcast skies and muggy atmosphere of the past few days, a record Tuesday throng entered the World's Fair gates yesterday" *New York Times* reporter Richard A. Tompkins wrote in August 21, 1940, editions. Although Margaret Ingels, in her review might claim that the "effect the visitor gets when in the Carrier exhibition is that of being out of doors on an ideal day," most people still used traditional criteria to judge the perfection of a summer afternoon. A quarter century later, Robert Moses, potentate of the 1964–1965 New York World's Fair, would publicly ask the Weather Bureau to avoid issuing forecasts that might discourage people from attending the city's first—and last—fair since 1940.[37] Compared to its own dramatic Futurama and the Chicago fair's futurist houses, this fair's displays of model houses and domestic technology were downright "homely," offering a utilitarian vision and a functional future that any visiting housewife could grasp. Fair visitors to the "Town of Tomorrow" paid an extra dime admission to view products they could buy today. There was no "House [or even Home] of Tomorrow" in this suburbanized Town. Ranging in price from $2,500 to $35,000, most of the fifteen models looked to the past for ways to sell houses in the present. "Gracious" was a favored descriptive.

Joseph C. Hazen Jr., associate editor of *Architectural Forum,* visited the Town on June 7 and 8, 1939, and asked four hundred visitors which houses they liked best. His rather slapdash poll showed that the $6,000 Bride's Home, a romantic cottage, came in first among 275 respondents. Placing second in Hazen's survey, conducted "during two of June's hottest days," was the $15,000 Kelvin Home, which, thanks to a contractual arrangement with the World's Fair corporation during the 1939 season, was the only house with working air-conditioning. "No other house in the Town boasted so cool an interior," Hazen commented in the July *Architectural Forum.* "The popularity of this house must in some measure reflect a growing public acceptance of this feature." A refrigerated drinking fountain installed in the laundry room also helped boost the Kelvin Home's ratings.[38]

Unlike Chicago's Keck house, Nash-Kelvinator's model residence sought to soothe and sell rather than provoke its visitors. *Architectural Forum* called the Kelvin Home the "most authentic Colonial design in the Town of Tomorrow." Declared a Town of Tomorrow press release, "With its quaint charm and quiet hospitality, the Kelvin Home breathes the spirit of New England's hallowed days. Yet stop inside—and the world of tomorrow awaits you!" From its dormers to its nonfunctional shutters to its columned veranda, the Kelvin Home laid claim to a conservative identity. Publicity literature invoked the blessing of Lord William Kelvin, who had died in 1907, and identified him as the "father of modern refrigeration and air-conditioning." The overtones of titled aristocracy presumably conferred a befitting graciousness on the new technology.[39]

When Kelvinator's exclusive right to use air-conditioning apparently expired in the 1940 fair season, other Town of Tomorrow houses were free to demonstrate cooling capabilities. General Electric's "Electric Home" was also grand in manner and Georgian in style. It was one of five houses, including the popular Bride's Home, renamed "The American Bungalow," that were equipped with an array of GE "electrical servants," often including air-conditioning (figure 18).

In a glass-sided "phantom" house, installed in General Electric's main exhibition building for the 1940 season, a "Happy Mother-in-Law Drama" was staged several times daily. Actors depicted the "felicities of married life in a modernly equipped home" including year-round central air-conditioning that presumably kept mother-in-law from complaining about the heat or anything else. Servel Electrolux demonstrated a prototype of its gas-powered air-conditioning system in Homewood, the *Good Housekeeping* model house in the Gas Industries' free exhibition area. Described as white stucco with Regency

THE TOWN OF TOMORROW IS REVISED FOR 1940 FAIR

REPRESENTATIVE CONDITIONING AND HEATING SYSTEMS SHOWN

"Packaged" Air Conditioning Unit Linked with Oil Furnace for "Split" System In Electric Home

All the houses in the "Town of Tomorrow" at the New York World's Fair have been completely refurnished and the automatic heating and air conditioning equipment in the five houses equipped by General Electric has been revised for 1940 to give a more representative picture of the various possible combinations of equipment to give winter or year-round comfort, using warm air systems or radiation, or both; using either gas or oil as fuel. Save this page and take it with you when you visit the "Town of Tomorrow" at the Fair this summer.

Electric Home

Equipped for what is known as "split" system—using both radiators and ductwork. Has automatic oil furnace and a new "packaged" air conditioning unit, equipped to provide both winter air conditioning and summer air conditioning. Represents ideal system for year-round comfort.

Fire Safe Home

This home also has a year-round "split" system. Heat is provided by an automatic gas-fired furnace. Another type of year-round air conditioner is shown. A separate refrigerating machine provides cooling for summer comfort.

Plywood House

This interesting small house is built throughout of plywood and is intended for use principally in milder climates. Its heating system is a horizontal gas-fired winter air conditioner. Additional equipment for summer cooling is not shown, but may be added easily at any time when the need arises.

Bride's Home

This compact little house was one of the most popular in the Town last year. It is equipped with a vertical model gas-fired winter air conditioner—the same equipment as shown in 1939.

House of Glass

The House of Glass, located down the street next to the Electric Home is one of the most unusual houses in the Town. Appropriate to its design for a mild climate, the air conditioning system is of the year-round type—using an oil-fired winter air conditioner, equipped with cooling coils and a compressor for summer cooling.

18. For the New York World's Fair's 1940 season, General Electric installed some of its latest air-conditioning equipment in some very conventional-looking houses in the "Town of Tomorrow."

touches, boasting ten rooms and three baths, Homewood was clearly not modernistic in the manner of *Good Housekeeping*'s Stran Steel House in Chicago, but rather shared the marketing aspirations of the nearby Town of Tomorrow.[40]

If the 1939 Town of Tomorrow had not exactly encouraged futuristic imaginings or challenged the single-family home, the 1940 season offered an even narrower vision of what was required to get the economically recovering middle class into a house of some kind as quickly as possible. In association with newspapers around the country, fair officials selected "typical" American families from each state to live for a week in "typical" American houses adjacent to the Town of Tomorrow. Selected families, all of them white, could bring only two children who had to share a bunk bed.

Long Island contractor Paul Roche built two houses at 25 and 31 Rainbow Drive to meet then-current eligibility standards for a Federal Housing Administration (FHA) insured mortgage. Priced at $2,500 and $3,100, these tiny houses foreshadowed the post–World War II Levittown developments. They necessarily lacked air-conditioning and a great many other appliances and details seen in the fancier Town of Tomorrow models. Luckily, the summer of 1940 was relatively cool.[41]

As it had in Chicago, one fair exhibitor, the state of Florida, preferred to soft-pedal its use of cooling technology at the New York exhibition. Florida's boosters and businessmen had priorities different from those of the air-conditioning engineer. At both fairs, Florida's official exhibits were equipped with central air-conditioning, but this modern improvement was artfully concealed rather than brashly promoted. As we have seen, the Florida Tropical House at the CPE was the only unairconditioned residence among the thirteen futuristic models. Florida's infamously humid heat, especially in summer, was described as "balmy," "healthful," and "ideal" in promotional materials offered visitors at both fairs. "The American Riviera," trumpeted one such brochure: "Where Summer Spends the Winter. . . . Far enough north to escape the enervating heat of the tropics . . . the home site ideal." Visitors interested in Miami were assured that "a heat prostration is unknown here—or elsewhere in Florida."

By 1939 Florida was only slightly more forthcoming. Florida's pavilion in the Amusement Zone at the New York World's Fair was one of just two state buildings equipped with an air-conditioning system. "Designed to duplicate the balmy atmosphere one actually encounters in Florida," this eighty-ton system was outfitted to perfume the air with the fragrance of orange blossoms. Even Westinghouse, builder and installer of the Florida air equipment, claimed it "simulates famous Florida weather."[42] A brochure boosting Sarasota suggested that air-conditioning was actually less necessary there than elsewhere in the United States:

If you want to escape excessive summer heat . . . and that oppressing humidity so typical of many communities during July, August, and September, come to Sarasota. You'll find Sarasota summers surprisingly cool. Fresh, tangy breezes sweeping in continuously from the Gulf of Mexico air-condition this year 'round playland. Houses are light and airy . . . and the average temperature is lower than most cities of the north.[43]

The Carrier Corporation had no such qualms about promoting products that in a generation would turn "balmy" Florida into the nation's most thoroughly air-conditioned state. Although still ailing from the effects of the Depression, the company made itself a prominent presence at the New York's World Fair. Carrier's Margaret Ingels would later claim that the company had misgivings about spending $200,000 on its 1939 fair exhibition. Considering that the seven-million dollar Futurama's design fee alone was $200,000, this figure seems improbably low.[44] Carrier's exhibition structure, located in the Production and Distribution Zone and designed by architects Reinhard and Hofmeister, was the only fair building devoted exclusively to air-conditioning. Somehow, a welter of contradictory messages about primitivism and progress, science and nature, ethnicity and climate overtook Willis Carrier's futuristic visions of an air-conditioned society. At the fair, Carrier chose to represent itself and its manufactured weather business with a five-story cone-shaped structure, dubbed the "Igloo of Tomorrow."

The igloo was coated inside and out with sparkling white stucco, in imitation of snow. Inside, "Northern Lights" were projected onto the walls of a central exhibition space, incongruously dominated by a palm tree (figure 19). Attached to the igloo by a glass arcade was a glass-walled "Hall of Weathermakers" featuring displays of air-conditioning equipment and tributes to the genius of Willis Carrier. Where other fair buildings had avoided glass because it posed too difficult a cooling problem, Carrier embraced the challenge, in defiance of the fair's predominantly windowless treatment of modernity. At the igloo's entrance stood a pair of 48-foot-tall thermometers. In one publicity photo, a thermometer labeled "Nature's temperature where you stand" read 90°; the second one labeled "Carrier Air-Conditioning in the Igloo" showed a temperature of 70 degrees. There is no evidence that Willis Carrier expressed his customary objections to such an extreme temperature differential as he enthusiastically took the lead in promoting his company's world's fair venture.

Actual igloos are built of ice and snow by the natives of climates that are life-threateningly cold most of the year, and their purpose is to keep their inhabitants as warm as possible. In E. L. Doctorow's *World's Fair*, a 1985 novel of New York in 1939, the protagonist, Edgar, helps his brother build an igloo one winter in their Bronx backyard. "I was further engrossed by the paradox of the

19. The Carrier Igloo at the 1939–40 New York World's Fair was one of several air-conditioned exhibits incongruously embellished with tropical vegetation.

warmth of a structure made of solid ice," he says. "You sweated in there, it was so hot . . . hot as on the hottest day of summer." Edgar's visits to the fair do not include the Carrier Igloo.[45]

The deliberate confusion of heat and cold, of comfort and survival, represented by the Igloo of Tomorrow seems not to have troubled press or visitors. Only David Irwin, an Arctic explorer who in 1935 had been dramatically rescued during a solo sled trip, protested. He threatened to sue Carrier because the igloo would prevent him from parlaying his ordeal into a world's fair attraction. A cartoon published in the *New York World-Telegram* after the igloo was announced in 1938 made fun of the igloo, but accepted Carrier's equation of "cold" and "igloo."[46]

Describing the exhibition on the day before the fair opened, the *New York Times* said, "Air-conditioning once consisted of opening a window or a damper, as the season might dictate. Now it's rather more complicated, mechanically speaking, but the results are better. To emphasize those results in terms of summer, Carrier Corporation houses its exhibition in a gigantic Eskimo igloo." An official Fair Guide Book called the igloo a "cool, comfortable, modernistic ice hut."[47]

20. The *New York World-Telegram* poked fun at the Carrier Igloo in 1938, but never quite figured out what was so peculiar about it.

As the 1939 fair season ended on October 31, the air-conditioning company staged the arrival by dog sled of "full-blooded Eskimo" Mayokok and his family. It is probable that the Mayokok family had spent the summer at the fair taking part in the Amusement Zone in a pseudo-anthropological display of "backward" or "exotic" peoples. This type of human display, with historical roots in the 1893 Columbian Exposition, was an easy-to-understand affirmation of modern white American progress. According to the caption on Carrier's publicity photo, the Alaska natives, bearlike, now sought to "bed down for the winter" in the igloo, presumably the only place in New York that would be cold enough for them. One can only wonder how they survived the summer outside it (figure 20).[48]

The igloo was not the only fair exhibition deliberately muddling modernist and primitive images of coolness and climatic control. Airtemp, Chrysler Motors' air-conditioning division, installed a "Frozen Forest" at the heart of its exhibition. There, according to a publicity folder, Airtemp technology had produced "an oasis of snowy palm trees in the midst of New York's summer heat . . . suggesting what city gardens of Tomorrow may become when today's science adds its inventiveness." Even *Refrigerating Engineering* was bemused. "Very pleasantly, though for no apparent reason, the Chrysler Company features frosted trees. They are not Arctic varieties but tropical ones, set in a cool, air-conditioneded, garden-like showroom otherwise given over to cars and comfortable seats," the journal reported.[49]

Jeffrey Meikle persuasively suggests that the Frozen Forest shows how designers had to struggle to impart spectacle to something like refrigeration, which is inherently motionless and essentially invisible. If the symbolism of exotic realms like the arctic or the tropics could be pressed into service, so much the better. Unlike these foreign hinterlands at the mercy of weather extremes, the air-conditioned venues of the fair aimed to provide a climate always constant and always under human control. Thanks to the magical mastery of the air-conditioning engineer, these exhibitions implied that the ordinary American—unlike the fur-swathed Eskimo and the near-naked tropical denizen—could live in civilized comfort.

These exhibitions also afford some additional insight into the larger issue of the New York World's Fair's fundamental attitude toward popular representations of science and technology. The promotion of air-conditioning by mystification, rather than clarification, was by no means unique to Carrier or Chrysler but prevailed among corporate exhibitors of technologically complex equipment. Scientists and engineers, although pleased by the attention paid to their work, were not necessarily happy about the way it was communicated to the fair-going public. In his keynote article, *Refrigerating Engineering* editor Fiske voiced serious reservations that were at odds with the issue's generally optimistic and self-congratulatory tone:

> The Fair is loaded with smiles, propaganda for capitalism, and extravagant claims for what science can do. Science, the essence of facts, of hard, inescapable reality, of common sense, becomes under this banner a sort of voodoo, medicine man, or charmer. Indeed, science is the god of the big business advertiser.

But, Fiske added, "They knew just how much ballyhoo and unreality people would absorb. . . . I like it, anyhow. I haven't heard of anybody who doesn't." He diplomatically refrained from criticizing any individual refrigeration exhibition, even the Igloo of Tomorrow.[50]

As Peter J. Kuznick has argued, the 1939–1940 World's Fair "venerated" science but this awestruck attitude if anything encouraged even greater use of "gadgets, commodities, and magic." Consequently, this fair, even more than Chicago's, was a showcase for "mystified and commodified" scientific spectacle. Scientists, says Kuznick, were themselves torn between wanting the fair to help ordinary Americans truly understand science's goals and methods and the more celebratory but less cerebral project of marketing science's "contributions" to the nation's material well-being. John C. Burnham sees in the fair experience an excellent instance of his argument that scientists, often socially disengaged and narrowly specialized, have surrendered their authority to gee-whiz journalism and preposterous advertising. The result, he says, has been an increased use of scientific language to foist magic thinking and folk beliefs on

21. Carrier's "Igloo of Tomorrow" opened on April 25, 1939 in 90° heat with scantily clad "snow bunnies" scooping manufactured slush under the benevolent supervision of thermometer-wielding founder Willis Haviland Carrier.

a gullible public. Thus is scientific prestige appropriated for promotional purposes, making the New York World's Fair a prime example.[51]

Willis Carrier had been portrayed in his firm's advertising as early as 1929 as a wielder of supernatural powers. "It was he who found the way to take humidity out of Summer air. . . . He creates the climate of Arizona in Maine — or the climate of Maine in Arizona. He even creates climates which do not prevail anywhere in nature. It is not a dream. It is a dream come true," gushed one such advertisement in the *Saturday Evening Post*.[52] Such unnatural dreams by 1939 informed most of the fair's treatment of science and invention. Even at the Chicago fair, where the scientific establishment had played an important consulting role, General Electric, as we have seen, framed its scientific research as a "House of Magic." GE brought the magic back, bigger and better, for both the New York and the smaller San Francisco world's fairs in 1939.

Many other companies followed suit. Revamping for the 1940 fair season, the natural gas industry promoted its "Gas Wonderland," featuring talking flagstones, singing trees and benches, and a talking model of a "typical American

22. Carrier closed the igloo for the season with the arrival by dog-sled of the fur-clad Mayokok family, who ostensibly planned to "hibernate" there until the Fair reopened in 1940.

suburb in miniature," in a press release studded with such words as "marvelous," "miracle," "magic," and "mystery." Servel Electrolux named its refrigerator display the "Magic Caves of Ice." At Westinghouse's "Scientific Curiosity Shop" visitors were encouraged to touch the exhibits, unleashing—without really understanding how—astounding special effects.[53]

The Carrier exhibition received its greatest publicity on August 23, 1939, when the company gathered seven hundred hay fever sufferers in the igloo to demonstrate the therapeutic value of air-conditioning. As reported in the August 24 *New York Times*, allergists selected eighteen sneezers for a demonstration of how to enhance the "air-conditioning function" of their noses. Said the *Times:* "The contestants could not sneeze in the Carrier Building, so the contest took place outdoors."

The igloo overall was not a major fair attraction of Democracity's or Futurama's magnitude. It was not mentioned in a *Business Week* article "What Shows Pulled at the Fair?" nor did it appear in a rigorous market analysis of the fair's seventeen top-attended industrial exhibits.[54] Yet Carrier president J. Irvine

Lyle enthusiastically renewed the lease of the igloo for the 1940 season. In a letter to fair president Grover A. Whalen, Lyle said two million people had visited the igloo. The fair, he added, had made people think about air-conditioning and had helped level out the usual seasonal sales peaks and valleys. "From a selfish standpoint, we are also pleased at the impetus this fair has given to the air-conditioning industry," Lyle wrote, adding "in fact, the New York World's Fair provides more air-conditioned comfort for visitors than all former fairs combined."[55] Who needed utopia, when a "modernistic" igloo in the World of Tomorrow held out such promise of comfortable profits?

6. No Place Like Home

The dream of owning a freestanding single-family house, a desire deferred by the Depression and World War II, was in 1946 for the first time a reality for more than half the families in the United States. As house ownership soared in the fifties, the powerful and much-abused idiom "home" was popularly applied to any and every rendition of the one-family domicile, even a 750-square-foot box under construction in a muddy potato field. This iconic "home," as Elaine Tyler May has shown, was a site of familial regulation in an era of global containment and a shelter against dangerous social forces. It was also armor against an array of equally threatening natural perils. Beset by noise, pollen, dirt, germs, and summer's pernicious heat, the American home needed help—or so the housing-industrial complex insisted—to fulfill its role as the only certain site of domestic tranquility in a risky world. This home needed every means of control modern science and engineering could provide. It needed air-conditioning.[1]

Eleven years after the first important installations of industrial air-conditioning and twenty-four years after Nikola Tesla and George Westinghouse marketed the first electrically powered portable fan, Minneapolis financier Charles G. Gates, son and heir of John "Bet-a-Million" Gates, in 1913 built his wife Florence a three-story Italian Renaissance mansion on East Lake of the Isles Boulevard at a cost of more than one million dollars (figure 23). The forty-bedroom mansion, with an entrance hall that

23. Completed in 1914, this forty-bedroom mansion on East Lake of the Isles Boulevard and 25th Street in Minneapolis was the nation's first private residence equipped with air-conditioning. The photograph was taken about 1920. Used for years for charity events, Charles Gates's million-dollar dream house was torn down in the fifties.

"simply screamed wealth and luxury," was equipped with an 840-cubic-foot air-conditioning unit that was personally designed by Willis Carrier at a cost of more than ten thousand dollars. "In those days only the very rich could afford Carrier air-conditioned homes, but it's different now," said Carrier Corporation cofounder and chronicler L. Logan Lewis in 1955. Lewis sensed the publicity potential in the transformation of nouveau riche excess into democratic accessibility. By 1955 a family could buy an entire house, complete with central air-conditioning, for ten thousand dollars.[2]

The Gates mansion, saved from the wreckers in 1932 but demolished in 1956 over the protests of local preservationists, proved to be a historical oddity, not a precursor. Charles Gates died on a trip to Wyoming before the mansion was completed in 1914. Florence Gates briefly occupied the house, but spent much time abroad and moved east when she remarried a few years later. A Saint Paul lumberman, D. F. Brooks, owned the house from 1923 until his death in 1929, but never lived in it, instead allowing the Junior League and other charitable groups to hold fundraisers there. It is possible that the mansion's climate control system was never used.[3]

Charles P. Steinmetz of General Electric, one of America's most lionized engineers, told *Ladies Home Journal* readers in 1915 that they would someday enjoy a "uniform temperature in our homes throughout the year," powered by electricity that he said would be cheaper than water. But middle-class housing trends in the first part of the century actually favored a more naturalized relationship between indoors and outdoors. Between the 1890s and 1920s, advocates of modern living promoted house designs meant to make the most of fine weather, rather than to escape weather's effects. Sleeping porches and sun parlors; larger windows, courtyards, and stucco exteriors were all aspects of the Americanized bungalow. The very term "bungalow," a borrowing from the Indian subcontinent, suggested tropical enjoyment rather than year-round uniformity of indoor conditions. This way of conceiving the interaction of house and environment persisted into the fifties and would complicate acceptance of air-conditioning by offering comfort strategies that did not require cooling machinery.[4]

Yet as air-conditioning began to gain an appreciative audience at the movie palace and department store, residential cooling seemed to a number of manufacturers and gas and electric utilities to be a logical next step. The Carrier Corporation set up the Carrier-Lyle subsidiary in 1929 to enhance its prospects in the home cooling market. One of the spin-off's first moves was to rehire mechanical engineer Margaret Ingels. She had been the University of Kentucky's first female engineering graduate in 1916, and was one of fewer than a hundred American women who earned engineering degrees prior to 1930. She also was a protégé of Kentucky engineering dean F. Paul Anderson, for whom the air-conditioning industry's highest honor would later be named. Ingels went to work for Carrier in Newark, taking a leave of absence in 1920 to join Anderson at ASHVE's new Bureau of Research, where she worked on dust filtration problems (figure 24).

Ingels worked briefly on C.-E. A. Winslow's second Ventilation Commission, leaving in 1929 to return to Carrier and its new residential air-conditioning endeavor. In her June 17 resignation letter to Winslow she said, "engineering is my profession. I believe absolutely in the principles of mechanical ventilation." The house organ "Carrier Courier" welcomed Ingels back, describing her as the "first woman air-conditioning engineer who is undertaking a program of educational work among women, designed to inform them of the advantages of Manufactured Weather in the home and how it can be made and controlled."

Margaret Ingels, over the next thirty years, would become the company's key link between its masculine "big iron" tradition of engineering and the ever more

24. Margaret Ingels, a pioneering heating and ventilating engineer, spent most of her career with the Carrier Corporation doing publicity work and promotion among women. This photograph was taken around the time that Ingels joined the ASHVE Bureau of Research in Pittsburgh. She and Carrier colleague L. Logan Lewis were named to the University of Kentucky's Hall of Distinguished Alumni in February 1965. Ingels died in 1971 at the age of 79.

important and ever more feminized domestic realm. Despite her obvious technical credentials, she spent most of her long career with Carrier as a publicist, publishing fifty articles, giving radio interviews, and delivering almost two hundred lectures to audiences comprising an estimated 12,000 people. Ingels also researched and wrote the only extant biography of Willis Carrier, published in 1952, two years after Carrier's death.[5]

Residential cooling efforts got off to a slow start in the thirties hampered both by the economic slump and a myriad of technical problems. Carrier cofounder

J. Irvine Lyle offered up his own house in Plainfield, New Jersey, as a testing site. The disappointing results included nasty drafts on lower floors and serious lags in cooling and dehumidifying the third floor. Carrier's initial venture into "portable" room cooling for residential hotels and apartment houses, advertised in *Time* and *Nation's Business* in 1932, hardly boded well for the company or the industry. For $255, the customer basically got a box on wheels that held 300 pounds of ice. Blowers powered by a one-horsepower motor moved air over the ice. The company, promising an extra 15 percent commission, implored employees to sell more of these Portable Room Coolers during the company's most dismal Depression year. Customers were told the units would cool a 300-square-foot room for up to 10 hours, provided sun exposure, electric lights, and crowds were kept to a reasonable minimum. Actress Jean Harlow used several of these rudimentary devices in her Park Avenue apartment "and, like the others, they had given so much trouble that [Carrier engineer Sam Shawhan's] visits had been frequent," Logan Lewis recalled in 1959. It was his recollection that Shawhan did not at all mind his many regular trips to Harlow's apartment.[6]

Chrysler Airtemp, Nash-Kelvinator, Servel Electrolux, and General Electric, all of them prominent presences at the world's fairs, also got involved in home air-conditioning at this time. GE built, in 1939, a $750 room unit housed in a radio cabinet, similar to the one that cooled Sally Rand in Chicago. It was designed to "match room furniture." The company sold about 50,000 of these and other types of units during the decade. In a paper written for presentation at a January 1932 professional meeting, three GE engineers linked their theories of indoor comfort to those of Ellsworth Huntington and warned against the "shock" of cold indoor settings during hot summer weather.

The public, they said, was not yet "sold" on the need for home cooling.[7] Airtemp and Servel made a major commitment to residential air-conditioning in 1936, as did American Radiator, John B. Pierce's company, and General Motors' Frigidaire division. Airtemp even placed full-page advertisements in late thirties' issues of the *Saturday Evening Post,* declaring that "residential cooling has arrived." But it was only after World War II that Airtemp or Servel sold more than a few hundred units a year. Beyond the grounds of the thirties' fairs, residential air-conditioning was still part of the "today" of only a very few wealthy urbanites.[8]

Metropolitan Life Insurance Company began in 1944 clearing seventy-five acres to build Stuyvesant Town in what was once east-side Manhattan's notorious Gashouse District. Residents—who were middle-class, mostly Jewish, mostly veterans, and at first all white—began moving into the rent-stabilized high-rise housing project's almost 9,000 apartments in 1947. Stuyvesant Town, and the smaller, classier Peter Cooper Village to its north, were immediate and continuing successes, providing a residential oasis in the big city. From the outset, Stuyvesant Town was equipped with trees, lawns, fountains, refrigerators, and trash incinerators, but no air-conditioning.

The insurance giant now known as MetLife had long been unusually active in studying the health of the living as well as underwriting their deaths. In the early twenties, the company's medical director was an active member of Ellsworth Huntington's Committee on the Atmosphere and Man. Metropolitan Life frequently published health bulletins and brochures including one in July 1950 titled "Air-Conditioning and the Comfort of Workers."[9] Yet air-conditioning was not even considered when Stuyvesant and Peter Cooper were built. Not until the early nineties did MetLife, at great expense, replace electrical wiring so that residents could install and run window air-conditioning units. Residents who did not want to share in the rewiring cost, and there were many of them, went to court and won the right to decline to air-condition.

Stuyvesant Town, writes Corinne Demas, who grew up there in the forties and fifties, was a "space capsule," "nature kept at bay." Yet the Demas family would retreat in July to a grandparent's vacation house in semirural Mount Kisco. Stuyvesant Town's reasonable rents and many amenities encouraged long residencies. Heat was a minor concern for families who could save enough on rent to pay for trips and outings, summer cottages and movie tickets. When other heat-beating strategies failed, there were local bars, ceiling fans, benches near the complex's grassy Oval, and spray fountains on the playgrounds.[10]

Air-conditioning manufacturers thus had good reason to be unsure about their residential prospects as they entered the fifties. Their experience with industrial and commercial installations had hardly prepared major manufacturers to deal with the space and cost strictures of the housing market. Nor were they skilled at the kind of marketing needed to sell air-conditioning to individual consumers. Air-conditioning was commodified in the fifties, but the process was neither certain nor simple. The loosely linked array of experts who took the lead in promoting air-conditioning in this decade would include manufacturers, advertisers, and dealers; architects, builders, and their publicists; authorities on health, physiology, and efficiency. They would at first underestimate the extent and strength of Americans' desire for air-conditioning. Later, they would be surprised to encounter any consumer resistance at all.

After a year-long study that cost a half-million dollars and included trial sales campaigns in New Orleans and the city of Washington, a four-man team of Carrier Corporation researchers concluded in 1948 that the only important foreseeable market for summer residential air-conditioning would be among southern households with incomes in excess of ten thousand dollars. Even when the engineers assumed home air-conditioning might become cheap enough to appeal to households in the $7,000 income bracket, they predicted that only 312,000 home air-conditioning systems would be sold in the United States between 1947 and 1961. As it happened, by 1960 more than six and a half million American households would own some kind of air-conditioning apparatus.[11]

The Carrier researchers postulated an upper-middle air-conditioning "class" that would use the technology to put the finishing touch of luxury on their ideal homes. But even among this limited set, they anticipated sales resistance. The kind of people who could afford air-conditioning, they argued, would most likely live in the suburbs where "whether it is actually true or not, most suburban home owners feel that their home is 'at least 10° cooler' than the city."

> Most people who can afford to own and operate air-conditioning can belong to country clubs, send their families away for summer vacation, or otherwise combine escape from the heat with recreation. The desire to live outdoors is another sales obstacle.[12]

Those most likely to be able to pay for air-conditioning were also the least likely to demand it for comfort, prestige, or an overall sense of family well-being. Like President Franklin Roosevelt—who air-conditioned Washington offices where lower-grade civil servants worked but disparaged the White House system available to cool him and his family—the most likely air-conditioning prospects, this study suggested, were likely to have a class bias against mechanical means of achieving living conditions appropriate to their birth, breeding, and income.

These were also the people who could afford larger houses. Robert and Helen Lynd's 1929 study of *Middletown* describes an interesting episode of class warfare that erupted in Muncie, Indiana, when enactment of daylight savings time was proposed there in 1925. Workers, whose tiny cottages remained hot long after midnight, forcefully protested losing an hour of cool morning sleep in order to give the more spaciously housed business class an extra hour to golf on summer afternoons.[13]

The housing available to the well off posed other challenges to the success of air-conditioning. Larger houses, far more readily than cramped cottages, could take advantage of such traditional cooling strategies as cross-ventilation, screened porches, and shady landscaping. And, as Carrier had so brutally discovered at J. I. Lyle's house and other ill-fated early ventures, the installation of air-conditioning in a sprawling or multistoried residence cost more and frequently worked less satisfactorily.

The Carrier engineers divided the United States into five climatic zones based on the number of hours between June and September when the temperature exceeded 65 degrees. The Gulf Coast and the Wheat Belt were adjudged the most promising markets. Zone 3, encompassing the city of Washington, where the federal government had been air-conditioned for two decades, was termed a region of only occasional discomfort. "The result is that many who could afford summer cooling will give priority to other luxuries," said the study. In the zone that included New York City and Chicago, "summer cooling for the home would be quite an extreme luxury."

The Carrier team estimated it would cost $1,350 to $2,500 to install three tons of central cooling at a time when the average price of a complete house was eight-nine hundred dollars. This was a bare minimum, only enough to cool a six-room house in Texas's climate or a "compact" seven-room house in Washington. They said it would take five costly tons of cooling to "carry a seven-room home, ranch type, in Texas and handle almost everything up to the mansion category in cooler climates." These, said the team, "are the size dwellings that house the greatest number of potential buyers of home air-conditioning at today's prices."[14]

The Carrier team was confident that their target market could afford to spend $100 a season to run their air-conditioning. But they were concerned that local electric utilities like New York's Consolidated Edison, already experiencing high summer load peaks due to widespread use of commercial air-conditioning, would view residential customers as a "highly *unattractive* load (emphasis in original)," and would express their antagonism with usage surcharges and installation assessments.[15] Nor were the Carrier engineers convinced that emerging architectural and design trends would be helpful or even compatible with air-conditioning:

> The architectural practices of today have not been shaped with any particular attention to paving the way for year round air-conditioning. It will probably be a period of some years before most modern homes are designed with summer air-conditioning in mind.

The emerging fashion for picture windows and huge expanses of glass was a decided negative. Radiant heating systems embedded in flooring were also more difficult to combine with air-conditioning than was traditional ductwork. On the plus side, the team told management, new houses tended to be smaller and better insulated. This could make air-conditioning more affordable and, although the engineers would not say so, enhanced the likelihood that systems would perform as advertised.[16]

So, despite the costs of installation, operation, and design, despite geographical and class limits on the extent to which consumer attitudes could be altered, Carrier researchers were cautiously optimistic that the right kinds of appeals could sell air-conditioning equipment:

The public—particularly in the South—sees both sensible cooling and dehumidification as major improvements in living comfort. Less important than comfort, but susceptible of future development, is the feature of health. . . . There are many people who, even though they enjoy air-conditioning in their offices and in the stores, theaters, and restaurants they patronize, do not want it in their homes. Many have the feeling that the 'shock effect' produces colds. . . . Others object to the thought of keeping doors and windows closed in the summertime.[17]

While Carrier researchers were gazing into a crystal ball clouded by what would prove to be a misapprehension of the fixed relationship between cost, climate, and comfort, other experts were stepping forward with alternative ways to achieve indoor comfort. Home building and ownership surged forward, released from the constraints of the Depression and war and encouraged by new federal programs. One such effort was the *House Beautiful* Climate Control Project.

House Beautiful—founded more than fifty years earlier by a civil engineer—had early established itself as the voice of a small "r" republican elite dedicated to "simplicity, economy, and appropriateness in the home" and committed to avoiding the sorts of excesses in house construction and decoration that comfortable finances might otherwise make possible. In the late forties, along with other home and garden magazines, *House Beautiful* enjoyed major circulation gains and had perhaps a half million readers at the time of the Climate Control Project.[18]

House Beautiful began its climate control research in 1947 in collaboration with the American Institute of Architects, the U.S. Weather Bureau, and the American Society of Heating & Ventilating Engineers. By the time the resulting project was introduced to readers in the magazine's October 1949 issue, it had taken on all the trappings of scientifically objective expertise. There were no heating or cooling engineers on the magazine's eight-man advisory board and just one architect. The panel was headed by Dr. Paul A. Siple, an Army climatologist and geographer. The other members were a Yale anthropologist, a climatologist and a physician-geographer both attached to the Army, a climatologist with a Weather Bureau background, and physiologist Lovic P. Herrington, C.-E. A. Winslow's associate at the Pierce Lab. The eighth panelist, technical writer and research pilot Wolfgang Langewiesche, would for the next three years write most of the Climate Control articles that appeared in *House Beautiful*. In the lead-off article, "What climate does to YOU and what you can do to CLIMATE," *House Beautiful* editor Elizabeth Gordon set the tone of the ensuing discussion and established herself as a lay person poised to personalize and popularize what this all-male panel of scientific experts would be telling readers was wrong with their habitats.[19]

The Climate Control Project was strongly grounded in the climatological assumptions of Ellsworth Huntington, but took a more activist approach to achieving the ideal Huntingtonian climate and a more lenient attitude toward thermal comfort, viewing it as beneficial in and of itself. Huntington had impracticably suggested seasonal relocation to maintain ideal conditions for physical and intellectual work; *House Beautiful*'s goal was a house for *all* seasons. Huntington linked weather changeability to human achievement; *House Beautiful* argued that modern life was difficult enough that "we don't need the weather to challenge us." The inaugural installment of the series repeatedly associated climate with, in Gordon's words,

> your energy, your ambition, and your efficiency. . . . You should know that those areas of the United States with the most *easily controlled* climates are also those with the highest income per capita, the best health, and the best intelligence and culture records. Clearly, there must be some relation between man's having an environment he can really control and his ability to make progress (page 131, emphasis in original).

In case readers missed the scientific saliency of Gordon's introduction, the message was reinforced throughout the 48-page section. On an early page, climatology tomes seem to march from a horizon massed with dark clouds into brilliant daylight (figure 25). This parade of expertise included all the big names: Huntington, Winslow, and Herrington, Sydney Markham, Clarence A. Mills, and *House Beautiful*'s own architectural editor, James Marston Fitch, who wrote the accompanying article "How You Can Use *House Beautiful*'s Climate Control Project." Fitch's 1948 book, *American Building,* found air-conditioning to be a lazy and ineffective way to provide indoor comfort, a view Fitch still held when *American Building* was reprinted a year before his death at age 90 in the year 2000.[20]

The project devoted far more attention to the perils of summer heat than it did to the problems of cold. Its experts warned that overheating taxed the heart, endangering the elderly especially, and portrayed heat as a merciless enemy of health and efficiency. Nevertheless, the overall message remained equivocal. On page 135 of the inaugural issue, for example, a full-page illustration showed two female forms side by side (figure 26). One is rectilinear and abstract, emerging from a background depicting laboratory equipment, molecular models, and algebraic formulae. The other is romantic, a curvilinear figure garbed in flowing robes bedecked with leaves and flowers. "You are two different personalities. Your hot self is the opposite of your cold self," the caption says, continuing:

> When you are *extremely hot* your body relaxes and your mind becomes contemplative, imaginative. You like flowing rounded lines, poetic ideas, shapes like a

25. This array of climatological expertise introduced *House Beautiful* readers to the magazine's Climate Control project in October 1949. Ellsworth Huntington and C.-E. A. Winslow are among the climate luminaries represented.

woman's. When you are *very cold* your body becomes tense and rigid. Your cool self becomes rational, energetic, efficient. You like things square, to fit exactly. If you had to design a building, it would come out engineered, functional, square-cornered, and factory-like (page 135, emphases in original).

26. *House Beautiful* used contrasting female forms to define "cold" and "hot" personalities in 1949, a time when it was not yet clear to the magazine or its readers which
personality would or should prevail.

This calculatedly ambiguous representation of the modern female form under
differing thermal conditions neatly evades the problem—raised by theorists of
human energy and fatigue—of where to locate the twentieth-century woman's
body on a spectrum from passive decorativeness to energetic efficiency, from
garden to machine. Clearly, the issue had not been settled in the generation since
the release of *The Science of Life*, a 1922–1937 U.S. Health Service film series
for high school biology classes. In these films, the "woman of tomorrow" was
depicted in "stark mechanical images" that likened her to a "sleek streamlined"

locomotive, while simultaneously offering soft-focus images of long-haired, apple-cheeked young women glowing in natural sunlight.[21]

It is not too surprising that *House Beautiful,* despite the Climate Control Project's anxiety about the dangers of summer heat, did not unreservedly embrace mechanical solutions. On the contrary, as in the case of the "warm" and "cold" women, romanticism regularly competed with modernism as the series attributed American summer discomfort to the loss of traditional construction practices and social customs that had once produced satisfactory thermal conditions in the home.

"So you think you're comfortable!" chief writer Wolfgang Langewiesche challenged in the October 1949 opener:

> How many hours a year are you really comfortable? You probably don't know. Because you have been trained not to notice. In our society, rooted in Puritanism, it is a sign of character to accept the pinpricks of discomfort. . . . Besides, we think weather discomfort is something we can't do anything about anyway. The truth is you are uncomfortable most of the time, for our houses are uncomfortable and not at all well adapted for the stresses and strains of the many climates in America (page 132).

If this, too, sounded like a prelude to an endorsement of air-conditioning, it proved to be otherwise. Langewiesche went on to criticize Americans for ignoring or forgetting the old ways of coping with summer heat. He blamed obedience to irrational design trends and misguided efforts at construction economy for creating a modern American house that was wrong for the climate of almost every part of the country and in almost all seasons:

> True, we now have better heating plants; we have cooling devices, insulation, electric fans, refrigerators, and swimming pools. These things do make our rough weather more tolerable. But we gloss over the fact that the house itself has not continued to evolve and improve as a weather shelter. . . . We have built, in the South, little, low-ceilinged hot-boxes. We have built, in the North, houses that are cold in winter and hot in summer. We have put Cape Cod houses into climates that are as different from Cape Cod as Cape Cod is from England (pages 133, 230).

Fitch pursued this argument in another article titled "Our ancestors had more savvy about climate," praising even the much-maligned nineteenth-century prairie sod hut for using the earth's constant temperature as effective insulation. Fitch continued:

> We act as though comfort-making machines would take the place of good siting, orientation, community planning. Nonsense! Air-conditioning in your house, for instance, means you've got to *pay more attention than ever* to wind and sun. Other-

wise, your operating costs will eat you out of house and home as the sun heats you while the machine cools you (emphasis in the original, pages 156–57).

Fitch here has clearly left the door open just slightly to "responsible" use of machinery to control the home climate where natural techniques have failed to achieve the higher standard of comfort propounded by *House Beautiful*.

As the series continued into the nineteen-fifties, natural strategies were emphasized and elaborated. In house designs prescribed for fifteen different climatic regions, ranging from Miami to Portland (Oregon), Columbus (Ohio), and Arizona, the magazine stressed wind direction, sun angles, room orientations, overhangs, and landscaping as viable alternatives to extravagant outlays for cooling and heating machinery. The designs featured huge window walls, simple rooflines, and ample opportunities for indoor-outdoor interaction. Articles might warn of the danger and discomfort of summer heat, but the designs that exemplified modern climate control favored "wall of glass" construction that allowed Americans living in colder regions to enjoy the "immense new freedom formerly possible only in warm climates" (page 138).

Although the readership of *House Beautiful* continued to grow, its Climate Control solutions would have minimal influence on American home building practice and home-owner habits. The magazine's "naturalism" ran counter to the circumstances under which most housing was actually being built in the United States. Its emphasis on careful site selection and construction planning, on "head work" rather than machines, fit neither the financial constraints nor the social attitudes of architects, builders, and utility companies or their customers in the swelling home-owner class. Between 1950 and 1955 there were more than a million housing starts each year.[22]

As early as 1951, local architects were writing to the American Institute of Architects *Bulletin* to criticize the Climate Control Project's lack of enthusiasm for mechanical air-conditioning. "Certainly air-conditioning has become almost standard equipment in hotels, restaurants, theaters, stores, banks, and many offices and is being adopted in the homes of those who can afford to pay for it," wrote an architect from Charleston, South Carolina. He wondered what medical evidence Project experts could possibly muster to make them so hesitant to recommend air-conditioning in Charleston. Two months later, an Albany, New York, architect accused the Project of taking summer in Albany "a little too lightly," adding "it's much harder to cool off in summer than to get warm in winter since few houses are cooled."[23]

House Beautiful might obstinately disregard or underrate mechanical air-conditioning but other publications were happy to take it more seriously. In 1952, its first year of publication, Henry Luce's *House & Home* mounted a national conference and devoted thirty pages to the question "Is air-conditioning in for a boom?" The magazine's answer, under the editorship of Joseph C. Hazen Jr., the Town of Tomorrow pollster, was an only slightly hedged "yes." Price, coupled with restrictions on FHA and VA mortgage allowances, was the "big stumbling block." But that was changing. Just six months earlier, builders had been hesitant to install central air in $25,000 houses. Now some Dallas builders were talking about making air-conditioning standard in $12,500 houses and "*House & Home* helped to spread their significant story to builders everywhere."[24]

The *House & Home* articles highlighted a number of interesting aspects of the pending boom. Regional climate did not seem to be the most important factor in the local success of installed residential air-conditioning. Next to Texas, the New York City suburbs were the "hottest" market for new systems. The relationship between the price of a house and the cost of installing air-conditioning varied significantly from region to region and even within the same region. In the New York metro area, a New Jersey contractor charged buyers a loss-leading $450 for a one-ton unit. At that price, all but one buyer wanted the air-conditioning, *House & Home* reported, but "families who used the equipment last summer say it does 'only a fair job of cooling.'" At 90°, the units—about half the size experts considered adequate for these 1,200-square-foot houses—struggled to reduce the temperature to 80 degrees. On especially humid days it took two hours for cooling effects to be noticeable. In Stamford, Connecticut, builder Carey Wellington, who sold his $40,000 to $60,000 air-conditioned houses to the likes of opera star Ezio Pinza, was having no success selling $12,000 houses with one-ton units that added $1,000 to the list price. "No one would pay that much extra," *House & Home* said of the 8 percent add-on.[25]

House & Home's review also disclosed that air-conditioning was lagging in regions that already had strong local traditions for keeping houses cool. Louisianans, it seemed, were attached to their big ceiling fans. In El Paso, virtually every house, from adobe shacks to mansions, used simpler and cheaper evaporative or "desert" coolers. Central system installations in Miami were so few that the local power company had no usage data. Window units were popular in places as diverse as Minneapolis and Albuquerque.[26]

When Irwin Jalonack, Levitt & Sons' chief mechanical engineer, said at a roundtable convened by *House & Home,* that air-conditioning should cost the builder "nothing," manufacturer representatives laughed but took notice. Carrier's 1948 research had suggested that speculative builders such as the "much-publicized Levitt Organization" might "*consider* air-conditioning if they can do so without risking too much of their own money."[27] Systems that took up little space, worked seamlessly with heating units, used less or no cooling water, and were sold to builders at a volume discount, said Jalonack, would persuade builders to make air-conditioning a customary new-house feature. "If you could put in an air-conditioner in a house for no more cost, I think that anybody would take it," he said. "Nobody would say, 'Just leave out the air-conditioning because I don't like it; my cat is allergic to it.'"[28]

During the very hot summer of 1952, air-conditioning advertising, even in the "agnostic" *House Beautiful,* became more abundant and more insistent in its claims. In the August 1952 issue, General Electric and Carrier both proclaimed a new affordability. "Why swelter? Complete home cooling is now within the reach of millions" declared General Electric, showing $12,500 houses in Dallas's East Ridge subdivision along with much fancier models in New Jersey and Kansas. "You can have a new kind of house," Carrier declared. Because "comfort is built in," the ad suggested, walls, doors, and windows could be located anywhere or even omitted. Cross-ventilation was portrayed as the luxury, not air-conditioning. It was the exact opposite of the message *House Beautiful* had been nurturing and promoting for three years.[29]

If *House Beautiful,* its presumed readers and its stable of experts wanted houses "at peace with nature," most young families starting out just wanted entry into the middle-class world of home ownership. They had neither the money, the time, nor the social status to hire architects, climatologists, and landscapers who would measure sun angles and wind speeds to assure the most environmentally attuned home. They were moving into suburban subdivisions where local ordinances and the postwar economics of construction dictated regularly arranged houses on lots where hills had been flattened, streams diverted or drained, and trees chopped down. To rotate a house plan on its axis to take advantage of prevailing winds, as *House Beautiful* frequently suggested, would have seemed in such subdivisions both pretentious and a stunning violation of neighborly and civic norms.

In her magazine's April 1953 issue, editor Elizabeth Gordon weighed in with an editorial titled "The Threat to the Next America." It was a surprisingly savage attack on the modernist and predominantly European architectural theory and practice generally known as International Style and foretold a new direction for *House Beautiful*'s own ideology of comfort. Gordon, it seems, had been approached by prominent Illinois physician Dr. Edith Farnsworth. Farnsworth had hired the famous International stylist Ludwig Mies van der Rohe to build her a weekend house in Plano, and now wanted to publicize her shock at its cost and her distress with its discomfort. Made almost entirely of glass, the house attracted insects when it was lit at night. Lacking both screens and air-conditioning, its windows could not be opened nor the interior cooled.

International Style and its perpetrators, proclaimed Gordon, were elitist, uncomfortable, empty, inhuman, and autocratic. Unlike the best of American design, she said, this import disregarded site and climate, paying no attention to sun, rain, heat, or cold. Couched in the language of Cold War Americanism, Gordon's article strongly suggested a menacing connection between International Style and international communism. It won her the devoted admiration of American architect Frank Lloyd Wright, who called Mies van der Rohe and his colleagues "totalitarians" who were "not wholesome people." The article also brought Gordon enduring cultural influence. Years later, author Tom Wolfe would caustically blame "respected instruments of architectural opinion and cultivated taste" for trying to persuade Americans that factory-like European modernism "was *living*."[30]

While seeming to reaffirm thoughtful climatic strategies and sparing use of household technology, Gordon's broadside signaled *House Beautiful*'s partial repudiation of its own home-grown but nonetheless elitist modernism. The magazine had deliberately ignored American popular tastes and had emphasized expert intervention in every phase of the home-building process. The Climate Control Project had conducted a love affair with huge areas of glass, flat roofs, and unornamented exteriors, all detested by most Americans. Its scornful attacks on the cozy Cape Cod and the imposing pseudo-Tudor or Regency did not reflect what was happening out in the mushrooming subdivisions. The *House Beautiful* aesthetic bore little relation to what might be called the Levittown pragmatic.

Henry N. Wright became the magazine's Climate Control and Air-Conditioning editor in November 1953. Wright, a former staff architect for the John B. Pierce Foundation, was heating engineer for a 1953 *House Beautiful* Pace Setter House described as "at peace with nature." In the early months of his editorship, the magazine published such articles as "Climate Control in the Kitchen Means Air-Conditioning." An April 1954 piece on a house in Louisville, Kentucky, focused on cross-ventilation but added "even with climate control, air-conditioning is a 'must' for real comfort." By the fall of 1954, air-conditioning maker Mueller Climatrol was publishing a promotional brochure for home owners in which the Climate Control series was gratefully acknowledged. Air-conditioning advertising in the magazine continued to increase and articles stressing the benefits of air-conditioning multiplied.[31]

After the war, many developers had set out to fulfill the modest promises of the American Family–FHA houses of the 1940 New York World's Fair, and one, Levitt & Sons, gained national fame (and a reputation for "ticky-tacky") for doing so.[32] Levitt & Sons had begun in 1929 as custom builders in Queens, Manhasset, and Long Island. Abraham Levitt, the Brooklyn-born son of a rabbi, and sons William and Alfred, in 1940 were advertising a $10,500 brick and stone semi-Tudor-style house that included General Electric air-conditioning and an array of name-brand appliances as well as automatic membership in a neighborhood country club that was closed to Jews, as was the entire development. After the war, the Levitts turned to mass housing that far more closely resembled the Town of Tomorrow's FHA models than did this spacious abode.[33]

Between 1947 and 1951, Levitt built 17,500 houses on approximately 2,700 acres of marginal farmland in Nassau County, Long Island. The first of these four-room, 750-square-foot "Cape Cod bungalows" situated rather incongruously on generous 6,000-square-foot plots, were geared to sell for $7,500 to war veterans and other young families who were white and had annual incomes of $3,750. At completion, 82,000 people would live in Levittown, New York. Says Levittown historian Barbara M. Kelly:

> Levitt's promise of postwar miracle houses, prefabricated with all new, built-in components and innovative materials, echoed those made during the World's Fair of 1939. The fair's "Home of Tomorrow" would be made from inexpensive, easy-care materials, it would be bathed in sunlight, and—thanks to modern technology—within the reach of "all but the lowest classes."[34]

The early Levitt houses were minimal even by the contemporaneous standards of the FHA and American Public Health Association.[35] They had no basements, no garages, a single bathroom, two bedrooms, and an unfinished, unheated, and uninsulated attic intended for future expansion. Yet, as Kelly points out, these cramped cottages were defiantly middle-class. Their interiors mapped the geography of the middle-class home, boasting a formal living room almost twice as large as the kitchen, and an expanse of lawn 2,000 square feet larger than required by town zoning ordinances. They had neither garage nor workshop.[36] A wood-burning fireplace and large picture window were added to the living rooms of the ranch-style 1949 models. The houses that completed Levittown in 1951 offered carports, a finished attic, and the hottest appliance of all, a television set built into the living room. Except for the attic, all these improvements added status to the public areas of the house, rather than comfort to the private and productive sectors. Notes Kelly, "Instead of rooms, the houses offered efficiency; instead of work space, they offered appliances (page 96)."

With their uninsulated attics and a size and floor plan that made cross-ventilation difficult, these first Levitt houses must have sweltered during Long Island summers. There are no obvious indications that this problem deterred or disappointed eager purchasers of these "cute" and affordable new houses, but it did sharpen the challenge to air-conditioning manufacturers posed by Levitt's Irwin Jalonack. In the sixties and seventies, a wave of Levittown remodeling transformed many of the humble Cape Cods: these projects would often include air-conditioning.[37]

The Carrier Corporation, apparently no longer content to wait for wealthy individuals to beat a path to their door, in 1952 commissioned an architectural firm to design a mass-producible house that would make optimal use of the firm's Weathermaker air-conditioning system. "This house started a revolution," Carrier declared in trade advertising that ran several years later:

> It need not depend on natural ventilation. Ells and wings wouldn't be necessary. Only a few windows need have movable sash. The bathrooms needn't require a window. Windows, doors, and even the rooms themselves could be placed to suit the convenience of the owner, *not* to catch a breeze (emphasis in original).[38]

Carrier followed up with a nationwide Weathermaker Home Competition, announced in ads in the 1953 *House & Home* and several other architectural publications.[39] A $5,000 grand prize attracted 861 entrants. Thirty smaller awards based on region, house size, and roof style were also given out. Five jurors, including veteran industrial engineer and efficiency expert Lillian M. Gilbreth, identified in Carrier publicity literature as "housewife, mother of 12, heroine of 'Cheaper by the Dozen,'" sifted the submissions.

The grand prize was awarded to two Argentinean architects based in Raleigh, North Carolina. Their design, later built, was a 1,000-square-foot house with huge areas of fixed glass on the north and south exposures, a flat roof, and generous overhang. The June 1953 *House & Home* complained that "most contestants showed only a rudimentary grasp of how to take advantage of air-conditioning." Specifically, the article criticized heavy reliance on flat roofs that absorb heat readily and shed it slowly, and a failure to consider trees and fencing as shading strategies:

> While high ribbon bedroom windows, tightly sealed and tucked under wide over-hangs, are fine from an air-conditioning viewpoint, they darken rooms, cause claustrophobia, and ride roughshod over most people's desire to keep windows open part of the year. Builders cannot sell houses in today's market with sealed windows. Many of the contest bedrooms are also far too small for public acceptance.[40]

Yet only a few months later *House & Home* was singing the praises of sealed houses. The summers of 1952 and 1953 had been unusually hot across the nation. Throughout the disappointingly cool summer of 1954, the mass media kept up a drumbeat of news that air-conditioning was no longer just a movie-palace treat, but now was available for the suburban home. That year's late spring and mild summer left 700,000 air-conditioning units unsold, despite frantic price-cutting. With an estimated forty "legitimate" air-conditioning manufacturers, and perhaps a hundred more brand-name boxes, consolidation was inevitable as the bad year helped "shake out the cats and dogs." In 1955, for example, Carrier acquired Bryant.[41]

In a special 24-page supplement to its March 1954 issue, *House & Home* hailed the benefits and affordability of air-conditioning. The magazine then went further than it ever had before by endorsing houses designed to be unlivable without mechanical air. "All the rooms are sealed with fixed windows against outside wind, dust, and weather," one article said approvingly of a house in Dallas featuring an "indoor garden." The magazine then described an even more expensive Dallas residence:

> Air-conditioning is bringing new ways of life in hot climates. Owner Herman Blum soon discovered that air-conditioning was so pleasant that he and his wife almost never use their outdoor terrace. Not only is it cooler inside but there is also an absence of mosquitoes and bugs. . . . As soon as it is warm enough for outdoor living it is time for air-conditioning. . . . When a woman stays indoors all day she enjoys looking out to a patio or garden.[42]

Before the war, women would find public opportunities for comfort and companionship in the movie palaces and department stores of the great downtowns. Now, this article implied, they should seek their comfort and enjoyment in a privatized suburban space made safe—by air-conditioning—from nature's intrusions or urban hazards.

The special *House & Home* supplement featured comments from home owners who had told the magazine their home air-conditioning was miraculous. Two months later, excerpts from the same survey appeared in *House Beautiful*.[43] "If you ring the doorbells of air-conditioned houses, this is what people say about summer cooling," the *House Beautiful* headline declared. On the page opposite, a full-page ad extolled the virtues of Frigidaire Conditioner's "One Temperature Home Summer and Winter," a house where "costly construction details" like breezeways, porches, screens, movable sashes, and high-pitched roofs had been eliminated.

The survey subjects were wealthy Dallas and Houston residents occupying new $35,000–$75,000 houses. They fit the by-now outdated profile of the ideal air-conditioning customer Carrier researchers had assumed in 1948. Both magazines treated the responses as if they were those of average middle-class Americans, even though many respondents focused on the relation between air-conditioning and the customary pleasures of their well-to-do lives.[44] "When we have a party now, the men leave on their coats," said one interviewee. Another said she no longer had to "worry about rain coming in the windows or about burglars." "When you advertise for a girl, they ask if you have air-conditioning," said a third. "We save the price of a summer home," one commented. "We run our machine twenty-four hours a day. It costs us much less than we'd thought, and we save part of the cost in fewer restaurant bills," said still another anonymous subject.

But the wealthy Texans also affirmed some of the more mundane virtues advertised by air-conditioning manufacturers. Mothers said air-conditioning gave them renewed enthusiasm for cooking hot meals and baking family treats. "We're healthier," "we sleep better," "we dust less," "no mildew," others added. "There is no doubt that air-conditioning is better for children," a Houston pediatrician opined. "He's a new man," said one woman of her husband.

Another woman astutely connected her experience to a larger social context. "The movies and the automobile broke up family life," she said, "but telvision and air-conditioning are bringing families together again." Movie palaces had drawn people out of their homes in search of communal comfort and entertainment in a relatively democratic public setting; both television and residential air-conditioning were privatizing comfort for those who could afford the capital expenditure and operating costs.

Those costs were not insignificant. *House & Home* spent a good deal of its March 1954 special section justifying the cost of operating air-conditioning. The opening article said that Dallas families, most of them living in 1,150-square-foot houses equipped with two-ton General Electric central air-conditioning units, had average electrical bills of thirteen dollars a month, sixty-five dollars for the season, during a summer when the temperature topped 100° on 34 days. The highest bill of $111.57 was ascribed to a family with big windows facing east and west and a preference for 68° all summer long. An indoor temperature of 74° was recommended. The magazine's own estimates indicated that the average Dallas household was using almost twice as many kilowatt-hours each month just for air-conditioning as for all other household uses combined.[45]

The bellwether Levitt organization, now under William Levitt's sole control, affirmed the ongoing commodification of residential air-conditioning in 1955, when it signed a huge contract to install Carrier air-conditioning units as standard equipment in hundreds of new houses:

In announcing this largest contract ever placed for residential air-conditioning, William J. Levitt stated: "It doesn't make any sense to heat a home in the winter and not cool it in the summer. Before very long we hope to be able to install central air-conditioning equipment in every home we produce."[46]

The 702 "Country-Clubbers" erected in Levittown, Pennsylvania, in the spring of 1955 were a big step up, in scale and amenity, from the Cape Cods and ranches built by the organization as recently as four years earlier on Long Island. On half-acre lots, with three bedrooms and space for two more, two baths, and a two-car garage, these $18,990 tract houses contended for custom-built status. At approximately 2,400 square feet, they were twice the size of the average 1955 house and three times larger than the original Levittown boxes. This deal with Levitt, Carrier bragged, proved "indisputably that home air-conditioning now has been brought within the reach of millions of Americans."[47]

Now that ownership of even the most modest house was de facto evidence of entry into the middle class, those who sought to consolidate their tenuous new status were well-advised to install whatever extra features and appliances were needed to differentiate their houses from those in their own and in other neighborhoods. Levittowns, and thousands of other similar subdivisions, were communities of emulation. New products meant tiny but important increments of status. One such product was the window air-conditioning unit. It was cheaper than central air and becoming more so as dozens of manufacturers rushed into a "chaotic" marketplace. It could be bought impulsively, when the weather turned torrid, and installed without a lot of special planning. Although clearly not as high status nor as effective as a central system, one or multiple window units were satisfyingly obvious to the passersby.

Sociologist William H. Whyte Jr. used patterns of window-mounted air-conditioner installations on blocks of new town houses in Philadelphia to demonstrate in 1954 how neighbors influenced each other to purchase certain kinds of goods. "The more similar most things are, the more important the minor differences become," Whyte said, noting elsewhere:

> Air-conditioners were chosen because they are currently the prime example of a new product climbing up the acceptance curve from the luxury to the necessity category. Not unimportantly, they also happen to be highly visible, and thus provide a convenient index of how people are influenced by one another.[48]

Of the 4,948 Philadelphia houses Whyte surveyed, 988—or 20 percent—had one window conditioner, compared to an estimated 3 percent of residences nationwide, and 395 or 8 percent had two window units. The Overbrook Park area where Whyte did his study was a modestly affluent urban neighborhood consisting primarily of white-collar couples aged 25 to 40, who earned $5,000 to $7,000 annually and lived in "nearly identical $12,000 houses." Interestingly, said Whyte, he found a stronger concentration of window units in row-house neighborhoods than in upper-income neighborhoods, adding: "Conditioner ownership, it would appear, is not something that is trickling down from the top income group."[49]

What was going on? Philadelphia's summers were often hot, but this could not explain why one block had only three air-conditioner–equipped houses while the adjacent block had eighteen. Whyte's thesis was based on "less logical forces" than a desire to keep cool. Women watching over children and men attending to their yards had many opportunities, he said, to chat informally about the advantages of their new air-conditioner, or simply to allow their neighbors to see—and hear—the units. The visibility of air-conditioning apparatus certainly played a key role in promoting neighborhood emulation. It would be years before the outdoor compressor, emblem of central air-conditioning, would become a neighborhood status symbol, trumping the cumbersome and unattractive window units. As clusters of air-conditioner–equipped town houses emerged, said Whyte, "on a hot night the whir of the motors" would become "psychologically deafening" to those who still needed to open their windows.

There was a delicate balance, Whyte observed, between the unseemly ostentation of being first on the block to buy an expensive new appliance and being unwilling to buy one after everyone else had done so. Such recalcitrance, he noted, might be perceived as an "unsociable" aspersion on neighbors' spending and lifestyle decisions. *It is the group that determines when a luxury becomes a necessity,"* he said (emphasis in original). Word-of-mouth, Whyte suggested, worked better than mass-market advertising to create customers who were pre-sold on air-conditioning. Neither mass-market ads nor dealers, he said, were doing an adequate job of helping customers transform their desire for what their neighbors had into an actual acquisition.

As Roland Marchand has pointed out, advertising never simply mirrors the social order but reflects advertisers' inevitably partial understanding of who their audience really is and what they can be persuaded to buy. The physical attributes of an advertised product become just the jumping-off point for a fantasy on the theme of how the product will change the customer's life for the better, or at the very least rescue him—or more often her—from an array of physical and social disasters. Although it is almost impossible to determine whether a specific ad has sold measurable quantities of a particular product, Marchand says, advertising is a historical text that can help us identify the framing assumptions within which public attitudes are formed and consumption decisions take place.[50]

Advertising does the important job of domesticating and normalizing the use of technologies that might at first be perceived as frightening. It can also ultimately marginalize those who still refuse to use them. Advertising also works to turn products of agreed-upon utility or necessity into "pleasures" by emphasizing their style, color, or some other extraneous new feature. "Luxuries" must be recast as urgent, even essential, requirements for modern living. The most serious concerns of daily life—health, family happiness, status—are marshaled to promote their consumption. Because the utilitarian purposes of air-conditioning were still viewed by many potential customers as a relative luxury, air-conditioning advertising partook of both these marketing strategies.

Air-conditioning manufacturers and dealers were by no means oblivious to the status appeal of their product; it became a central component of early advertising efforts. By focusing on the mythical "Joneses," advertisers could address the perceived vanity of women and the self-importance of male householders concerned about property values. A shift in air-conditioning advertising from engineering, architectural, and specialty trade and industrial journals to mass-market newspapers and magazines—and later to television—bore witness to its emergence as a consumer commodity.

Although still primarily focusing sales efforts on their strong commercial-industrial sector, the Carrier Corporation in 1945 chose N. W. Ayer, a consumer-oriented old-line Philadelphia ad agency, to position the company for residential marketing in the postwar period.[51] Especially in the early Ayer ads, distinctions were clearly drawn between the elite class of home owners who might install central air, and customers looking for the limited relief of a room unit. A 1947 ad in *Time* and the *Saturday Evening Post,* for example, depicted an elegant couple enjoying an upper-middle-class holiday. "'Weather' stole the show at Radio City. . . . Added zest to dining at Stouffer's. . . . Right there we 'bought' it for our living room. So now we're comfortable at home." Ads promoting Carrier's room air-conditioner, prepared by Ayer for the same two magazines, used a completely different visual vocabulary that stressed humor over drama, economy over luxury, and perspiration over refinement. In these ads, cartoon figures whimsically demonstrated such traditional methods of keeping cool as frequent baths, haircuts, loose clothing, drinking (but not gulping) cool (not icy) water and "the best of all! Get a Carrier Room Air-Conditioner to keep you cool as a cucumber . . . gives you a holiday from heat . . . feel like a million at work or play!" The room unit, not Radio City, would be this family's summer vacation.[52]

Not that appeals to prestige in humbler settings were entirely overlooked. A 1950 Carrier newspaper cartoon showed a man watching the television ball game all alone, surrounded by empty chairs, as a neighbor stuck his head in to say, "They're all next door enjoying Carrier air-conditioning." This association of air-conditioning with television suggested that neighborhood status could only be assured by ownership of both new technological marvels. The Carrier Corporation began advertising in 1956 on NBC's "Today Show" with David Garroway and "Home Show" with Arlene Francis.[53]

Advertising generally has long catered to the perceived desires and frailties of women. As competition in the air-conditioning market increased, fifties ad campaigns refined these traditional gender appeals by incorporating appeals to family "togetherness" within the walls of the single-family suburban home. As supervisors of this home, guardians of its health, and caretakers of their family's emotional well-being, women would need to be persuaded that air-conditioning, which many found chilly and stagnant, could make the whole family function properly and protect it from whatever lurked outdoors. If this were not enough to motivate mother, the ads also promised that air-conditioning would reduce house cleaning, affording her more ease without guilt.

Trade publications forthrightly advised dealers that it was impossible to sell the man of the house without first persuading his wife. "A year or more ago when builders first began air-conditioning their houses they expected it to work miracles," *House & Home* told its builder-readers in March 1954:

> The trouble has been that air-conditioning is hard to sell to families who have no experience with it. Many women still associate it with chilly, drafty movie theaters and restaurants. Yet women who have had it in their homes for two summers are its greatest boosters.

Carrier used an ad in the June 1954 *House & Home* to tell the trade "what women want." Las Vegas contractor Helen Boris "Sells Them as Fast as She Builds Them!" the ad proclaimed, continuing archly:

> The woman's touch is proving mighty profitable. Helen Boris gives the girls natural birch kitchen cabinets, mahogany slab doors . . . and Carrier air-conditioning. She says, 'A woman spends twice as much time at home as her man. So she appreciates that Carrier comfort on hot days.'[54]

Air-conditioning took full advantage of an advertising genre that connected home appliances with yearnings for devices that could produce not just a well-cooked dinner, clean floor, or cool house but healthier, better-behaved children, and happier, more attentive husbands. Only an air-conditioned home, the ads suggested, could fulfill the suburban promise of sanctuary from a hot and dangerous world. It would be a haven for men returning home from hot city streets and would give those who worked in air-conditioned city offices no excuse for straying from the family fold. Many ads featured a perfectly groomed woman at her ease reading a book or magazine on a couch near a curtained window equipped with an air-conditioning unit. Perhaps she had just finished mopping the kitchen floor in pearls and heels, in the manner of contemporary television ads. Or perhaps air-conditioning had made it unnecessary for her to clean at all. "Make your home a Castle—not a workshop . . . why clean mountains of dust and dirt?" declared one such 1954 ad for the General Electric room air conditioner.[55]

The perfection of the living room was further assured by manufacturers' mindfulness of home decor. An extreme example was a 1954 ad for International Harvester's "Decorator" air-conditioner, a "fashion first" and the "only air-conditioner you can decorate to match your room." With less than a yard of fabric, the imaginative homemaker could turn a room cooler made by a company best known for farm machinery into a decorating triumph. Here an evening-gowned woman reclines uncomfortably in a modern chair. Her vivid orange lipstick perfectly matches both the bold orange draperies and, of course, the front panel of the air conditioner.[56]

Family "togetherness" ads showed nuclear families at very close quarters, each engaged in gender and age-appropriate leisure pursuits, including decorous play, games, reading, needlework, but very rarely television viewing. Typical of these was a series of full-page magazine ads developed by Ayer for Carrier that ran in 1955 and 1956 in *Time* and *Newsweek*. "Your children are more fun in a Weathermaker Home" shows a girl playing with a doll as her brother rides a rocking horse. In another, headlined "You enjoy your children more in a Weathermaker Home," a mother plays with a chuckling infant. Sharpening the point, the ad continues, "And watch what happens when Dad steps inside after a steaming day at the office! Two breaths of cool air and he's ready to tumble with his youngsters."[57]

A 1955 Mueller Climatrol booklet aimed at "Mr. Builder" rather than "Mrs. Housewife" also incorporated images of prestige and togetherness. In one illustration, an obviously sweltering handyman pushes a lawnmower outside while inside the crisp, cool family clusters around the air-conditioner. In this rare instance, the draperies are actually drawn apart to reveal the scorching outdoors just beyond the window air-conditioning unit (figure 27).[58]

The smiles of satisfied families were certainly easier to convey than air-conditioning itself. As had been true at the World's Fairs, the invisibility of air-conditioning posed marketing problems. In their eagerness to make the cooling *equipment* unobtrusive, fifties marketers were in danger of making its *effects* disappear into the background as well. Seasonal amnesia about hot weather was a persistent challenge—almost no one, then or now, thought about buying an air-conditioner in the winter. *House & Home* counseled builders on how to dramatize their air-conditioned models during the summer house-hunting season. These recommendations included posting a large sign or thermometer comparing indoor and outdoor temperatures and humidities (à la the Carrier igloo at the 1939–1940 World's Fair); secreting a pair of mildewed shoes in a closet to show the failings of an unairconditioned house; soaking a huge sponge in water condensed from an operating unit; and finally "frame a color photograph or drawing from a magazine showing home entertaining. Caption: 'Everyone

27. If the subtext of air-conditioning advertising was "never let them see you sweat," this page from a 1955 Mueller Climatrol booklet strongly suggested that keeping cool was a reward for those who could hire others to do the hot work.

enjoys inviting in old friends. For new summer popularity there's nothing like a cool, comfortable house.'"[59]

Some of air-conditioning's less salable effects were quite apparent and already well known to potential customers. Implicit in every ad was a subtext that whispered air-conditioning's flaws, drawbacks, and inadequacies. Were air-conditioners, especially window units, bulky and unattractive? Ads focused, at times to the exclusion of all other features, on elegance, slim lines, and unobtrusiveness. Were they noisy and annoying to neighbors? General Electric, for one, referred to its units as "kitten quiet" and ads generally highlighted the exclusion rather than the creation of outdoor noises. Did air-conditioners make your house smell funny and exclude wholesome fresh air? Remington offered optional odor control to "bring the true sweet breath of spring into your home." Philco was exceptional in scorning the almost universal emphasis on cabinet design. Its promotional material stressed fresh air and claimed to have corrected problems of condensation drip, a defect virtually never admitted by other manufacturers.[60] Were air-conditioners tricky to use? The finger on the "finger-tip control" was almost always that of a woman. This also helped assuage women's concerns that they might be unable to keep their houses from getting too cold.

The question of temperature preference, a long-standing concern of physiologists and engineers, mostly got short shrift in home building media and its advertising. An article in *House & Home*'s March 1954 special section alluded to surveys showing that

> . . . young people want more cooling. Middle-aged and older people want less cooling. Men usually prefer a 2° cooler house than women. . . . As to the difference between the sexes, a woman who shivers all summer in a 72° house says: "Just right for my husband but, my gracious! Too cold for me. I wear a sweater."

The question of why a woman home all day would suffer in her husband's absence is neither asked nor answered. Presumably this woman felt unqualified to manipulate the controls.[61]

While advertisers of air-conditioning trained their sights on suburban housewives, these "typical" American women were not, it seems, looking to air-conditioning to solve all their housekeeping and familial problems. When 103 female delegates gathered in Washington on April 23–25, 1956, for the Women's Congress on Housing that would tell federal agencies, belatedly, what women wanted in a home, indoor cooling was very low on the agenda. Its desirability was acknowledged but overshadowed by calls for more space and greater privacy; the inclusion of such traditional, if extraneous, niceties as fireplaces and parlors; and demands for more consumer say-so over the number and kind of installed appliances.[62]

The congress, which took place after the postwar housing boom had already peaked, was organized by climate and region. Its delegates, selected from 4,300 who had applied to the Housing and Home Finance Agency, were sorted into nine geographic areas, roughly corresponding to Census divisions. A tenth "control" group consisted of women from northern California, Florida, Missouri, Oklahoma, Texas, western Washington, and Long Island. The participants were almost certainly all white. The women ranged in age from 25 to 45 and 87 percent had at least two children. Almost half were college graduates, but only a dozen held jobs outside their homes. Fifty-eight percent had household incomes in excess of $8,000 and only 15 percent had incomes below $5,000. Ninety-five percent were already living in single-family houses.

Demographically, these women might have stepped directly from the air-conditioning ads of the fifties into a government conference room. They were asked to reach a consensus on what a $10,000 house must include, and then propose what amenities and features should be added, given a $20,000 budget.

The average house in 1955 had 1,170 square feet, making it 36 percent larger than Levitt's first Long Island tract houses and 15 percent larger than Carrier's 1953 national award winner. Congress participants declared themselves willing to sacrifice many appliances, at least temporarily, in return for more roominess, and expressed a strong preference for purchasing their own appliances rather than having builders like Levitt select and pre-install them. Congress members wanted basements, fireplaces, dining rooms. They loathed floor-to-ceiling glass window walls and open-plan living rooms.

The ten groups were asked specifically to give their views on "interior weather conditioning." Two groups, one representing the mid-Atlantic states centered on the District of Columbia and the other composed of women from Michigan, Minnesota, and Wisconsin failed to address the question at all. Of the eight groups that did respond, five felt air-conditioning was desirable enough that houses should be constructed to make future addition possible. The women from Illinois, Indiana, Ohio, and West Virginia called for fresh air and attic fans. Air-conditioning, they said, was a luxury and provisions for its future installation were unnecessary. The group from the deep South and Border States "divides evenly on a choice of installing air-conditioning initially, if money is available." Only the control group and women from Texas and the desert Southwest argued that new houses should have air-conditioning already installed. Asked to select the most important of twelve household appliances, half the groups did not even mention air-conditioning. Only deep freezers had a lower priority ranking.

As efforts to "sell" women on air-conditioning continued through the fifties, manufacturers and dealers began to worry that over-feminization of the product was driving away male customers. This concern was not entirely new. Although advertisers had come to see women as their primary audience in the early years of the twentieth century, they had never satisfactorily decided the extent to which women made or strongly influenced decisions regarding capital outlays for major household machinery.[63]

Home air-conditioning occupied an unsettled position in the gendered hierarchy of domestic appliances. Was it a "white good," an appliance that, like refrigerators and washers, enabled women to perform their duties efficiently within their sphere of production? Or was it a "brown good," much as a television or record player, purchased by the male breadwinner for his and the family's pleasure?[64] Or, in these years of Cold War and nuclear anxiety, was air-conditioning really a fortification against literal or symbolic invasion?

Advertising reflected inherent anxiety about appropriate gender messages. In 1958, Carrier plugged its $149.95 Portable Year-Round Air-Conditioner in both trade and mass publications, including Sunday newspaper supplements. Although the focus remained new color styling—the choice was mocha and sand beige or turquoise and colonial white—a June 2, 1958, ad in *Home Furnishings Daily* carefully hedged its appeal:

> Let's face it. In most cases it's the man of the house who first makes up his mind to buy a room air-conditioner. But on the other hand, let's not sell the little lady short.

The accompanying photo showed a white-gloved, braceleted hand toting this sixty-pound "portable" with the greatest of ease. In other versions a man in a suit carried the portable as if it were luggage.[65]

Ads running in the summer of 1959 made an almost absurd effort not to alienate the important male target audience of builders and installers or their primary customers, male heads of household. A June ad published in several trade publications, including *American Builder,* shows a man in shirt and tie smiling in front of his air-conditioning's elaborate instrument panel as his wife, carrying a tea tray, gazes at him admiringly (figure 28):

> Here are the biggest 112 square inches in air-conditioning. . . . There's something masterful about flipping switches and turning knobs. And then feeling and seeing how your air-conditioning responds.

A September 1959 ad depicted the centrally air-conditioned house as a male domain scientifically controlled by Mr. Home Owner, winning him the adoration of his family and admiration of his friends. No longer was a mere switch "flipped" by a painted fingertip. Instead the "handsome" Carrier Climate panel was overtly likened to the instruments on a ship's bridge or airplane cockpit. Comfort could be masculine, too.[66]

If the air-conditioning manufacturers were committed to persuading women through appeals to family happiness and social success, and swaying their hus-

Here are the biggest 112 square inches in air conditioning...
the revolutionary panel that gives new mastery of indoor climate!

NEW CARRIER CLIMATE CENTER

There's something masterful about flipping switches and turning knobs. And then feeling and seeing how your air conditioning responds. That's part of the mastery a homeowner can now enjoy with the revolutionary Carrier Climate Center.

But on this 8 x 14 inch satin aluminum wall panel (which mounts between studs), he also sees what the weather is outside—and what it will be tomorrow. Here he sees how his Carrier air conditioning system is operating. These things, too, make up the new mastery he has in a Carrier Weathermaker* home.

Now he can custom-tailor indoor climate to the preferences of his family. He can also operate his system more economically. For example, a timer can be preset to lower the indoor temperature automatically during sleeping hours. There's also a signal light† to show when filters should be replaced for top efficiency.

A Carrier Weathermaker home now becomes a new experience in comfort, health and cleanliness. And to make it a new experience in economy, Carrier also offers the 63D Horizontal Weathermaker. It's a complete central cooling system, but supplied in one compact package that's ready to operate as soon as it's connected to electricity and air ducts. In homes with wet heat, special prefabricated ducts can be installed in a jiffy.

The Horizontal Weathermaker can be installed indoors or outdoors in dozens of different ways.

Phone your Carrier distributor today for details about these products ... plus the triple advantages of a Carrier franchise.

MORE PROOF OF
BETTER AIR CONDITIONING FOR EVERYBODY   EVERYWHERE

Carrier

†Optional   *Reg. U.S. Pat. Off.

28. Was comfort too feminine? Carrier apparently thought so when its agency created this trade ad in 1959. One can only speculate how the target audience understood copy and images that would now seem laughably Freudian.

bands with pride, power, and promises of control, their attitude toward potential residential customers who were black was one of benign neglect, at least in terms of advertising. The South, air-conditioning's most likely market, was still home to a large part of the nation's black population. Blacks in northern cities often occupied cramped apartments or modest houses that could decidedly benefit from compact cooling equipment. As air-conditioning prices declined in the fifties amid ferocious competition, failure to pursue African American customers was only partly a question of their disposable income.

Theories such as those of Ellsworth Huntington and S. Colum GilFillan that associated undesirable racial characteristics with hot climates were by no means defunct by the fifties. The idea that dark-skinned people suffered less from heat than did whites was a central tenet of racialist thought. A Carrier ad that appeared in *Time* and *National Geographic* in April 1950 shows a cartoon Englishman, nattily dressed in safari shirt and sun helmet, followed by two smiling, near-naked, dark-skinned natives bearing a room unit. "Twombley won't go anywhere without his new Carrier Room Air-conditioner," two fellow "great white hunters" comment. In a similarly colonial spirit, *House Beautiful* Climate Control Project staff writer Wolfgang Langewiesche traveled to Africa in 1951 to learn "How the White Man Keeps Cool in the Congo." In this article, Belgian colonists were credited with discovering how to have cool houses in darkest Africa. "Everything the Belgians use in the Congo is simple! You will find no mention of air-conditioning or air drying. Even electric fans are rare," Langewiesche effused.[67]

The next year Langewiesche was prepared to admit that natives of hot regions might have at least as much climatic understanding as their colonial masters. Americans, he wrote, must be willing to take lessons from places like Zanzibar, Dakar, French West Africa, the Belgian Congo, Timbuktu, and the West Indies. Congo natives, Langewiesche now reported, used brick and metal-roofed dwellings provided by white bosses to house their livestock, while they and their families continued to occupy cooler lean-tos of branches and leaves. "But the Black Man has got something here. His house ideas were developed in this climate. . . . If the ignorant native can avoid summer heat discomfort why can't we?"[68]

There is no reason to believe that black Americans were any less interested in home ownership and better indoor comfort than their white counterparts, but there is ample evidence that builders and appliance makers were less interested in them. A review of the first ten years of *Ebony,* the large-format photo monthly frankly modeled on *Life* magazine and aimed at the emerging black urban middle class, reveals attitudes towards air-conditioning closely resembling those of the white mainstream.[69] In the early fifties, air-conditioning was, for blacks as for whites, a marker of status and success, clearly desirable but not yet intrinsic to the definition of home comfort.

Ebony took a special interest in housing. Trenchant editorials about housing shortages and the poor physical condition of much of the housing available to African Americans vied with lavishly illustrated features on black celebrities whose deluxe homes were material proof of their success in white-dominated society. The March 1949 issue of *Ebony* managed to combine both themes in a feature on architect Paul Williams. The Los Angeles–based Williams earned

$140,000 a year and supervised a staff of twenty. But his race, *Ebony* made clear, meant Williams could not stay at many of the hotels or buy virtually any of the 3,000 houses he had designed for wealthy white clients.[70]

Now Williams had turned his attention to the housing needs of his own people and had designed two models especially for *Ebony* readers. What they saw was a 625-square-foot house (nearly 20 percent smaller than the early Levitt houses) at a price of $5,000 that included heating equipment but not the cost of the lot. Purchasing real property was a major impediment to black home ownership. On Long Island, the Levitt organization in 1950 would evict two white families that had the temerity to invite black children over to play, and continued to exclude black home buyers well into the sixties. Williams recommended that "Negroes who are stymied by restrictive covenants" pool their resources to buy unsubdivided blocks of land less likely to carry restrictions.[71]

The architect called his expandable designs "conservative modern." These were no "Cape Cod bungalows" but rather miniaturized versions of the "new-look" house with its flat or low-pitched roof, wide overhangs, and expanses of window glass. Most of the front porch had been eliminated as well as the basement. Impatient with tradition "unless useful," Williams retained the "open fireplace, one carryover he likes and designs into most of his homes." He advocated an array of kitchen appliances, including a larger refrigerator, dishwasher, and garbage disposal, but made no mention of air-conditioning.

Air-conditioning was often mentioned in *Ebony*'s regular features on the African American rich and famous. In February 1954, a seven-page feature on opera diva Marian Anderson and her architect husband lovingly described each room in her new Connecticut mansion. "While the entire house is air-conditioned, Miss Anderson's room has a specially designed individual air-conditioning unit to protect her voice," the article reported. It did not say whether the singer used the unit to keep the bedroom cooler or warmer than the rest of the house. A December 1954 photo feature on James Alexander Franklin of Mobile, the "South's Richest Negro Doctor," shows his Cadillac and, in side-by-side pictures, his modest original office and his new quarters, a "three-room, air-conditioned suite equipped with the latest of modern equipment."

"Push Button Home," a November 1954 feature on surgeon Howard H. McNeill's 29-acre all-electric estate in previously all-white Bloomfield Hills, Michigan, made no mention of cooling capacity. Outfitted with a three-car garage, bomb shelter, floodlights, driveway ice-melter, electric gate controller, radiant heating system connected to seven thermostats, and remote control movie screen, the $200,000 house used four times the electricity of the average house and almost certainly would have been air-conditioned. But compared to the house's exotic gadgetry—reminiscent of the airplane hangar-equipped Keck

House at the 1933 Chicago Fair—and the scale of McNeill's obvious wealth and technological appetite, it must have seemed unworthy of mention.

Some air-conditioning advertising, almost exclusively for smaller room units, meanwhile was beginning to show up in *Ebony*. Missing were the dramas of family togetherness, marital satisfaction, and admiring friends. The ads bluntly stressed cost and physical relief. A May 1954 ad for a Fedders air conditioner showed a black man reading in a flowered easy chair in a room with blinds drawn around a room unit. "Finds sleep after 30 years . . . with Cool, Cool Fedders!," it proclaimed. The man was identified as Atlanta railroad fireman Will Ray. He had written the company that he had slept badly every summer until the remarkably low price allowed him to install a Fedders unit. Although the ad went on to mention the usual boons— sleek styling, touch of a button controls, humidity and smoke reduction—overall it seemed to recognize that home might be the only place where black customers who labored in hot jobs could recover.

A full-page June 1954 ad for the International Harvester room unit is instructively less glamorous, in imagery and information, than the contemporaneous Harvester ad in a publication aimed at a white audience. "Now you can cool more air for less (quieter, too)" was the central message. The unit's "one yard of fabric" decorator potential was relegated to fine print and the unit shown did not seem to match the decor. The ad aimed at white suburbanites had provided specifications but no prices; the *Ebony* ad declared "You can own one for a little as $2.24 a week." This base price apparently procured a unit less powerful than any of those offered to white customers. The smiling female model in the *Ebony* ad was seated in an ordinary chair in a simple housedress. She actually had her hand up to the outlet of her window unit. The unsmiling marcelled blonde in International Harvester's "white" ad had not deigned to interact with her air conditioner except to match it to her lipstick.

The *Ebony* ad in fact most closely resembling air-conditioner ads in the white media appeared in the June 1955 issue. A black model in a fancy dress and earrings promoted "Resort Coolness Day and Night." The apparatus was described as quiet, handsome, sturdy, "colored in beautiful blended champagne," with "fingertip control." It was a twenty-inch Kisco electric window fan.

The U.S. Census Bureau's housing survey of 1960 was the first to inquire about air-conditioning. It showed that nearly a million occupied housing units were equipped with central cooling systems. Almost six million residences had one or more room air-conditioning units. "Although regarded as a luxury item not many years ago, air-conditioning was reported for approximately 6.5 million occupied housing units," said the Summary of Findings.[72] This represented 12.4 percent of all households in the nation. Regional penetration ranged from less than 5 percent in New England to more than 27 percent in the Census's

West South Central division comprising Texas, Oklahoma, Louisiana, and Arkansas. The 1960 Census found air-conditioning in just 4 percent of nonwhite households or less than a third of the national rate. The racial disparity was even more obvious in the South. There, the overall air-conditioning ratio was 18 percent; it was just 3.8 percent for households headed by nonwhites. Even in the most air-conditioned West South Central division, fewer than 7 percent of nonwhite households reported either central systems or room units.[73]

The Census offered two kinds of good news to air-conditioning manufacturers. Both consumer awareness and sales had stunningly exceeded the kinds of projections companies like Carrier had made a decade earlier. And there was so much room yet to grow. After all, 87.6 percent of all households, 46.4 million of them, were still unairconditioned. At the right price and with the right kind of advertising appeals, the industry knew that residential air-conditioning would become not only universally affordable but also irresistible.

7. The Air-Conditioned Nightmare

Ten months after the outbreak of World War II had forced him to flee Paris, expatriate Brooklyn-born author Henry Miller in October 1940 set out on a 10,000-mile American road odyssey in an eight-year-old Buick he had just learned to drive. Turned down for a Guggenheim grant, the chronically penniless Miller organized his trip to spend as much of it as possible with wealthy friends at their mansions, townhouses, and plantations. His resulting 292-page book, published in 1945 to scant and generally scathing reviews, discovered an America in thrall to "little comforts," synthetic, sexless, anxious, sterile, terrifyingly divorced from nature. "Our instruments," said Miller, "are but crutches which have paralyzed us. We have not grown more human through our discoveries and inventions, but more inhuman." He called his extended complaint *The Air-Conditioned Nightmare*.[1]

Miller's choice of air-conditioning to epitomize everything he loathed about America is curious. He had begun referring to the United States as an "air-conditioned nightmare" during his decade in Paris, although at the time of his departure for France in 1930 air-conditioning had hardly begun to penetrate his New York. Air-conditioning's public presence had grown dramatically by 1940, but it was not yet a ubiquitous feature of American daily life. Perhaps air-conditioning was simply as distant as any moral climate could possibly be from the "Tropics" of Miller's two most famous books, published in France in the thirties but not until the sixties in his native land.

Henry Miller's trip notebook, a mélange of drawings, addresses, inscriptions, notations, and anecdotes, reveals even more clearly than his book how much this Brooklyn German boy romanticized American Indians and blacks, and how much he generally preferred southern cities to the industrial centers of the Northeast and Midwest. To Miller's delight, the temperature in Charleston, South Carolina, was 70° when he arrived on a December evening. "Note: Had to travel 3,000 miles before striking *one* interesting city! What a comment on America!"[2]

Detroit, on the other hand, was "The Duraluminum City: A nightmare in stone and steel. Terrifyingly new, bright, hard . . . . The city of the future! God help us!" St. Louis was "a city embalmed and entombed." Miller overall denounced his country's "frigid, moral aspect . . . which chilled me to the bone." Nowhere but in his title did he complain in his book of actual air-conditioning or its effects. By 1963, the late-blooming success of Miller's "dirty" writings had catapulted him into a suburban two-story white colonial house of movie-star proportions in Pacific Palisades, California, equipped with an enormous fireplace, a heated swimming pool, and almost certainly air-conditioning. Miller himself was well aware of the incongruity, writing in 1971, "People say, 'Oh, he must be sitting pretty now. He's got money, that beautiful house, swimming pool. . . .' Well, that's an illusion" (figure 29).[3]

Miller's "premature" denunciation of air-conditioning represents but one of several important strands in how ideas of comfort, consumption, and the benefits of technology were evolving in American society. Air-conditioning was a highly successful instance of a mass-market product that used sophisticated technology to produce comfort. Its makers, marketers, and sometimes even its users were uneasy participants in a developing discussion that sharply questioned the habits and expectations of various groups of Americans and the proper role of technology in satisfying those expectations.

Such bourgeois-bashers as Henry Miller, or the more widely read H. L. Mencken and Sinclair Lewis, focused their critical wrath on the perceived complacency of a surging middle class full of Babbitts who smugly added foolish comforts to their way of life. Increased American affluence might seem to offer a way out of the pinched self-denial these critics identified, accurately or not, with the legacy of Puritanism. Yet Miller, Lewis, and their sort of writer seemed to fear that unthinking acquisition of enslaving comforts—just as surely as Puritan prudery or Jeffersonian self-restraint—would banish from American life all that was natural, passionate, and spontaneous. Pervasive technologies, of which air-conditioning was one, presaged a totalizing uniformity that would deform social institutions and smother American individualism.

A broader and more overtly political critique, labeled the "new moralism" by

29. Author Henry Miller's last home at 444 Ocampo
Drive, Pacific Palisades, California, featured picture win-
dows, a huge fireplace, and a heated outdoor pool in which
he swam daily. It was a far cry from the Big Sur shack
Miller moved to in 1944 soon after completing *The Air-
Conditioned Nightmare*.

Daniel Horowitz, also emerged after the First World War. This new moralism
was not a call for individual liberation or artistic expression but an exhortation
to social responsibility. Built on venerable republican forms of American self-
criticism, it was willing to accept the fruits of American economic success in
ways that redefined traditional republicanism's profound distaste for "luxury."[4]

"Luxury," as Christopher Berry has pointed out, is an enduring moral and
political category. Although the term is usually used pejoratively, historical
shifts in how it is defined provide a measure of a society's relationship to its
own modernity and an index to the values of its social system. Redefinitions
of "luxury" have proved useful in celebrating and vindicating the successes of
technological and commercial society, blunting some of its older connotations
of sin or immorality.[5]

In a "world where yesterday's luxuries seemed to become today's necessities," says Horowitz, the critics of the twenties and thirties did not oppose the

idea of consumption itself, and generally applauded improvements in the American standard of living. Nineteenth-century moralists had feared that the working poor and immigrants might be corrupted by abundance; the new moralists worried instead that the emerging middle class was losing sight of life's "higher" purpose amid the welter of material goods.[6]

Robert and Helen Lynd's 1929 study *Middletown,* called by Horowitz the central text of modern American moralism, used the techniques of anthropology to indict consumer culture generally and the automobile in particular for replacing the small-town values of Muncie, Indiana, with alienation, commercialization, and generational conflict. The Lynds were not alone in implicitly attributing "authenticity" to the poor, workers, and others seemingly uncontaminated by consumer culture. At the other end of the class continuum, the consumption decisions made by the truly wealthy were presumably redeemed by their inborn taste and educated sensibility. Only the middle class, precarious as the Depression would prove it to be, was adjudged guilty of wallowing in showy and useless consumption.

New moralists might, within limits, accept consumerism as a path toward social progress and the fulfillment of America's material promises. But many also saw in the proliferating array of machines and their products both constant dangers to individual virtue and threats of national corruption and decline. The enduring conflict between burgeoning technology and republican values, John Kasson writes, has helped shape an ideology of American progress at once self-satisfied and fearful of its own inventions. At the nation's first world's fair in New York in 1853, a Unitarian clergyman boldly suggested that "luxury" would cease to be a moral threat once it was diffused to the mass of Americans. "By ostensibly providing the means of wealth for all, technology has made luxury safe for democracy," Kasson explains.[7]

This sort of optimism about the affinity of moral and material progress, brokered by technological advances, never really took hold among American intellectuals. The educated and affluent turn-of-the-century cohort that T. J. Jackson Lears has characterized as "antimodernist" might have personally enjoyed many modern comforts. Yet they were troubled by the vision of a docile, sensually sated mass society in which medical or therapeutic definitions of well-being seemed to displace moral or religious convictions. Prefiguring the new moralists, these critics feared Americans had made the wrong choice between "authentic experience" and the "false comforts of modernity."[8]

Stuart Chase, a Thorstein Veblen disciple who worked in the twenties with the League of Industrial Democracy, was an influential new moralist who explored connections between passive consumerism and technological dependency. Chase's 1922 attack on the perceived wastefulness of the capitalist economy, a pamphlet entitled "The Challenge of Waste," was succeeded in 1927 by the more dramatically named "The Tragedy of Waste." A founder of the consumers' union movement, Chase was ideally positioned to say "I told you so" when the nation's economy declined precipitously after 1929. The league republished in 1931 two earlier Chase pamphlets as *Waste and the Machine Age*. In this 63-page booklet Chase assailed the "menace of technological tenuousness" stemming from "dependence on an unknown technology." "When a fuse blows out in my suburban home," he noted, "we can neither see, cook, nor keep warm." Chase warned that technology could produce "more geographical uniformity in dress, habits, manners, and a faster turnover in such standards." He associated this unwelcome possibility with an Ellsworth Huntington–tinged "softening of racial stock due to high levels of comfort long maintained."[9]

As the Depression deepened, even engineers were not immune from such misgivings. "Has the Engineer Benefitted Mankind?" asked C. E. Kenneth Mees, the British-born director of research at Eastman Kodak, in a trade journal article. He took issue with a recent declaration by leaders of civil, mining, mechanical, and electrical engineering groups "that the machine age had promoted human happiness." Mees disputed the idea that happiness arose from more plentiful material possessions or more comfortable physical conditions. Machines, he argued, had diminished the farmer's social status and economic importance and had replaced skilled craftsmen with interchangeable industrial laborers.[10]

The influential social critic Lewis Mumford in 1934 offered probably the widest ranging examination of the relationship between technology and its human creators and users. In *Technics and Civilization,* Mumford criticized many prevailing antimachine utterances as simplistic and romanticized. Bourgeois adherents of such views, he wrote, fancy themselves opponents of modern culture but had, in fact, "retreated from the factory or the office into a fake, nonmechanical environment, in which the past was modified by the addition of physical comforts, such as tropical temperatures in the winter" (figure 30).[11]

Mumford did see real dangers in the heedless application of powerful machinery to human problems and processes. Technology, he argued, tends to overpower common sense and undercut traditional practices, actually encouraging social inefficiency. New tools like telephones supplant equally effective if somewhat slower methods of communication. Commercially canned foods make eating fresh produce in the country in the summertime seem provincial and outmoded. "One is faced here with a magnified form of danger common to all inventions: a tendency to use them whether or not the occasion demands," Mumford wrote (page 240).

The habit of dependence on new technologies and the machines that imple-

30. Lewis Mumford began his long career as a social critic with a generally positive if cautious view of the potential benefits of technology. He would later change his mind.

ment them, Mumford argued, loosens the contingencies of time and season, ultimately causing the atrophy of the human function. A "purposeless materialism" develops, placing a "disproportionate emphasis on the physical means of living" (page 273). Comfort seems to be modern man's greatest achievement, but it multiplies his desire for goods and dangerously increases his reliance on living conditions that are no longer produced by his own exertions (page 391).

Given the critique embedded in both republican tradition and the new moralism, it was inevitable that air-conditioning would come in for its share of attack, by inference if not always by name. Potential accusations of luxury and demoralizing dependency were bugaboos of which air-conditioning pioneers were themselves keenly aware. The publication of Kodak engineer Mees's criticisms in the professional journal of the heating and cooling industry suggests that these engineers expected the critique to be applied to their endeavors.

Questioning the "genuine need" for air-conditioning had a well-established history of its own. Yale geographer and part-time air-conditioning advocate Ellsworth Huntington vacillated about the morality and desirability of comfort. Although he endorsed cooler indoor temperatures, he was equally convinced that the uniformity of conditions promised by air-conditioning could seriously impair human achievement. Huntington saved a 1930 Bruce Catton column on the "ideal home" that challenged the benefits of burgeoning domestic technology:

> We seem to have made up our minds definitely that the machine is to be our salvation. The luxuries of a former day are the necessities of the present. . . . We elevate incidentals, meant to iron out the minor rough places in life's pathway, into items of major importance, ends in themselves.[12]

Almost a decade later, Huntington was still worrying about the effects of man's increasing divorcement from nature:

> We tend more and more to live in a purely artificial environment. We cease to increase our physiological adaptation to environmental conditions, and thereby encourage the propagation of types that can live only under the optimum conditions. . . . We put our species more than ever at the mercy of natural disasters. . . . Thus each advance in our so-called control of nature makes us more dependent than before upon the continued existence not only of the artificial conditions which we create, but upon the natural conditions which alone make it possible to create the artificial conditions.[13]

Since the early twenties, when his invention of a new auditorium air-bypass system for movie palaces helped air-conditioning succeed in the public comfort market, Carrier Corporation executive Logan Lewis had fretted over the "luxury" label that he himself tended to associate with his industry's products. In a continuing project of personal and corporate justification, Lewis labored until his death in 1965 to link the idea of indoor comfort to the more politically and morally persuasive claims of health and efficiency, and to answer the critics of environmental uniformity. "No, our ultimate objective is not comfort," Lewis declared characteristically at a 1943 industry panel discussion. "It is to give man or woman a fair chance to apply the fundamental of creating wealth by producing up to the limit of his latent capacity" (figure 31).[14]

As the sacrificial public spirit of wartime receded in 1948, Lewis drafted a speech entitled "Is Air-Conditioning a Luxury?" Thermal comfort, he said, might suggest "luxury, idleness, nonproductivity" but was in fact a maximizer of human effort. In offices, said Lewis, air-conditioning would reduce errors, absenteeism, employee turnover, trips to the water cooler, conversations about the weather, and the "nuisance and spoilage of perspiration." Even in the home, "cooling for a bedroom looks like pure unadulterated luxury" but must instead be understood as a wellspring of worker renewal and reinvigoration.[15]

Although the economic boom of the fifties meant that more goods came within the reach of more Americans, shifting the boundaries between luxury, comfort, and need, it took industry veterans like Lewis to remind his colleagues that there was nothing inevitable or irreversible about air-conditioning's mi-

31. Leo Logan Lewis, a University of Kentucky–trained engineer, inventor, and cofounder of the Carrier Corporation, shown here in 1907, spent his later years at its Syracuse headquarters preserving and promoting air-conditioning history. He died in 1965 at age 77.

gration from the realm of desire to that of necessity. In his celebratory 1957 booklet "The Romance of Air-Conditioning," Lewis told new hires and veteran Carrier employees that it had taken twenty-five years of "concentrated effort" to overcome the idea that air-conditioning was an "extravagant luxury" and "raise it up into its present state of widespread acceptance." This effort, Lewis intimated, surely included his by now seemingly old-fashioned insistence on staking a claim to the "virtuous" zone between need and desire.[16]

While Lewis charted the somewhat capricious course of air-conditioning's successful "romance" with the American public, the public was fulfilling the new moralists' "worst expectations about America as a mass consumer society."[17] An emerging generation of social critics gazed with alarm at the seeming victory of affluence in American society. They used a neo-Malthusian language of waste and looming scarcity to attack growing consumption and to revive the claims made by Stuart Chase and others that deceptive advertising and other nefarious practices were victimizing the American middle class, making it dependent on inessential products and profligate with vanishing resources.

Historian David M. Potter in 1954 sounded a warning about American consumerism that would influence many subsequent critics. Economic abundance was altering the historical American character, he argued, and not for the better. Advertising, although not intrinsically evil, would inevitably progress from meeting wants or needs to creating desires in a society sated with material possessions and comforts. He raised the specter of waste, well on its way to becoming a central complaint of the new generation of critics:

> In contrast to other peoples who keep their bodies warm primarily by wearing clothes, Americans keep their bodies warm primarily by a far more expensive and even wasteful method. . . . The oil furnace has not only displaced the open fireplace; it has also displaced the woolen undergarment and the vest.[18]

Although Potter did not include cooling in his condemnation, the air-conditioning industry was sensitive to his study's ideological implications. In a February 1954 article, Arthur J. Hess, president of the American Society of Refrigerating Engineers, took it upon himself to debunk the debunkers, while conceding the responsibility of makers and installers to make air-conditioning work better.[19]

Opponents of air-conditioning, wrote Hess, were a "malcontented minority." They were less than 20 percent of those who had experienced the technology but "critical and vociferous" enough to create the impression of general discontent. Unfortunately, he added, the vast majority who liked air-conditioning felt no need to express themselves on the subject. The doubters, said Hess, could be divided into three basic types. "Spartans" were people, mainly men, who cling to the old spartan belief that discomfort without complaint proves virile manhood and superior physical power. . . . Practical women see no value in being uncomfortable as compared to bragging that one can stand discomfort. The spartans will always have a cult and some of them will choose air-conditioning as the villain in their campaign against change (page 82).

"Nature worshipers," continued Hess, "believe that conditions of living as supplied by nature are better for mankind than any we can manufacture with machines." Although they would eventually be won over, he predicted, they would continue to object to the most recently developed product. Finally, air-conditioning "complainers" imagine they are uncomfortable owing to mental or physical problems unrelated to their actual surroundings. Hess conceded that clothing customs "make it impossible to make both men and women in the same space completely comfortable simultaneously" and proposed that men wear "proper clothing" rather than adhering to the "old, conservative, and generally uncomfortable standards." In the photograph that accompanies his essay, Hess wears a long-sleeved shirt, double-breasted jacket, and firmly knotted tie.

Hess included in his "malcontented minority" chronically dissatisfied people or those easily swayed by "pseudoscientific" writers to believe any technological system inadequate or even dangerous. Hess might have been talking about notoriously quirky architect Frank Lloyd Wright who, by the mid-fifties, was joining *House Beautiful* in attacking International Style and questioning the healthfulness and desirability of air-conditioning, at least in residences. It was quite a conversion for the designer famous for the windowless S. C. Johnson & Son office building in Racine, Wisconsin, a building utterly dependent on a year-round air-conditioning system. Henry Miller had visited the then-year-old Johnson building during his "Nightmare" tour and was both impressed and horrified. "This place is flawless—deathlike. Man has no chance to create once inside this mausoleum," he wrote in his notebook. "Down with Frank Lloyd Wright! He's an inhuman bugger masquerading as a practical aesthete. He should build Henry Ford's tomb." Instead, Wright told readers of his 1954 book, *The Natural House,* that "to me air-conditioning is a dangerous circumstance." It was "far better," he added, "to go with the natural climate than try to fix a special artificial climate of your own."[20]

John Kenneth Galbraith's 1958 *The Affluent Society* took strong exception to the increasing use of technology to satisfy private wants while public needs were ignored. The Harvard economist argued that abundance was deforming American values, upsetting the balance between public good and private selfishness. His book was widely influential, going through four editions and becoming a byword in a few years as a new generation of environmentalists would denounce a polluted America as the "effluent society."[21]

Affluence, said Galbraith, was a historically unprecedented economic condition peculiar to the United States and western Europe. It both fulfilled and aroused desires that were "sensuous, edifying, and lethal" (page 140). In a chapter entitled "The Dependence Effect," Galbraith argued that once wants had been created by producers and their advertising minions, it was foolish to believe that the public would ever willingly "un-want" them, even in times of national crisis. As an example, he mentioned an outcry in New York City when a 1950 water shortage forced temporary limits on air cooling. The *New York Times* accorded Galbraith a reverential front-page review that asked "Are We Living Too High on the Hog?" The answer to Americans of like mind was obviously "yes."[22]

Vance Packard made this new moralist discourse of affluence and its discontents available to a mass audience. A magazine journalist turned social critic, Packard spoke to a middle class ready to be horrified and titillated by its own indulgence. During his earlier career with the middle-brow *American Magazine,* Vance Packard had asked Ellsworth Huntington for an article on the relationship between geography and American leadership. Interviewed by biographer Daniel Horowitz forty years later, Packard named Huntington's *Mainsprings of Civilization* as one of the two books that most influenced his thinking about American society in the forties.[23]

Affluence, Packard suggested, was a curse of modernity from which America's sheepish consumers could save themselves and the nation only by stern vigilance. Although Packard focused on flashier consumables, like automobiles and television sets, his criticisms of waste and false pleasures were aimed at the very families most likely to use air-conditioning both to bolster their status and to overcome the comfort deficiencies of the era's mass-produced housing. Packard's 1960 "jeremiad," *The Wastemakers,* spent 31 weeks on the *New York Times* bestseller list, making it the third of his "scathing, nostalgic, humorous, moralistic, ambivalent, and influential" books to attract a mass readership. By 1963 Packard was one of the nation's most widely read writers of nonfiction.[24]

Packard gloried in his reputation as a "public scold" and "anxiety maker." His book was a restatement, in a more popular style and more fervid tone, of the criticisms of Potter and Galbraith; it drew heavily on the admonitions of Stuart Chase who wrote an approving blurb for *The Wastemakers.* Upton Sinclair, dean of American muckrakers, also provided a plug. Attacking the tendency to equate goods with the good life, Packard complained that two-fifths of the things the average American owns "are things that are not essential to his physical well-being. They are optional or luxury items."[25]

Like the social critics he admired, Packard placed much of the blame for

American consumerism on advertising, calling it the "machinery of desire stimulation" (page 288), disparaging technology and desire in a single phrase. Although Packard, like Galbraith, favored the pursuit of large national objectives and public projects over the gratification of trivial and—by definition— indulgent personal desires, he warned, even these could result in the irreversible waste of materials and energy. "If the nation's exploding population is to settle the nation's open arid areas, then air conditioners will be a required amenity of life. And air conditioners are substantial water users" (page 208).

Packard was especially critical of the ways in which Americans used their newly acquired houses to achieve trivial increments in social status and, in that connection, viewed air-conditioning as an expression of social climbing. A fierce critic of auto makers' superficial model changes in this era of the giant tail-fin, Packard lumped the new option of auto air-conditioning with other status add-ons designed to "blur still further the already blurred line that distinguishes Americans' luxuries and Americans' necessities."[26]

As a popularizer of a pervasive trend in American social criticism, Packard spoke for a "considerable number of puritanically minded people who stood against the tide of America's growing affluence."[27] His distinctions between needs and desires, necessities and luxuries, were often naive and nostalgic, overstating the power of advertising, uncritically extolling small-town virtues, and understating the inconveniences of the past. Yet he helped enlarge the audience for a great deal of oppositional thinking, providing—in his 1957 *Hidden Persuaders,* according to Daniel Horowitz—the first important attack on advertising since the thirties. Many reviewers saw Packard's book as a useful corrective to what he called, with some irony, the "golden sixties" and others dubbed the "spending" or "soaring" sixties; opponents, like the *Chicago Tribune,* called it "socialistic happy talk" meant to "protect us from enjoying this lovely life too much."

The debate spearheaded by Galbraith and Packard helped popularize and refashion republican values and virtues in a way that made sense to many in a new era of white middle-class affluence. At the same time, a developing discourse and style of "cool" would resonate in interesting ways with air-conditioning in the American social imagination. Use of the word "cool" to mean controlled composure and grace under pressure had certainly emerged by the twenties in the predominantly black and urban jazz milieu and had, by the fifties, "crossed over" to the majority white society by way of beatnik culture. By the mid-sixties, "cool" was a mainstream way of defining what Peter N. Stearns calls America's "twentieth century emotional style." He writes:

> Cool. The concept is distinctly American, and it permeates almost every aspect of contemporary American Culture. From Kool cigarettes . . . and urban slang . . . the

idea of cool, in its many manifestations, has seized a central place in the American imagination.[28]

Stearns argues that middle-class Americans have forsaken the passionate if often veiled emotionalism of the Victorian era for a disciplined impersonality that requires men, women, and children to avoid embarrassing excesses of anger, jealousy, fear, and even grief and love. Emerging in the 1920s, and achieving dominion in the sixties, the trajectory of this notion of "cool" seems to parallel the awakening of the American public to the pleasures and possibilities of air-conditioning. Although Stearns does not propose such a literal conjunction of mental and physical states, he does suggest a correlation between the management of emotion and the discipline of bodily functions, almost all of which—think perspiration—were embarrassing to middle-class Americans by the twenties.

It seems unlikely, at least early on, that those black musicians and artists who daily experienced racist provocations on the sweltering summer streets of expanding northern ghettoes associated their mode of "cool" self-presentation with actual air-conditioning. The creators of urban "cool," both black and white, rejected the proposition that it could somehow be manufactured or imposed. "Cool" emanated from the souls of truly self-possessed human beings. Southern black émigrés were developing their "cool" style at the very same time that "tropical" stereotypes were being propounded by such Anglo-Saxon climatic authorities as Ellsworth Huntington and Colum GilFillan. True "cool" came from within. Mechanical devices would not be needed to control "fiery and volatile" temperaments, nor the hot conditions encountered in the ghetto housing of crowded northern cities.

In his 1955 "Lament for New York's Night Life," *New York Times Magazine* writer Gilbert Millstein bemoaned the demise of city night life, done in, he said, by "television and suburbanism." Like Henry Miller, Millstein saw excessive emotional and artistic restraint as the wrong kind of "cool." Such dispassion was a bland affront to unrestrained human nature, a nature stripped of the "heat" of natural passion. The "wan gentility" of an early show at an East Side "art movie theater," said Millstein, had replaced late, hot nights of dancing and drinking in Harlem. Recalling a New York that had once been both hotter and "cooler," Millstein said, "maybe it's all these new buildings breeding more of these cool Brooks Brothers cats. They're too cool." He referred to the totally air-conditioned skyscrapers then turning Manhattan's grubby Sixth Avenue into a gentrified Avenue of the Americas where businessmen in suits could fancy that they were hip.[29]

To black poet and nationalist LeRoi Jones (later Imamu Amiri Baraka) air-conditioning represented not just the manufacture of artificial "cool" but also the misapplication of technology in a larger and ultimately more dangerous project of tighter social control. Writing critically in 1963 of Martin Luther King Jr.'s nonviolent campaign for black civil rights, Jones invoked air-conditioning to describe the colonized status of American blacks. Jones, ironically like Huntington, perceived that air-conditioning was a way of erasing or trying to erase racial difference:

> The emphasis on passive resistance and moral suasion is an undiluted leftover from the missionary era, and its intentions are exactly the same. Only God has been replaced, as he has all over the West, with respectability and air-conditioning. The Negro must have both before he is "ready" for equality. . . . To enter into the mainstream of American society, the Negro must lose all identity as a Negro, as a carrier of possible dissent.[30]

Stearns's 1994 book sees the persistence and expansion of African American emotional assertiveness, expressed in sports, religion, and politics, even in new forms of music, like rap, as a sign that the era of "American Cool" as the national emotional orthodoxy may be fraying.[31]

Galbraith's and Millstein's admonishments might have sparked arguments at Manhattan cocktail parties while Vance Packard's best-sellers might motivate suburban homeowners to choose their home appliances with greater care, but few who could afford them proposed to forego conveniences and comforts altogether. While a new generation of moral muckrakers continued to question the effects of technology and rampant consumerism, air-conditioning's presence on the American landscape became ever more pervasive as makers and marketers looked for new challenges. Air-conditioning the outdoors, or at least controlling exposure to summer heat in settings previously perceived as "outdoors" was one of them. The automobile, long advertised as the means of escaping hot city streets for the presumably cooler countryside, became one such opportunity for the expansion of controlled environment.

R. Buckminster Fuller's air-conditioned Dymaxion car had attracted crowds but no imitators at the Chicago Century of Progress Exposition. The refrigerated car—featured in *Popular Science* at about the same time—disappeared, its grandiose marketing plans apparently a casualty of the Depression. Air-conditioning in private automobiles prior to 1953 was a luxury that offered high status but dismal performance. The car for many years remained—in comparison to airplanes, passenger trains, and even interstate buses—the most thermally uncomfortable mode of transportation. The opulent 1939 Packard was the first production vehicle to be "cooled by mechanical refrigeration," which added about 25 percent to its price tag. General Motors in 1941 equipped three hundred Cadillacs with a similarly costly but flawed cooling option. Early compressor units added hundreds of pounds to the weight of vehicles, impairing style, spaciousness, and efficiency. These car air conditioners either had no controls or had controls that were virtually impossible to adjust while driving. Poorly designed seals allowed refrigerant to leak readily from auto systems, quickly incapacitating them and adding to driver expense. Between 1939 and 1953, just 10,500 air-conditioned cars were manufactured.[32]

There were certainly indications that drivers wanted cars to be cooler than open windows, highly touted "flow-through" ventilation systems, and fans could make them. Some Continental Oil Company service stations in the early fifties in Texas advertised that they would pump any car that pulled in full of cold compressed air, using a pump-side three-ton air-conditioning unit to lower the car's temperature 20 degrees in two minutes. If the driver rolled up the windows fast enough this "free shot" of cooled air would supposedly keep the car comfortable until the next stop. As air-conditioning became more commonplace, Raymond Arsenault writes, some status-hungry Texans would keep their windows rolled up despite the heat to make people think their cars were air-conditioned[33] (figure 32).

Consumer Reports for the first time in 1954 discussed auto air-conditioning as part of its annual review of new car models. After listing all the aforementioned drawbacks, the consumer advocacy publication declared auto air-conditioning to be well worth the money. "Members of CU's staff who have driven air-conditioned cars agree that, in very hot weather, they would rather drive the cheapest car on the market with air-conditioning, than the most luxurious car without it," the editors uncharacteristically effused.[34]

There were not many "cheap" air-conditioned cars on the market and no stampede to buy those available. As *Consumer Reports* had noted, most systems added roughly an extra passenger's weight to the car and cost $600 at a time when most cars cost less than $3,000. Just 14 percent of passenger cars sold in the United States in 1963 were equipped with factory-installed air-conditioners. Virtually all of these were in the South and the Southwest. The July 1963 issue of *Popular Science* reported that just 10 percent of the two million Chevrolets sold nationwide in 1962 had air-conditioning, and almost half of them were sold to Oklahomans and Texans. Because prices and weight were down and reliability up, a boom was in the offing, the magazine predicted, adding pugnaciously: "If you're not tempted to order a cooling system for your new car . . . you're not with it, Buster."[35]

The air-conditioned share of the car market passed 50 percent for the first time in 1969 even though, priced at about $400, air-conditioning still represented a fifteen percent add-on for an average car. Auto air-conditioning grew

32. Offices as well as automobiles lacked air-conditioning in 1950s Texas. Dallas secretary Mildred Walston kicked off her pumps and employed two fans and a basin of cold water to keep cool on an August day in 1951 when the temperature hit 103 degrees.

almost continuously thereafter. By 2000, it was no longer a regional phenomenon but was installed in 98.4 percent of new cars.[36]

The triumph of auto air-conditioning significantly coincides almost exactly with what a number of commentators have called the "post-love affair" era of

Americans' relationship with their cars.[37] As rising gas prices sparked new concerns for fuel economy, as safety features shouldered aside sexy styling, as the price of cars, equipped with once inconceivable amenities like cruise control, stereo systems, and carpeting, far exceeded what older drivers had once paid for their Levittown Cape Cods, air-conditioning helped make the car a private extension of home rather than an escape from it. In these windless, gritless, and noise-free capsules, a driver could traverse the interstate, or risk the urban ghetto, but remain as if at home, making phone calls, accessing global positioning satellites, or spinning compact discs behind locked doors and rolled-up, dark-tinted windows. Daniel L. Guillory would compare the windshield of the modern car to the living room television screen, affording a view of pollution and crime but shielded from their effects.[38]

Volkswagen, the German American auto maker, in 1995 launched a "Drivers Wanted" television campaign that aimed to reglamorize the escapist, wind-in-your-hair aspects of automobile ownership and use. In the thirty-second "Windows" spot, developed for VW by Arnold Worldwide of Boston, a young executive gloats about his automated, air-conditioned skyscraper office. "I am in complete control," he declares, adding plaintively, "I just wish I could open these windows." Moments later, he escapes in a sporty red Volkswagen. "Open up a Volkswagen Jetta," the supertitles proclaim. "It invigorates, never Isolates." Ironically, as several models of the Jetta zoom by, even the quick-cut editing cannot hide the fact that their windows are rolled up, although a sunroof seems to be cracked open in several shots.[39]

As air-conditioning pervaded private as well as public spaces, and the means of getting from one to the other, traditional outdoor activities fought to retain summer patronage. Air-conditioning manufacturers were quick to attribute fall-off in summer theater, big-top circus, and minor league baseball attendance to excessive heat and propose their products as the "cure." Air-conditioning often appeared to be the simplest, and possibly cheapest, solution for providers of traditional entertainment struggling with changes in public taste, television, and suburbanization in addition to summer heat. In Connecticut, one theater manager facing summer ruin persuaded the town of Clinton to use tax money to install playhouse cooling and then economized by hiring lesser-known stars to perform in the air-conditioned space.[40]

Even financially thriving summer recreations used the installation of air-conditioning to garner publicity and enhance their reputation for staying abreast if not ahead of popular preferences. In 1956, the pennant-contending Cincinnati Reds baseball club installed cooling equipment in the player dugouts, the broadcasting booths, and two-thirds of the press box "because some sportswriters still prefer to hear the noise of the crowd and feel the midsummer heat."

Fans in the stands still had to be satisfied with water coolers and the breeze but, predicted a refrigerating trade journal, "ultimately, entire stadiums may be air-conditioned for the comfort of the fans as well as of the players and press."[41]

The prophecy was more or less fulfilled in 1965 with the construction of the ten-acre, 56,000-seat Harris County Stadium, soon renamed the Houston Astrodome. The January 1966 meeting of the American Society of Heating, Refrigerating, and Air-Conditioning (ASHRAE) was held in Houston so members could inspect the entirely air-conditioned facility first hand. The Astrodome was built with 4,600 translucent skylights, in expectation that the light thereby admitted would allow grass to grow. It did not work. Fly balls got lost in the glare and the skylights were removed.[42]

Although the Astrodome was still a Houston entertainment destination in 2001, the Houston Astros baseball club had deserted it for Enron Field. This $248 million showcase has real grass and a retractable roof that at least occasionally offers Houstonites, accustomed to air-conditioned tunnels between major downtown buildings, a rare experience with unmanufactured weather. An odd sidelight to this discussion is the case of the Carrier Dome, Syracuse University's 50,000-seat football stadium. Built, as its name implies, in the Carrier Corporation's home town with a grant from Carrier of $2.75 million, the Carrier Dome was not air-conditioned when it opened in 1980, and so it remains. The original twenty-seven-million-dollar construction budget did not provide enough money. In 1983 the Dome hosted its first and last summer function, a Willie Nelson Fourth of July Picnic. In the wake of that sweltering experience, the facility stopped booking July and August events. Today, it would cost seven million dollars to add air-conditioning, said assistant facility director Peter E. Sala, adding, "I don't see it ever happening."[43]

When Herbert L. Laube, a veteran air-conditioning engineer who saw himself as a "constructive dissenter," asked his colleagues in July 1967 "how vulnerable is today's comfort industry?" he was not defending the industry against the objections of the various "spartans," "nature lovers," and "complainers" identified in 1954 by engineer Arthur Hess, nor the recent critics of selfish consumerism—be they artistic nonconformists or social moralists. Rather, in this article and a later book, Laube criticized his industry for disappointing a public he believed to be nearly won over to the kind of comfort that air-conditioning, properly planned, installed, and operated, could indeed provide. "Yes, warmth and coolth, as desired, should make us completely unaware of our indoor environment," Laube declared in the book. "Between them they can free our minds for more productive matters. That is the implicit promise of air-conditioning."[44]

33. Critics of American consumerism have not been alone
in disliking air-conditioning.

Laube understood that differing versions of thermal comfort pitted men versus women, started fights between office and shop floor mates of different races and regions, and set bosses against employees. One unnamed opera star, he reported, refused to perform at a Miami concert until the air-conditioning was shut off. Agents for Frank Sinatra and Lawrence Welk had refused to book either star at the Rochester, New York, War Memorial in the summer of 1969 because they thought the unairconditioned arena would not sell out. Laube was confident such frictions would be overcome and predicted a bright future for air-conditioning. "Confucius say 'the superior man thinks always of virtue; the common man thinks of comfort,'" the engineer concluded archly (figure 33).

Lewis Mumford had never been the "common man" air-conditioning engineers like Laube had in mind. Mumford's view by 1970 of the prospects for the peaceful coexistence of technology and humanity had turned more darkly pessimistic than it had been in the thirties. Like Potter, Galbraith, and Packard, all of whom he cited, Mumford, in *The Pentagon of Power,* held affluence for its own sake in disdain. Far more dangerous than indulgence in petty comforts was American society's apparently willing acceptance of a monstrous technology that was being imposed on modern life by profit-seeking corporate exploiters of human invention.[45]

There was little to choose, said Mumford, between environmental conditioning and psychological conditioning: both required dependence and conformity to the dictates of various machines that had "liberated" humankind from a "varied and responsive 'unprogrammed' environment, human and natural — an environment full of difficulties, temptations, hard choices, challenges, lovely surprises, and unexpected rewards" (page 284).

This time, air-conditioning was an explicit part of Mumford's dismaying vision. In a section entitled "The Technique of Total Control," Mumford imagined how astonished Leo Tolstoy would have been by the realization of his mocking prediction:

> He pictured modern man ingeniously sealing up the windows of his house and mechanically exhausting the air so that he might, by utilizing a still more extravagant mechanical apparatus, pump air back again — instead of merely opening the window. Tolstoi did not suspect that within a generation this folly would actually be committed . . . even . . . in the midst of open country, where fresh air is available, and where the natural noises are at a lower level than that of the exhaust fans used by a ventilating system (pages 286–87).

In his next chapter, "The Megatechnic Wasteland," Mumford called the modern skyscraper an air-conditioned pyramid that, like those of the Pharaohs, asserted its society's false claims of divinity and immortality. Within this skyscraper and the nuclear reactor needed to power it, said Mumford, a megalomaniac technocrat class was working to impose on humanity the most tyrannical system of control ever devised. Air-conditioning was just one aspect of a larger design meant to ensure "that no part of a man's life shall be free from external control" (page 287).

Willis Carrier's optimistic 1936 dream of the American businessman's wholly air-conditioned life had, within a generation, become Mumford's version of the "air-conditioned nightmare." Only after events of the seventies and beyond triggered global energy shortfalls, economic concerns, and health anxieties would Laube's archetypal "common man," and American society at large, begin to find reasons more compelling than virtue or civic discipline to reexamine the costs and benefits of air-conditioning.

8. And the Air-Conditioned Malaise

onsumer Reports, monthly publication of the 800,000-member Consumers Union, in July 1953 omitted its traditional summer review of electric fans to make room for the results of the first-ever tests of room air-conditioning units. The units, readers learned, required special window fittings and brawnier electric wiring. They could be annoyingly noisy, costly to run, and might make indoor air seem stale. But, said the review, "such drawbacks may seem as nothing compared to the prospect of some cool, dehumidified air on a hot day."[1]

Every second year from then on until 1973 when it began annual reports, the consumer guide with a reputation for impartiality revisited mechanical cooling, noting improvements and singling out reliability and value. The articles took for granted that just about every American would want an air-conditioner. The only questions were how much it would cost and how well it would work. *Consumer Reports* of May 1965 surveyed residential central air-conditioning for the first time, noting that the Federal Housing Administration would provide low-interest home improvement loans for its installation. "America seems to be moving rapidly from an era when only sybarites had air-conditioning to an era when only stoics willingly do without it," the consumer advocacy group once headed by social critic Stuart Chase said with uncommon enthusiasm.[2]

Consumer Reports' tone had changed by 1973 from enthusiasm to disgust. The true price of comfort, that year's air-conditioner survey maintained, was energy waste and environmental degradation. Air-conditioners were the cause of unbearable weather rather than its cure:

> So a multitude of appliances providing "air-conditioned comfort" for home or office might make a significant contribution to overall discomfort by heating up the outdoors. . . . There appears to be, in short, *an air-conditioned nightmare* in the future of many urban areas. . . . Whenever possible, use a fan, rather than an air-conditioner. If you *must* use an air-conditioner, try to limit its use to night cooling only (emphasis added).[3]

Similarly harsh criticism continued for the next two summers. *Consumer Reports* in July 1974 called air-conditioners "major energy hogs of the American household" that gobbled up 47.6 billion kilowatt-hours of electricity a year. The publication urged consumers to consult their consciences before deciding whether their "bedroom, guest room, or den really needs air-conditioning." Abstinence was a recommended choice again in July 1975:

> Electric rates are zooming. The nation's energy resources continue to shrink. Prices for air-conditioners are up 20 to 30 percent this year. . . . Must you buy one? Only you can say.[4]

The Consumers Union's hostility toward a product it had once hailed as proof of the superiority of the American way of life was just one manifestation of a broader reaction to social and economic crises of the seventies and beyond. Although the United States remained an "affluent society" by John Kenneth Galbraith's definition, a large number of middle-class Americans were, for the first time since the Depression and World War II, rocked by self-doubt and shocked by geopolitical events that seemed to challenge their comfortable lifestyle. The abstract moralizing of neo-Malthusians and the alarm of environmentalists took on a concrete and disagreeable reality for Americans during and after the 1973–1974 Middle East oil embargo. As utility costs climbed, the gasoline pump and the thermostat became the real battle lines in the federally declared "war" for energy independence.

Air-conditioning was by no measure the predominant user of energy resources. Winter heating and automobiles were far more culpable in this regard; summer cooling in this uneasy climate gained unwelcome visibility in the debate over waste. Now that air-conditioning could be found in so many places, *having* it was no longer necessarily considered a luxury. But *using* air-conditioning might be a different matter. Temperature settings, long a cause for private disagreement, became the stuff of public conflict as well. Air-conditioning also readily provoked regional muttering about which Americans were the worst squanderers of energy resources only now recognized as expensive and scarce.

As the energy crisis loomed, Yale sociologist Dorothy K. Newman and a team of researchers set out in search of the typical "American energy consumer." Her resulting study for the Ford Foundation was infused with "new moralism" and clearly motivated by growing energy concerns. This survey of 1,500 households and 125 public utilities made clear, said Newman, "how quickly we have become an energy-devouring people." Americans in 1975, she reported, used twice as much energy per person as they had in 1920. The United States, with 6 percent of the world's population, consumed a third of its energy resources. A great deal of this growth represented more automobiles traveling more miles, but appliances and air-conditioning were also implicated in America's voracious energy appetite.[5]

Newman's case studies of six couples and their families showed wide variations in energy use and desires across generations, incomes, and races. The parents of a young couple living in Washington, D.C., on $8,000 a year gave them a window air-conditioner to use in their Capitol Hill basement apartment, but they ran it sparingly. "Shelly does not turn the air-conditioner on until Peter comes home," said one "vignette" in the chapter "The Way Some People Live." David and Gloria M, a rural West Virginia–born couple in their sixties, lived in a prewar Alexandria, Virginia, apartment on an income of $11,000 annually. They had to pay the landlord an extra $29 a month to run their window air conditioner. "The M's have come from kerosene lamps and wood stoves to color television and air-conditioning," the study noted.[6]

The cooling strategy of Edward and Mabel A, a black couple living in Baltimore on $3,000 a year, was to keep shades drawn and lights dim against the heat. They chose to spend their modest electricity budget to power a washer, a frost-free refrigerator, and a black-and-white television. Bill and Susan F, at the scale's other end, were art dealers earning $100,000 annually. They owned a five-story centrally air-conditioned gallery and brownstone in Manhattan's East 70s. Their fourteen-room, six-bath summer home in Connecticut, a refurbished eighteenth-century stable, was also centrally cooled. When "asked how in theory he would adjust to an America that suddenly had no air-conditioning and no jet planes," Bill F "said without hesitation that he'd move to London."[7]

Americans' careless self-indulgence and short-sightedness, epitomized by their waste of energy and other natural resources, had long inspired gloomy handwringing. When major oil producers imposed restrictions on exports, in the wake of the 1973 Arab-Israeli war, these warnings exploded into mass consciousness. The crisis flared anew in 1979–1980 when Iran took American embassy personnel hostage and cut petroleum exports. As prices of fuels soared and the television news showed panicky drivers lined up at neighborhood gas stations, environmentalists and their allies in the scientific establishment were transformed from Cassandras to experts.[8]

By virtually any measure, the United States used—and uses—more energy per capita than any other industrial nation. One study of nine industrialized nations, based on 1972 statistics, showed that the United States used almost twice as much fossil fuel to produce each million dollars in Gross Domestic Product as did France, the most frugal nation analyzed. The United States was the *only* nation to use a significant percentage of its energy resources for cooling. Climate could not adequately explain the magnitude of the difference, the study said. Heating and cooling customs accounted for fully half the reason why the United States was the largest consumer of heating and cooling energy, "with a consumption level generally 40 percent higher than many Western European countries."[9]

Until the nineteen seventies, such extravagance had been a source of pride, not shame, for most Americans, providing clear evidence of the world's highest standard of living. In his classic 1961 essay, "The Beer Can by the Highway," John A. Kouwenhoven offered a paean to the type of wastefulness symbolized by discarded consumer products, seeing them as an affirmation of America's abundance, mobility, and opportunity. Conservationists' "dread of wastefulness," Kouwenhoven asserted, was an overwrought attempt to curb the nation's joyous sense of limitless possibility.[10]

Limitless possibility certainly included the expectation of consistent indoor comfort. For several reasons, air-conditioning, although a relatively minor component of overall energy use, attracted a disproportionate amount of attention during the seventies. Although air-conditioning consumed less than 3 percent of the nation's total energy derived from all sources in 1978, according to the U.S. Department of Energy, it made extremely intense demands on electrical power supplies. In the seventies, cooling machines used almost 14 percent of the nation's annual electrical generation during a very concentrated period during the summer.

Auguring many such emergencies to come, during a five-day hot spell late in August 1948, New York City experienced its first-ever "brownout" attributed to air-conditioning demand. As temperatures exceeded 100° on August 27, several Consolidated Edison generators burned out under the strain. Subways slowed to half-speed, traffic lights blinked out, and some department stores lost lighting, elevator service, and air-conditioning. In response to pleas for conservation, less severely affected buildings made voluntary reductions. Their priorities were a measure of public wants. "Seventy theaters above the downtown area turned off their marquees and dimmed lights elsewhere. Many of them kept the air-conditioning systems going, including Radio City's Music Hall," the *New York Times* of August 28 reported. The outages were the "greatest emergency to face the Edison Company since the hurricane of 1938," the front-page article declared.

New York City, like the city of Washington in 1942, had joined the summer peak load vanguard. In most of the nation—according to the Edison Electric Institute, a national umbrella organization for investor-owned electric utilities—winter usage of electricity continued to exceed summer usage until 1963.[11] By the seventies, air-conditioning was the predictable culprit in summer brownouts and blackouts that regularly afflicted major urban areas across the country and made it easy to tell when cooling demand exceeded power supplies. Electric utilities had little trouble persuading state rate commissions to allow surcharges for summer electric use, even when overall rate hikes were denied.

The use of air-conditioning also exacerbated tensions between regions. It was a symbolically and rhetorically convenient way to express the differing interests and economic trajectories of the Rust Belt and the Sun Belt. Although the 1970 Census showed that air-conditioning was installed in a majority of homes only in the Census division comprising Texas, Oklahoma, Louisiana, and Arkansas, critics found it easy to attribute the population and job shifts they deplored to the availability of air-conditioning throughout the South and southwest. Interestingly, author J. Kirkpatrick Sale—whose much-quoted 1975 book, *Power Shift,* added "sunbelt" to the popular lexicon—saw sunshine as a more salient factor than air-conditioning in the ascendancy of what he called the "Southern Rim." The South and southwest had always had sunshine; it took air-conditioning to make all that sun tolerable. San Diego, once cooled by Pacific breezes, as Sale noted, now featured the "ever-present air conditioner."[12]

Air-conditioning restriction, especially during Jimmy Carter's 1977–1981 presidency, became a key component of the federal government's symbolic effort to convince Americans of the severity and permanence of the energy crisis. Months before his resignation, President Richard M. Nixon in 1974 urged Americans to reduce indoor temperatures to 68° in winter. In 1975 President Gerald R. Ford also proposed national standards for heating and cooling new residential and commercial structures. But not until President Carter pushed stringent regulations did the public begin to recognize home and workplace energy conservation as both intrusive and controversial. Like a long line at the gas station, an uncomfortably hot house or office was something every American could experience and understand.

Just two days after his inauguration in a bitterly cold January 1977, Carter, dressed in a cardigan, asked Americans to turn their home thermostats down to 65 degrees. Three months later, the president summoned the nation to the "moral equivalent of war," saying failure to end energy waste would lead to a "national catastrophe." Everyone would be required to make sacrifices in lifestyle habits and convenience, Carter said in a somber television speech. "Ours is the most wasteful nation on earth," he said.[13]

By 1979 both the energy crisis and the president's rhetoric had escalated. In a 23-minute nationally televised speech that April, Carter told Americans to prepare to shiver more in winter and sweat more in summer, to drive less, and in smaller cars. The temperature in Washington hit 90° on July 15, the same day that new federal heating and cooling restrictions were to take effect. Carter picked that evening to give a nationally televised speech from the Oval Office in which he placed United States's energy woes in the larger context of national "paralysis and stagnation and drift." The real threat, the president told the nation, was a "crisis of the American spirit":

> Too many of us now tend to worship self-indulgence and consumption. Human identity is no longer defined by what one does but by what one owns. But we've discovered that owning things and consuming things does not satisfy our longing for meaning.

Carter's concern that the nation faced a spiritual crisis as well as an economic one garnered an initially positive response. "Jimmy Carter found his voice again last night," *Washington Post* pundit David Broder wrote the next day. Carter's languishing approval ratings rose nine points to a meager 30 percent in overnight polls. But within days, other columnists, apparently inspired by the spin that Carter pollster Patrick Caddell gave the speech, were deriding Carter as a preacher of "malaise," who had capitulated to an un-American state of doubt and anxiety. Although Carter himself never used the word, this address is still best known as his "Malaise Speech."[14]

Carter's appeals for sacrifice and voluntary discomfort were not words Americans wanted to hear. A law requiring that thermostats in all air-conditioned public and commercial buildings be set no lower than 80° had been enacted in May. Defiant federal judges in Texas and New Mexico set their courtroom thermostats at 74° and 70° respectively. Barraged with complaints from owners and managers of museums, restaurants, department stores, and a broad array of other commercial enterprises, the federal Energy Department said in June that thermostats could be lowered to a psychologically cooler 78 degrees. This was the law that went into effect the day of Carter's speech. Riddled with loopholes and exceptions, it also ordered thermostat settings of 65° in winter until April 1980. Although fines of up to $10,000 a day for violators were threatened and a hotline was set up to report cheating, there is little evidence that any real enforcement was consistently attempted. The day the law took effect, the

Energy Department announced a thirty-day grace period. Only two hundred agents, the department disclosed, would be hired to monitor five million buildings nationwide.

There appears to have been no time during the energy crisis that a significant majority of Americans really believed that the crisis was much more than a plot by oil companies and electric utilities to guarantee themselves higher profits. A November 1977 *New York Times/CBS* poll found that 51 percent of Americans did not believe their president when he said the energy shortage was real. The energy crisis gave Americans a new way to talk about their energy habits, but it was not clear what effects the new vocabulary of conservation and privation actually had on social attitudes and individual conduct. Governor David Boren of oil-producing Oklahoma took note of this resistance early on:

> It is not easy for us to go to the American people and say, "All right, cut back drastically on your use of energy consumption. Keep your car in the garage. Turn the thermostat down.". . . If the American people can be convinced that they must really do these things, they will do them. . . . But I think the people have trouble believing that there is a necessity.[15]

If many Americans did turn their thermostats up in summer—and down in winter—it was probably because they simply could not or would not afford the rising cost of energy. A sweaty sense of grievance pervaded public discussions of energy issues throughout the summer of 1979. In the spring of 1980, Carter extended temperature controls for nine months, despite polls showing that the nation's fifty-five million white-collar workers were complaining more and working less productively. That July, as his city suffered through a record heat wave, a *St. Louis Post–Dispatch* columnist heaped scorn on "Big Brother" government agencies for telling workers they could cope with higher air-conditioner settings by wearing lighter clothing. "Don't you feel stupid that you didn't think of it yourself?" he jeered.[16]

President Carter's pessimism about America's energy future generated virtually no support on the producer or "right wing" side of the energy debate. Nor did his austere outlook really inspire the conservationists and environmentalists who comprised the energy "left." Across this broad ideological spectrum, early talk of America's energy future rarely challenged current definitions of comfort or questioned the multiplication of energy-consuming desires. Some "small is beautiful" adherents predicted future misery but most critics of United States energy policy, on both left and right, appeared to favor a language of reassurance, a sort of conservation through joy. Although the two sides disagreed sharply on where future energy would come from, how it would get to consumers, and at what cost, few really took issue with the idea that energy should be and would be used to do all the things Americans already did. In fundamental ways, both groups endorsed standards of comfort and physical well-being assumed to be innate and immutable when they were, in fact, not even as old as the century.[17]

A 1981 essay collection titled *Resettling America* provides a useful overview of then-current environmentalist literature. Editor Gary Coates sounded an initial note of gloom, saying that "there is a growing sense that something has gone wrong . . . that the road toward a future of unlimited wealth and happiness through science, technology, and the American Way of Life may, in fact, be a dead end." Contributor Tom Bender emphasized the ironies of mismanaged affluence:

> Freeways use so much land that places are farther apart and require more freeways to get to. Air-conditioning makes cities hotter, necessitating more air-conditioning.[18]

But most of the essayists readily endorsed "appropriate technologies" such as solar and hydro power, and conservation techniques like insulation and more efficient appliances, all of which would allow life to go on more or less as before. In the book's introduction, Amory Lovins, the influential proponent of "soft energy"—energy that would come from safe, renewable sources and be distributed in a decentralized and egalitarian manner—offered an almost delectable energy-saving scenario that sounded like *House Beautiful*'s Climate Control project revisited:

> It is not only savings in money that lead people to build houses so heat-tight that they need little or no heating or cooling energy even in our worst climates. Other motives matter too, such as greater comfort and beauty, independence from distrusted institutions, better rapport with natural rhythms, more scope for sitting in the sunspace in February munching fresh tomatoes, and greater resilience (page xvii).

Lovins also forecast continued population shifts from the Northeast and Midwest to the South and the southwest, where both highways and air-conditioning were already rampant.

Energy producers and marketers, forced by the energy squeeze to downplay their historic predilection for "maximum growth" in favor of "quality growth," predicted that the American standard of living would continue to improve, just more slowly. A 1976 study by the Edison Institute conceded that "materialistic values" rooted in human desires for health, wealth, consumption, and physical comfort were under pressure from "no-growth" forces.[19] The eighteen-month study suggested levels of affluence already achieved would keep American society from falling backwards. Looking towards 2000, Edison Institute's new "moderate" scenario projected that increases in energy demand could be trimmed, primarily by market forces, without conspicuously altering the consumption patterns and lifestyles of the free-spending maximum growth era of the fifties and sixties. Intrusive government regulation of lighting, heating, and cooling levels would be unnecessary.

The people who actually made and marketed air-conditioning equipment and installations responded in two main ways to the energy crisis and criticisms of their products. Under some duress, the industry cooperated with efforts to make cooling more energy-efficient. Faced with the revelation that room air-conditioner energy usage had surged 22 percent between 1959 and 1969, the U.S. Commerce Department's National Bureau of Standards in 1974 decreed that air-conditioners would be the first consumer appliance labeled with energy consumption information. As a result, air-conditioner prices rose but the operating efficiency of most models also improved.[20]

At the same time, the Heating, Ventilating, and Air-Conditioning establishment's decades-long debate about what it really meant to be comfortable within a building took a sharp turn towards relativism. Physiological experiments conducted on predominantly young, predominantly male subjects under laboratory conditions took a back seat as researchers began to focus on the psychological comfort reactions of "real" people working or living in actual buildings.

The Comfort Zone was first calculated in 1923 by research engineers F. C. Houghten and Constantin Yaglou at the Pittsburgh laboratory of the American Society of Heating and Ventilating Engineers (ASHVE). They created and used a new variable: effective temperature, which took both heat and humidity into account. It required measurements to be taken by two kinds of thermometers, dry-bulb and wet-bulb, and use of the psychrometric chart, developed by Willis Carrier in the teens, to calculate properly the indoor temperature and humidity. Comfort, they announced to their colleagues at a meeting in Chicago that May and in the paper they published in September in the ASHVE *Journal,* was an effective indoor temperature between 61.8° and 68.8° with 64.5° the optimal temperature for most people.

Houghten, who was the laboratory's research head, used himself as an experimental subject. Like eight other men and five women, he spent ninety minutes in each of two chambers set to deliver different combinations of heat and humidity. Houghten felt "too warm" after spending twenty-five minutes in a room at an effective temperature of 68.8 degrees. Transferred to a room where the effective temperature was 58.6°, Houghten felt refreshed at first but "too cool for comfort" after an hour and twenty minutes. Although the article does not say whether these comfort experiments were done in winter or summer, other evidence indicates that the scientists were establishing a zone of winter indoor comfort.

The experimenters used 130 subjects overall, trying hard to get a "representative group of people." There were men and women in clothing that ranged, one engineer later commented, "from the flapper to the hack driver." Some effort was made to select people with varied occupations, apparently as a surrogate for education and social class. Many were students from the nearby Carnegie Institute of Technology, and most of the rest were professionals and support staff affiliated with the ASHVE Lab or Pittsburgh-area federal agencies. If the photograph that accompanies the *Journal* article is representative, all of them were white.[21]

The American Society of Heating, Refrigerating & Air-Conditioning Engineers (ASHRAE) by 1966 was defining thermal comfort as "that state of mind which expresses satisfaction with the thermal environment." Compared to the carefully measured precision of the twenties' Comfort Zone calculation, it was an extraordinarily inexact and subjective definition. MIT-trained architect Lisa Heschong in a 1979 book pointed out that the indoor temperature range considered acceptable in Britain was 58° to 70° and, in the tropics, 74° to 85 degrees. In the United States, she reported, the comfort zone was now 69° to 80°, quite remarkably warmer than the 1923 calculation. Psychologist and mechanical engineer Frederick H. Rohles Jr. noted in 1980 that winter comfort recommendations promulgated by American engineers had risen steadily from 64° in 1923 to 68° in 1941 to 77° in 1960.[22] The comfort analysts of the nineteen seventies and eighties saw in this obvious elasticity a key to making the new energy strictures more acceptable. Their purpose was certainly not to repudiate air-conditioning but to enhance its status as the only reliable means of indoor environmental regulation in a waste-watching world.

A symposium on "Thermal Discomfort in the Name of Energy Conservation" was held during ASHRAE's 1979 annual meeting in Detroit. "From all sides we are told that we can no longer enjoy the luxury of being comfortable. . . . Must we sacrifice comfort to conserve energy? *No!*" declared Michigan architect Joseph B. Olivieri. He went on to recommend that glass be used less and insulation more, and that sections of houses, such as bedrooms, be placed underground because "we don't need large windows when we're asleep. "Stressing winter comfort needs, Olivieri considered but seemed to reject such options as changing thermostat settings or wearing more or heavier clothing indoors. Such low-tech solutions would not require the expertise of an engineer or architect.[23]

As heating and cooling restrictions became fodder for the nightly news, practitioners in the recently recognized realm of environmental psychology weighed in with techniques for making people believe they were comfortable under conditions of energy restraint. Psychologist Rohles asserted at a 1980 seminar that comfort was a "condition of mind" not always perfectly correlated with physiology or "condition of body." Wood paneling, carpets, and plushly upholstered furnishings helped people feel warmer in their offices, he said.

In one of his experiments, Rohles deliberately misled secretaries by telling them there were space heaters under their desks; most said they felt comfortable when the office temperature was only 65 degrees. Other office workers were told the room temperature was 74° when it was actually 68° — as many said they were comfortable as they did when the room temperature actually was 74 degrees. Deliberate misinformation, he suggested, could trick office workers into accepting unpopular federal guidelines. A skeptical Pierce Lab scientist asked Rohles how long these psychological stratagems could possibly work before losing their credibility. Rohles called for more experimentation.[24]

Rice University psychologists William Howell and Carlla S. Stramler in 1981 reported to the heating and cooling industry on three workplace studies: one done before federal temperature regulations were publicized; one after imposition of the regulations, with public awareness at its height; and a third after the "initial furor" had died down. They found that psychological variables, including a factor they called "coldnaturedness," were more important than demographics or even the actual temperature at a study site. They defined "coldnaturedness" as the extent to which people perceive that they tend to feel warmer or cooler than the people around them do. Howell and Stramler suggested that a better understanding of such psychological variables as temperature tolerance and willingness to adjust to temperatures, presumably without complaining, might be used to ease adjustment to mandated indoor settings.[25]

The journal *Energy and Buildings* in 1992 devoted an entire issue to the tangled links between air-conditioning technology and the varying cultures within which it was used. The centerpiece of this special issue was a provocative essay by British scholar Gwyn Prins, who used saucy language reminiscent of Henry Miller's to accuse "asexual" Americans of actual addiction to the unnatural state of "coolth" produced by their omnipresent air-conditioners. Seven respondents, all but one an American, generally agreed that air-conditioning could be more selectively and less wastefully used. But most defended manufactured comfort, in the United States and elsewhere, against Prin's postcolonial condescension. "It's O.K. to want to be cool," said California energy researcher Carl Blumstein. The problem, he noted, lies not in a desire for coolness, but in the means of its achievement.[26]

If Americans really were "addicts" to their air conditioners, heat waves might still force them to go cold, or perhaps "hot," turkey.

When St. Louis was the nation's fourth largest city in 1902, muckraker Lincoln Steffens came calling. He held the city up as a prime example of everything wrong in his influential municipal corruption casebook, *The Shame of the Cities*. The visitor to St. Louis, Steffens wrote, hears the boasts of its citizens, but sees a "ramshackle firetrap crowded with the sick, and learns that it is the City Hospital."[27] That particular City Hospital was replaced in 1905, a year after Steffens's book came out. Its 120-bed successor was still serving the poor of St. Louis in 1980 when a month-long heat wave killed 1,265 people in the central and southern United States, 311 of them in Missouri, and 112 in St. Louis alone. The "new" City Hospital proved to be about the nastiest place to be in St. Louis during the nation's first "air-conditioned heat wave."

On July 10, 1980, the temperature in the general medical wards at City Hospital was 95° for the sixth straight night. Relatives of the more fortunate patients brought in small fans to supplement floor-mounted blowers installed in the wards. Medical residents spent the nights packing the sickest elderly patients in ice. Local voters in 1974 had rejected as too expensive plans to air-condition the hospital. "Air conditioners are not a luxury at hospitals," said Dr. Stephen Ayres, head of City Hospital's medical staff, as heat conditions there worsened six summers later (figure 34).

Not everyone agreed. When it was discovered that only 36 of the 600 elderly and chronically ill patients at Robert Koch Hospital—another ramshackle city health facility—were housed in air-conditioned rooms, and that a patient in an unairconditioned ward had died of heat stroke, the superintendent was quoted as saying, "I really don't think chronic patients require air-conditioning. . . . Old people take the heat well." An irate St. Louis doctor complained that City Hospital had not improved since the "hot summers of 1954 and 1955 when I worked there as a medical student. Lack of air-conditioning was the rule then all over St. Louis, but nowadays all other important public and private facilities . . . are well provided with cooling systems. Not old City Number One. It remains a monument to the rule that sick, poor people are the last priority."[28]

These charity hospitals notwithstanding, air-conditioning was ubiquitous in Missouri's major cities. The 1980 U.S. Census would reveal that 70 percent of Missouri's households were equipped with some form of refrigerated cooling, a higher proportion than in 38 other states.[29] *Kansas City Star* columnist Jerry Heaster thought the region was handling the heat wave admirably as he wrote on the seventeenth day of temperatures over 100°:

Thanks to central air-conditioning, many in these parts will remember the brutal heat wave as nothing more than a minor inconvenience. It is a life-and-death matter only for those who can't afford the luxury of an air-conditioned existence.[30]

Heaster's peculiar characterization of air-conditioning as both "life-and-death" and a "luxury" should not obscure his larger point. It seems fair to say that without modern air-conditioning even more people would have died of heat effects during the 1980 heat wave. Although more than a hundred did die in St. Louis, a city once dubbed the "center of the cooling belt" by the air-conditioning industry, 470 St. Louisans had died from heat during the scorching Depression summer of 1936. In the thirties, fewer than a hundred buildings in the entire city, only a handful of them residences, had been equipped with air-conditioning.[31]

It must also be said that the 1980 heat wave demonstrated dramatically that the ability of air-conditioning to shield Americans from the effects of extreme heat was limited by an array of factors both social and technological. Those in "life-and-death" need of cooling were also those least likely to have access to it, primarily for economic reasons but also because of habit, fear, and social isolation. The more fortunate who both had and used air-conditioning soon discovered that the appliances were inadequate to cope with constant temperatures over 100 degrees.

For Missourians of 1980, Willis Carrier's 1936 prophecy of a seamlessly cool "air-conditioned life of the future" proved to be not only physically unachievable but psychologically unbearable. Just days after the heat wave settled in, an occupational therapist told *Kansas City Star* readers that even 24-hour air-conditioning would not shield them from the "stupefying effects" of persistent 100° heat. "Even if you go from air-conditioned home to air-conditioned car to air-conditioned office, the heat probably is affecting the way you're spending your time," she said. "You probably are giving up outdoor activities that might otherwise be your pleasure, your release."[32]

The 1980 heat wave was not only Missouri's worst since the thirties but also its longest hot spell since the 1973 onset of the energy crisis and the accompanying rise in electric rates. In the state's two major metropolitan areas, the newspapers kept up a drumbeat of anecdote, advice, alarm, and astonishment. This was "mid-America" where July temperatures in the 90s were expected, but 100s were uncommon. "Kansas City is not a hot-weather city," its health director Richard M. Biery told the *Star,* adding rather inaccurately:

> It's a temperate city, and probably the air-conditioning level in the city is not substantially high. . . . People in upper-economic levels take air-conditioning for granted. But there are a large number who can neither afford air conditioners nor feel they need them.[33]

The "weather story," a staple of American journalism, is ordinarily a colorful and anecdote-packed description of an extreme but short-lived weather incident, written in a tone that mingles amusement and irritation. As a high-pressure sys-

34. After much political finger-pointing, Air Force and Army Reserve units were called up on July 11, 1980, to pump cool air into St. Louis's sweltering City Hospital at 1515 Lafayette. Gasoline-powered generators were parked in these trucks outside. The hospital complex closed in 1985, but still stood, stripped and crumbling, in 2001 as St. Louis pondered options for its centrally located but asbestos-tainted site.

tem stalled over the continent, pushing temperatures above 100° day after day and preventing them from falling below 85° night after night, the heat wave as "weather story" long outlived its novelty. Searching for new angles, newspapers milked the story for dramatic detail.[34]

Over the weeks, a portrait of the typical heat-wave victim gradually accumulated. The "magic" of air-conditioning "seems to be everywhere but it isn't," the *Star* reported on July 8.[35] In a melodramatic feature on July 17 another *Star* reporter found a disaster lurking behind the "serenity of air-conditioners humming in the palpable July night." It is "Heat Wave 1980, inner-city style. Old people dying in front of pint-size fans blowing warm air. Bodies decomposing in front of blaring television sets."[36] Most older people interviewed by reporters blamed high electric rates for their refusal to own or use air conditioners or even fans. Many took pride in making do with traditional cooling techniques like porch sitting, iced-tea sipping, and damp clothing. But those who were dying were not the ones being interviewed. As the heat wave continued, it became clear that those found dead were usually not merely or even necessarily poor or old, but rather people fearful of any contact with authorities and estranged from family or friends.

Public and private groups trying to help soon learned that simply passing out fans and other cooling devices was useless if people did not know how to use them effectively. Despite a break in the weather, it was still 100° at one woman's house, related the Rev. Larry Rice whose evangelical church passed out 2,500 window fans in St. Louis and East St. Louis. A parishioner's windows had been nailed shut after the theft of a television years earlier. A fan sat on the floor, blowing hot air around. Volunteers persuaded the woman to open a window and had to show her how to blow the fan across a tray of ice from the refrigerator.[37]

Other such anecdotes raised doubts whether some elderly and chronically ill people even knew they were hot. In Kansas City, an 87-year-old man donned his customary long underwear and refused to let his niece plug in the fan for fear he would catch cold.[38] Whether mental confusion in such cases was caused by the extreme heat or preceded it, it provided a convenient explanation for some victims' seemingly willful refusal to be cool.

A 65-year-old woman in suburban Webster Groves was found dead on July 15 at her dining room table. Authorities could not explain why the window units and fans found there were not in use. The next day, another suburban St. Louis woman with heart trouble was found dead in her unairconditioned house by her cleaning woman. Health authorities in St. Louis and Kansas City speculated that more affluent victims such as these died of "hopelessness that made them not want to make it through the heat wave—they really didn't care."[39]

The attribution of deaths to heat rather than other factors is itself not an exact science. Dr. Bonita Peterson, medical examiner for Jackson County, Kansas, admitted to the *Star* that rulings of death by heat could be arbitrary especially since bodies were arriving at the morgue faster than autopsies could be performed. Body temperatures in excess of 105°—one victim had a temperature of 109.5°—were determinative of heat stroke, she said, but other signs were less clear-cut. Peterson said she presumed that heat was the main reason why there were more than three times as many "natural" deaths in July 1980 as in July 1979.

An Environmental Protection Agency study would predict twenty years later that climate changes in North America could double weather-related mortality in St. Louis by 2050. This study—much like the 1923 mortality study by Ellsworth Huntington's Atmosphere and Man panel—summed the effects of summer and winter and did not "fully account for air-conditioning use." Predictions for Dallas, Chicago, Atlanta, Los Angeles, New York, and Minneapolis were similarly bleak.[40]

In Missouri's continuing heat emergency it was obvious that the poorest city dwellers, like those in St. Louis's City and Robert Koch hospitals, were effectively denied access to the air-conditioned culture all around them. When the air-conditioning broke down at Kansas City's privately run Martin Luther King Memorial Hospital, the hundred-bed health facility continued to admit patients, including some already suffering from heat stroke, even though repair parts had not yet arrived from New Jersey. On July 11, the temperature in one patient's room stood at 96°. The city health department had not been informed. Asked how he planned to remedy this situation, the city health director pointed out "there is no law that says a hospital has to have air-conditioning. . . . In the old days, no one had it." The hospital remained without air-conditioning for eight days.[41]

Old-timers incessantly recalled how, during the heat waves of the thirties, forty-eight movie houses in Kansas City, almost all of them air-conditioned, had provided crowds with coolness unavailable anywhere else. Yet in July 1980, movie attendance actually declined. "Movie theaters, which were havens for the weary during the years when air-conditioning was a novelty, suffered Tuesday," the July 2 *Star* reported. Theater managers speculated that people were refusing to leave their presumably air-conditioned houses once they got home from their air-conditioned offices. The experience of one St. Louis man showed that even movies, even in 1980, might not be a reliable refuge. At a second-run movie house in a low-income neighborhood where he had gone to get cool, he found that the only "air" was a "large electric fan in the lobby." A movie house employee was unsympathetic:

> Forty years ago, this was normal weather in St. Louis and you didn't have air-conditioned theaters, barbershops, and stores like you have now. Places were kept cool by ceiling fans. Older people have far more problems, and they suffer far more in weather like this. I doubt if you'll hear them complaining the way young people do.[42]

Public transit users in St. Louis and Kansas City soon learned the difference between air-conditioning's promises of comfort and its ability to deliver comfort when needed. In St. Louis, a record-setting temperature of 105° on July 1 coincided with a rate increase that doubled the basic fare on Bi-State transit system buses. They would not mind the increase from a quarter to 50¢, riders told the newspaper, if it meant clean, cool transportation. Claims by Bi-State that the air-conditioning was working on at least 85 percent of the 775-bus fleet were so obviously untrue that officials soon had to concede that the number was closer to 54 percent. For two years, Bi-State admitted, broken bus cooling systems had been deliberately ignored in an effort to save fuel and maintenance costs. Drivers on buses with air-conditioners that actually worked were under orders not to turn them on until explicit complaints were voiced.

While Bi-State hired emergency repair crews, some commuters mounted a small but well-publicized fare strike against buses on which the air-conditioning had failed. At the mercy of stop-and-go driving, jarring, vibration, dirty air, and a constant influx of hot passengers, city buses had difficulty maintaining cool interiors even under ordinary conditions. With temperatures so consistently high, even buses that normally met federal standards requiring interiors to be 15° cooler than outdoors had trouble producing noticeable cooling effects.[43]

The aging St. Louis bus fleet was fortunate to have windows that could be opened to admit air, no matter how warm it was. In wealthier and more up-to-date Kansas City, sixty-two brand-new Grumman buses, almost a fifth of the city's fleet, had windows that could not be opened at all. When the air-conditioning failed, these sealed buses were intolerable and had to be taken off the streets. "Hisses on buses whose air-conditioners break down, and double hisses when it happens on those new ATA buses with windows that won't open. Talk about microwave cooking," on July 11 the *Star* editorialized.

Kansas City Area Transportation Authority manager Richard F. Davis responded almost a month later. "Your complaints were on target," he said, adding humbly, "We offer our apologies to our customers who have had to tolerate non-air-conditioned buses. We will do better." During the heat wave, only about 65 to 70 percent of air-conditioners on the system's 343 buses had worked, he reported. Because the new buses were unusable without air-conditioning, maintenance crews were pulled off repair jobs on older but usable buses so the ATA could get the sealed Grummans back on the road.[44]

Buses were, for the most part, the urban transit choice of people too poor to have other choices. Better-off commuters had their air-conditioned cars. By isolating themselves in air-conditioned cars, houses, and workplaces, middle- and upper-class Missourians were less likely than ever to perceive the heat wave as a communal event. During the Depression, or so the nostalgists argued, people of all classes had flocked to the movies and slept in their yards or in the parks. They could see one another's suffering as they endured the same heat.

"For the most part, everyone suffered equally regardless of their station in life," said *Star* columnist Jerry Heaster about the Depression-era experience. Now the parks were too dangerous and were in any case ruled off-limits for sleeping by city ordinances. Only facilities primarily used by the poor still lacked air-conditioning. In both generations, the same class of people—poor, older, alone, and without air-conditioning—were at risk but in 1980 they were even less visible. Twelve corpses were discovered on July 11 in Kansas City. Meanwhile, just twenty-eight fans and three room units were donated at local fire stations in response to pleas for cooling equipment.

For Missourians of adequate means the "luxury" was not air-conditioning it-self, but the opportunity it gave those who had it to choose when and where to stay cool, or to voluntarily endure the unprecedented heat. Although newspa-pers in both major cities wrote vividly about how the heat was keeping people "virtual prisoners" in their air-conditioned homes and offices, not all outdoor activities went begging. The pennant-contending Kansas City Royals baseball team drew large crowds throughout the heat wave, despite well-publicized tem-perature readings ranging from 97° in the stands to 136° on the artificial turf. Even the mediocre St. Louis Cardinals maintained respectable attendance num-bers. Malls were crowded with shoppers who probably consumed more air-conditioning than they purchased goods, but several Kansas City–area malls held successful annual sidewalk sales outdoors. Free outdoor concerts were well-attended; drive-in movies, already heading toward extinction, did even worse than usual.[45]

The summer of 1980 forced even Missouri's suburban middle and upper class to face the limits of air-conditioning's dependability and to question its cost. Power outages occurred regularly, disrupting service in scattered areas. Drought and illegal use of city hydrants lowered water pressure, shutting down large air-cooling systems, including the air-conditioning at St. Louis's Veterans Admin-istration Hospital on July 9. On July 14, federal workers in Kansas City were sent home, with pay, for the third time in three weeks, because of malfunction-ing office air-conditioning.

Air conditioners were difficult to procure and even harder to get repaired. On July 3, Kansas City Montgomery Ward stores ran out of advertised room units. A $69.88 ceiling fan was also unavailable. By mid-July in St. Louis it was tak-ing three days to three weeks to get service on a central air conditioner. Win-dow units were out of stock everywhere. Callers, said one air-conditioning dealer, were not just impatient but afraid. "The news media have scared people about the heat," she said.[46]

In both Kansas City and St. Louis, electricity usage set new records during the heat wave. In a single hour on July 2, customers of Kansas City Power & Light drew down 2.13 million kilowatts. On July 7, Union Electric's 689,000 St. Louis–area customers, 90 percent of them residential, used six million kilo-watts in a single day. Within a week this all-time record was broken when 6.33 million kilowatts were consumed.

A utility spokesman in Kansas City put it bluntly. It hardly mattered whether a home owner set his thermostat to a civic-minded 78° or 80° or a hoggish 72 degrees. With daily temperatures over 100°, the unit would have to run twenty-four hours a day just to keep the house at 80 or 85 degrees. Kansas City customers were warned to expect bills 50 to 60 percent higher than those of July 1979. In St. Louis, Union Electric said bills might triple. Fully half the electricity Union Electric customers used in summertime was used to run air-conditioning, an engineer reported.[47]

In the state and national election year of 1980, heat of this magnitude and utility bills of this size were politically irresistible issues. The national energy crisis had already pushed the federal government to help the shivering poor buy heating fuel. Politicians from the hotter parts of the nation used the 1980 heat wave to justify federal aid for summer cooling and to strengthen their view that heat was equally as threatening to human health and well-being: heat was, in fact, the moral equivalent of cold.

The new Home Energy Assistance Act, signed in April 1980 by President Carter, substituted "aggregate residential energy expenditures" for "heating costs" in aid formulas currently providing a $1.6 billion annual subsidy for utility bills. This, said the *Kansas City Times,* meant states could use federal money to pay the summer electric bills of elderly and low-income residents but, significantly, the "government will only pitch in for air that's cooled on doctors' orders." Recipients would have to show evidence of asthma or a heart condition. Still this was a breakthrough for arguments that air-conditioning was a necessity. "I thought the idea of helping people pay their air-conditioning bills was kind of funny, until the heat hit Texas," an aide to Missouri Senator Thomas Eagleton told the *Times*.[48]

Facing a nasty Democratic primary in the fall, Missouri Governor Joseph P. Teasdale used the heat wave to garner headlines and refurbish his sagging popularity with state voters. Teasdale campaigned in favor of massive federal aid, melodramatically describing the heat as a "plague" visited on the innocent people of Missouri. When, on the twelfth day of Kansas City's ordeal, the White House announced $6.7 million in grants for six heat-afflicted states, including $1,250,000 for Missouri, Teasdale just escalated his demands. Federal bureaucrats, the governor charged, were disregarding "death by heat" in the heartland while preparing to spend hundreds of millions to fix damage caused by the May 18 explosion of Washington State's Mount Saint Helens volcano.[49]

St. Louis Mayor Jim Conway was a star witness when the U.S. Senate's Select Committee on Aging held a well-attended hearing in Washington on July 25.[50] Describing the 112 heat-linked deaths in his city, Conway conjured up the horror of bodies piling up in the morgue while confused old people sweltered in their homes, reluctant to leave and unsure what to do to cool off. The mayor did not blame high utility costs or the lack of air-conditioning for these deaths. He focused rather on some structural problems peculiar but not unique to St. Louis, including a disproportionately high elderly population, customarily oppressive summer humidity, and an aging housing stock built of brick that retained heat especially well.

The hearing was a fresh opportunity for senators from the warmer regions of the United States to display bipartisan concern for the costs and casualties of hot weather. Then-Senator Lawton Chiles of Florida and Missouri's Eagleton declared it was time elected officials realized that heat victims suffered as much as those exposed to cold weather.[51] Congress was not prepared to rebuild St. Louis, nor any of the nation's other obsolescent inner cities. Nor was Washington proposing to decree the reinstitution of social arrangements that had once kept old people in the bosom of their families rather than living alone in fear and confusion in stuffy rooms. Providing air-conditioning, or at least the wherewithal to pay for it, struck many politicians as a straightforward technological solution to problems that, until a heat wave struck, seemed to be a relic of the Depression years.

Could heat waves be "solved" by making sure everyone had an air-conditioner and could pay for the electricity to run it? If the heat wave experience itself had not already revealed the pitfalls in such a simple proposal, the political struggle that ensued certainly did. Opposition to a large infusion of state money to pay summer electric bills for the poor and elderly came primarily from Teasdale's fellow Democrats, and involved issues of fairness and necessity.[52] A number of legislators pointed out that helping people pay electric bills for cooling provided no help at all to those who had no fans or air conditioners to run or had declined to use them. The ability to cool was much more unevenly distributed than the ability to heat. Decisions about air-conditioning use were still perceived as voluntary. By the time the legislature was done with Teasdale's "Cool Aid" plan in September, the governor's package had been pared from five million dollars to two million and the individual benefit from $100 to $50 or half the July electric bill, whichever was less. The great Missouri heat wave of 1980 had ended not with a bang but with a whimper.

Air-conditioning became even more ubiquitous in houses, cars, and large buildings in the years following the 1980 heat wave. The growing availability of cooling increased the marginalization of those poor and dysfunctional persons and neighborhoods that did without it. The political benefits to be gained from advocacy on behalf of the sweltering poor declined even further. A six-day heat wave in July l995 that included two consecutive days over 100° was blamed for causing or contributing to the deaths of more than seven hundred people in Chicago and environs.

Why did so many die in so short a time? Coverage by the *Chicago Tribune* made a rather compelling case that many of the victims were, as in 1980, old, ailing, estranged, alone, perhaps even ready to succumb to emotional, mental,

35. During the three days Doris Rederer spent without electricity, all the food in her refrigerator spoiled, and she was unable to run her fan. Few Chicagoans sought relief in neighborhood cooling centers during the 1995 heat wave that killed hundreds of people.

or physical exhaustion magnified by the extreme heat. Nine *Tribune* reporters collaborated in November 1995 on a series of vignettes limning the lives of eleven heat fatalities. "See how some of them lived, and it is clear that, although the summer heat was a terrible problem in their lives, it wasn't the only terrible problem," the article declared (figure 35).

Tribune columnist Mike Royko pointed out that in the days before universal air-conditioning, heat deaths provoked less attention because they seemed more normal. He wrote "when poor Gramps croaked in those days, nobody got to see him being wheeled into the morgue on the 10 o'clock news." A September 22 article compared the 1995 death toll to that of 1955, Chicago's hottest summer on record. Experts speculated that with fewer ways to escape from heat in the fifties, healthy Chicagoans managed to acclimate themselves to it. Reporter Nancy Ryan wrote, "despite all the hardships then, there was generally far less whining. . . . That's mainly because there were fewer technological wonders to get angry at for failing to insulate people from the heat."[53]

Letting nature take its course is hardly a politically astute response to disaster in a technological age. As in Missouri in 1980, the 1995 Chicago heat episode brought about a brief period of partisan invective. In Lake County, where twenty-two died in the heat wave, the village of Vernon Hills that August

36. In the fifties and sixties, air-conditioning engineers conducted research projects at dairy farms and hog lots to show that air-conditioned cows would produce more milk and cooled swine more meat. But when a major heat wave struck Chicagoland in July 1995, fans were the best that farmer Lee Hennig of Huntley, Illinois, could afford his sweltering herd.

adopted an air-conditioning rights ordinance that mandated at least one working air conditioner in the bedroom, living room, or dining room of all fifteen hundred rental units in the village. Landlords objected and experts quoted by the *Chicago Tribune*'s environmental writer were skeptical (figure 36):

> Neither Orlando nor Phoenix—hot weather meccas for retirees—require air-conditioning because other, less expensive ways to stay cool are available. Said Scott Greene, a climatologist, "Air-conditioning is not a necessity."[54]

"Thank God for air conditioning."

37. At last someone figured out the thermodynamics of an igloo. This cartoon originally appeared in Sunday newspaper comic supplements on November 12, 1995.

Greene prescribed open windows, lots of liquids, cool baths, movies, and shopping malls. Only the shopping malls might have puzzled Chicagoans of the thirties (figure 37).

Although air-conditioning use—at home, at work, in the car—continued to
climb during the brisk economy of the late nineties and the early years of the
twenty-first century, America's age of energy innocence appears to be over. Despite the emergence in recent years of an overwhelming lust for gas-guzzling
Sport Utility Vehicles and trucks, and the prodigious multiplication of consumer
appliances, gadgets, and toys powered by electricity, the "malaise" that dared
not speak its name in 1979 still resonates. When President George W. Bush introduced his administration's energy plan in May 2001, he was careful, the *New
York Times* reported, "to separate his approach from President Jimmy Carter's
politically disastrous calls for household austerity." Both advocates and foes
of the president's plan explicitly connected current problems of rolling blackouts, high prices for gasoline, electricity, and natural gas, and overdependence
on imported oil to those problems of the seventies.[55]

Intermittent weather and environmental panics continue to affect the way
makers and users of summer cooling think about its costs and benefits. The concept of "global warming," as scientific evidence mounts almost daily, has made
air-conditioning seem even more necessary but also more suspect. For a small
number of Americans, giving up air-conditioning has become a moral or aesthetic choice. In humid Houston, self-proclaimed "air-conditioning capital of
the world," the *Wall Street Journal* claimed in 1994 to have found young people
who had stopped using it because it made them feel "sort of alone and cut off."[56]

Architect and energy consultant Lisa Heschong's 1979 meditation on the joys of thermal inconsistency is still available in paperback and attracts an active online following among advocates of sustainable resource use and human scale. In just 78 pages, Heschong considers what we lose in "sensual delight" as we perfect our control of built environments. We have used our heating and cooling systems, says Heschong, to homogenize and erase culturally linked responses to seasonality in food, clothing, activities, festivals, and building design. Our systems are mundane, functional, convenient, and, perhaps worst of all, unchallenging. Heschong argues that some degree of thermal distress fulfils the human desire for extreme—but not necessarily dangerous—sensual experience.[57]

Publications devoted to alternative lifestyles, such as the *Tightwad Gazette*, regularly pick air-conditioning to represent everything that has made American life less "natural" and more uniformly stressful. The *Country Journal* detected a conspiratorial dimension:

> We and our employers finally absorbed the message of air-conditioning: There is absolutely no reason to loll around in August. Besides, while making it so much pleasanter indoors, air-conditioning has made the outdoors rather horrid. The summer idler sits on his front steps rocked by the pulsing roar and fetid breath of a million room coolers.[58]

Even as air-conditioning engineers and trade organizations helped underwrite a 1999–2000 exhibition titled "Stay Cool! Air-Conditioning America" at the National Building Museum in Washington, all was not celebratory. Exhibition cocurator Donald Albrecht noted that windows that can be opened and open-air porches were making a comeback as air-conditioning users at least symbolically strove to reassert a connection to the weather. In offices as well as houses, a *New York Times* feature reported that a "deep yearning for fresh air and the open window" was changing building design and use.[59]

At the end of air-conditioning's first century, it would seem that cooling technology is omnipresent but not beloved. Even those Americans who switch from heating season to cooling season without ever opening a window are among those who worry about it. Some are concerned with waste and diminishing energy resources. Others, since the identification in 1976 of Legionnaire's Disease and, in 1978, of Sick Building Syndrome, suspect that airborne dangers lurk inside air-conditioned buildings. Perhaps air-conditioning's very invisibility has made it harder to love—and easier to fear.

Conclusion

For Willis Carrier, air-conditioning was a dream of social perfection; for Henry Miller and Lewis Mumford, it was a nightmare that sucked the very air out of life while imposing a new kind of social control. We are heirs to both of these visions of an air-conditioned America. If all our air-conditioning machines by some peculiar accident or rolling blackout were to stop working tomorrow, American life as we have come to know it would be altered irrevocably. The ramifications are almost endless, but some should now be more immediately evident. Most of our large buildings would be uninhabitable in summer; our trains, buses, and planes would be intolerable in hot weather. People might once again drive their automobiles with their windows rolled down and their sleeves rolled up. Electric utilities would need to promote new summertime uses for their output. Blockbuster movies would be released in the fall. Much of our computer and communications equipment, engineered for thermal consistency, would behave more erratically, if able to function at all. The productivity of both white- and blue-collar workers would likely display seasonal cycles of efficiency and stagnation. Congressmen and congresswomen might leave Washington between Memorial Day and Labor Day. More people, not all of them poor or elderly, would die of heat stroke.

This grab bag of repercussions emphasizes the "reality" of hot weather in the United States and the "real" differences air-conditioning has made in dealing with it. To place quotation marks around "real" is not to deny that heat can be dangerous—even fatal—to human life. The concept of what it means to be comfortable may be culturally contingent, but that does not mean that C.-E. A. Winslow was mistaken about the probable deadliness of the Black Hole of Calcutta. When, in April 2001, China briefly held twenty-four crew members from a United States surveillance plane after an air incident that killed a Chinese pilot, the media took note that *this* despotic power detained Americans humanely in an air-conditioned hotel.

Nor does the story told in this book deny the physical reality of the United States's climate and its grave effects on human life. It has asked why certain aspects of that climate came to be considered problematic and has shown how air-conditioning, with all its defects, annoyances, inequities, and compromises, proved to be one of the technologies Americans use to fix the defects they found in their new Eden. As Thomas P. Hughes has pointed out, European observers understood the United States to be technology's nation long before Americans were ready to give up on their "Nature's Nation" conceit.[1]

In 2000, the National Academy of Engineering named air-conditioning and refrigeration tenth among the twenty most important achievements of the twentieth century. Air-conditioning has certainly been a major technical advancement and a marketing triumph. In the process, it has also provoked opposition and uneasiness. People who dislike air-conditioning—and I count myself among that number—tend to portray an unairconditioned America as simpler, purer, more sensual, more natural, more neighborly. Yet the introduction of air-conditioning, initially in public urban spaces and later in private suburban realms, significantly democratized opportunities for physical comfort that had previously been available in summertime only to the wealthy. For all the racism and sexism implicit in air-conditioning advertising, especially in the nineteen-fifties—as cooling machines became cheaper and some actually worked better—more and more Americans of all races, regions, and incomes could purchase the means to work more comfortably in the daytime and sleep through nights when the temperature might never fall below 80 degrees.

For every Ellsworth Huntington or Colum GilFillan who believed that only superior races and classes of people would spearhead the "coldward course of progress," there were those like Winslow or Sydney Markham who were convinced that manufactured cooling could make every American a more productive member of a happier, healthier society. Although hundreds died, air-conditioning certainly saved lives in Missouri, Chicago, and elsewhere in the eighties and nineties and continues to do so to this day. To expect that any technology's effects could be distributed with absolute and perfect equity to every single American in every place at all times is to propose a utopia beyond the wildest dreams even of American utopians.

But if the unairconditioned America could not be utopia, neither can the air-conditioned. Thoughtful advocates of air-conditioning technology, people like the editors of *House Beautiful* or engineer-gadfly Herbert Laube, even Carrier's Logan Lewis, tried without much success to persuade the public that true comfort did not come in a box, but was part of a much broader and also subtler conception of the good life. The quick fix usually won instead. When you "came on in," it was "Kold" inside. Before recurring energy crises made people at least pause to consider cost, air-conditioning was almost always too cold, too noisy, too quickly pressed into service when an open window, or fan, or just lighter clothing would have been more effective and pleasanter.

As Lewis Mumford pointed out in the bleak book he wrote when he was 75, air-conditioning is deeply complicit in our society's authoritarian tendencies toward control. It can be and has been used to discipline both the individual human body and the social order, forbidding sweat, enforcing uniform and continuous productivity, and muddling traditional human connections with time, weather, and season. Daniel J. Boorstin has put it this way:

> There was less difference than ever before between what man could do indoors and what he had to go outdoors and brave the weather for. . . . Americans began to carry their indoors with them. . . . The commonsense distinction between outdoors and in, between the world Nature's God had made and man's little artificial worlds was blurred as never before, leaving Americans more disoriented than they commonly realized.[2]

The counterpart of technologically enabled control is dependency, and the history of air-conditioning provides it in full measure. Air-conditioning has made it possible to erect structures that must be evacuated when the power fails, to make buildings in which people get sick. It gulps electricity; roars, wheezes, and whines; makes urban heat islands even hotter with the exhaust of a million air-conditioned cars and thousands of sealed buildings.

Technology, by allowing humans to evade "environmental insults" they once had to deal with physiologically has, René Dubos reminds us, exposed human life itself to new physical and moral perils:

> Human history shows . . . that the same kind of knowledge that permits man to alter his environment for the purpose of minimizing effort, achieving comfort, and avoiding exposure to stress also gives him the power to change his environment and ways of life in a manner that often entails unpredictable dangers. . . . The state of adaptedness to the world of today may be incompatible with survival in the world of tomorrow.[3]

For better and for worse, our world of tomorrow will be air-conditioned.

Notes

Shortened Titles

Ayer. N. W. Ayer Advertising Agency Records, 1889–1972. Archives Center, National Museum of American History, Smithsonian Institution, Washington, D.C.

Carrier. Carrier Corporation, Records, Number 2511. Division of Rare and Manuscript Collections, Cornell University Library, Ithaca, New York.

HB. House Beautiful magazine.

HPAC. Heating, Piping, & Air-Conditioning (Journal of HVAC Engineering, April 1929 to May 1999).

Huntington. Ellsworth Huntington Papers. Manuscripts and Archives, Yale University Library, New Haven, Connecticut.

NYPL. New York World's Fair, 1939, Inc., and 1940, New York's World Fair, 1940, Inc. Records. Rare Books and Manuscripts Division, New York Public Library.

Orth. Edward J. Orth Memorial Archives of the World's Fair, 1939–1940. Archives Center, National Museum of American History, Smithsonian Institution, Washington, D.C.

Warshaw. Warshaw Collection of Business Americana: Air-Conditioning. Archives Center, National Museum of American History, Smithsonian Institution, Washington, D.C.

Winslow. Charles-Edward Amory Winslow Papers, Manuscript Group 749. Manuscripts and Archives, Yale University Library, New Haven, Connecticut.

Yale Series I (CPE) and Yale Series II (NYWF). Manuscript Group 820, Century of Progress/World's Fair Collection. Manuscripts and Archives, Yale University Library, New Haven, Connecticut.

Introduction

1. René Dubos, *Man Adapting,* enlarged ed. (New Haven: Yale University Press, 1980), xviii. See also his *Mirage of Health: Utopias, Progress & Biological Change* (New York: Doubleday, 1961).
2. Marsha E. Ackermann, "Air Conditioners: Send Them Back," *Buffalo Courier-Express,* 12 July 1981, C1.
3. Perry Miller, *Nature's Nation* (Cambridge, Mass.: Belknap Press, 1967). Connections between social contexts and "common sense" are distilled in Peter L. Berger and Thomas Luckmann, *The Social Construction of Reality: A Treatise in the Sociology of Knowledge* (Garden City, N.Y.: Doubleday/Anchor Books, 1967). In the inaugural issue of *Technology and Culture,* Melvin Kranzberg exhorted historians to be concerned "with the relations of technology to science, politics, social change, economics, and the arts and humanities." ["At the Start," *Technology and Culture* 1 (Winter, 1959:1–10). The quotation is on p. 1.]
4. Raymond Arsenault, *Journal of Southern History* 50:597–628 (Nov. 1984).
5. Gail A. Cooper, *Air-Conditioning America* (Baltimore: Johns Hopkins Press, 1998).
6. Witold Rybczynski, *Home: A Short History of an Idea* (New York: Penguin Books, 1986), esp. 224–32.
7. Michel Foucault, *Discipline and Punish,* trans. by Alan Sheridan (New York: Vintage Books, 1979), 149–56.
8. Thomas P. Hughes, *American Genesis,* 1.
9. Andrew Ross, *Strange Weather* (London: Verso, 1991), esp. chap. 6, "The Drought This Time," 193–249.

1. The Coldward Course of Progress

1. Proof sheets for all three ads, the first scheduled for publication in the 13 Aug. 1949 *Saturday Evening Post,* the second undated, the third dated 25 Feb. 1950, are in Ayer, Box 94/Folder 1.
2. "President's Address," *ASHVE Transactions* 1:55 (New York: Published by the Society, 1895). On turn-of-the century engineers, see Cecilia Tichi, *Shifting Gears: Technology, Literature, Culture in Modernist America* (Chapel Hill: University of North Carolina Press, 1987). For the early history of air-conditioning, see Cooper's *Air-Conditioning America* (Baltimore: Johns Hopkins Press, 1998) and her 1987 Ph.D. dissertation, "'Manufactured Weather': A History of Air-Conditioning in the United States, 1902–1955," University of California, Santa Barbara.
3. Karen Ordahl Kupperman, "Fear of Hot Climates in the Anglo-American Colonial Experience," *William and Mary Quarterly* 41:213–40 (Apr. 1984).
4. See Reyner Banham, *The Architecture of the Well-tempered Environment,* 2d ed. (Chicago: University of Chicago Press, 1984), 25–27, 45–52. Also, Rybczynski, *Home,* and Siegfried Giedion, *Mechanization Takes Command* (London: Oxford University Press, 1948; repr., New York: Norton, 1975).

5. Charles Dickens, Boston, to John Forster, London, 29 Jan. 1842, quoted in *Charles Dickens American Notes,* Arnold Goldman and John Whitley, ed. (Baltimore: Penguin Books, 1972), 306. Leeds's letter to the editor in *The Manufacturer and Builder* 1 (April 1869:107–8) is available in facsimile at Cornell University's "Making of America" website, http://cdl.library.cornell.edu/moa/ (30 Nov. 2000).

6. Max O'Rell (pseud.) and Jack Allyn, *Jonathan and His Continent,* trans. by Mme. Paul Blouët (Bristol: J. W. Arrowsmith, 1889) 18:234–37.

7. William Stanton, *The Leopard's Spots: Scientific Attitudes Toward Race in America 1815–59* (Chicago: University of Chicago Press, 1960).

8. The shaping force of climate was a theme in the work of twentieth-century southern historians Wilbur J. Cash and Ulrich B. Phillips. See A. Cash Koeniger, "Climate and Southern Distinctiveness," *Journal of Southern History* 54:29 (Feb. 1988), and Dane Kennedy, "The Perils of the Midday Sun: Climatic Anxieties in the Colonial Tropics," in John M. MacKenzie, ed., *Imperialism and the Natural World* (Manchester: Manchester University Press, 1990), 118–40.

9. Charles Stelzle, *A Son of the Bowery: The Life Story of an East Side American* (New York: Doran, 1926), 284–85.

10. Lily B. Merman's 1999 oral history, "Growing Up on the Lower East Side" (RG 3.7.6 Folder 8) and Josephine Baldizzi Esposito's 10 July 1989 interview are in the collection of the Lower East Side Tenement Museum. The museum offers tours of the 97 Orchard Street tenement.

11. George Rosen provides a panoramic view of American public health in *A History of Public Health* (New York: MD Publications, 1958). On New York City's experience, see John Duffy, *A History of Public Health in New York City, 1866–1966* (New York: Russell Sage Foundation, 1974.) Also James H. Cassedy, "The Flamboyant Colonel Waring: An Anticontagionist Holds the American Stage in the Age of Pasteur and Koch," in J. W. Leavitt and Ronald L. Numbers, ed., *Sickness & Health in America*, 2d. ed. (Madison: University of Wisconsin Press, 1985), 451–58.

12. Duffy, 71–72.

13. This excerpt from Lady Hardy's 1881 travel memoir *Through Cities and Prairie Lands* appears in Bayrd Still, *Mirror for Gotham* (New York: New York University Press, 1956; repr. Westport, Conn.: Greenwood Press, 1980), 235–36.

14. Stelzle, 25.

15. Cooper, *Air-Conditioning America,* 10–11.

16. John E. Chappell Jr., "Huntington and His Critics: The Influence of Climate on Civilization," Ph.D. dissertation, University of Kansas, 1968; Geoffrey J. Martin, *Ellsworth Huntington: His Life and Thought* (Hamden, Conn.: Archon Books, 1973). Huntington's influence is recognized in George Carter, *Man and the Land: A Cultural Geography* (New York: Holt, Rinehart and Winston, 1968), 7. The "high priest" label is from Koeniger, 27.

17. *Civilization and Climate,* 3d ed. (New Haven: Yale University Press, 1924), 6. All page references are to this edition.

18. For a discussion, see T. J. Jackson Lears, *No Place of Grace: Anti-Modernism and*

the Transformation of American Culture, 1880–1920 (New York: Pantheon Books, 1981) and William Cronon, *Nature's Metropolis* (New York: Norton, 1991), 38–46.

19. Cronon, 36. Berkeley's poem was titled "On the Prospect of Planting Arts and Learning in America."

20. Pitirim Sorokin, *Contemporary Sociological Theories* (New York: Harper, 1928). The quotations are on 138, 153, and 193. On Sorokin's turbulent early life and controversial career, mainly at Harvard, see J. B. Ford, et al., eds., *Sorokin & Civilization: A Centennial Assessment* (New Brunswick, N.J.: Transaction Publishers, 1996). Sorokin died in 1968 at age 79.

21. Jared Diamond's 480-page book, issued in paperback by Norton in 1998, spent more than two years on the *New York Times* bestseller list. His discussion of climate appears on 22.

22. Chappell, 175.

23. The article appeared in *Political Science Quarterly* 35 :12 (Sept. 1920). GilFillan (b.1889–d.1987) was also a self-styled spelling reformer who variously spelled his names "Colum" and "Columb"; "Gilfillan" and "GilFillan."

24. The letter, dated 22 June 1931, is in Huntington, Series III/Box 66/Folder 2411.

25. The Australia draft is in Huntington, Series V/Box 61/Folder 532.

26. The Huntington archives are replete with examples. This one is in Series III/Box 39/Folder 993. The clipping from England's *Weekly News* is in Series X/Box 20/Folder 195.

27. Robert W. Rydell, *World of Fairs: The Century-of-Progress Expositions* (Chicago: University of Chicago Press, 1993), 93–99, and David F. Noble, *American by Design* (New York: Knopf, 1977), 229.

28. The Committee on Atmosphere and Man's statement and budget, dated 1 Feb. 1922, are in Huntington, Series IV/Box 2/Folder 9.

29. Series IV/Box 2/Folders 10–11. Berryman's letter is dated 12 May 1922.

30. The 1956 statistic is in *HPAC* 28:70 (Oct. 1956). Thrift told her mill experience to her daughter, Victoria Byerly, author of *Hard Times Cotton Mill Girls: Personal Histories of Womanhood and Poverty in the South* (Ithaca: ILR Press/Cornell University, 1986), 116–17.

31. Anson Rabinbach, *The Human Motor* (New York: Basic Books, 1990).

32. Frederick W. Taylor, *The Principles of Scientific Management* and Frank G. Gilbreth, *Primer of Scientific Management*, 2d ed., Hive Management History Series, no. 86 (Easton, Md: Hive Publishing Co., facsimile repr., 1985) and Frank and Lillian Gilbreth, *Fatigue Study* (New York: Sturgis & Walton, 1916), chap. 5. On Taylor, see Robert Kanigel, *The One Best Way : Frederick Winslow Taylor and the Enigma of Efficiency* (New York: Viking, 1997). The sweatshop worker is quoted in Leon Stein, ed., *Out of the Sweatshop* (New York: Quadrangle/New York Times Books, 1977), 354.

33. The Temperature and Mortality study is in Huntington, Series IV/Box 44/Folder 484.

34. GilFillan, 396. The *Washington Evening Star* article of 29 Aug. 1930 is in Huntington, Series V/Box 43/Folder 320.

2. No Calcutta

1. Rosen calls Winslow a "truly outstanding leader of public health in the United States and in the world" (*A History of Public Health*, 515.) For biographical details, see the *National Cyclopedia of American Biography,* vol. D (New York: James T. White, 1934), 443, and John A. Garraty, ed., *Dictionary of American Biography* (New York: Scribner's, 1980), 701–3.

2. Winslow's article appeared in *Transactions of the Sixth International Congress on Tuberculosis*, 4, pt. 1 (Philadelphia: W. F. Fell Company, 1908), 184–89 (Winslow, Series V/Box 118/Folder 60). The quotations are on 187 and 189.

3. Winslow presented his paper, "The New Art of Ventilation," at the International Congress on Hygiene and Demography in Washington, D.C., in Sept. 1912. Versions appeared in *Medical Review of Reviews* 18 (Oct. 1912) and *Engineering News* 68 (Nov. 1912; Winslow, Series V/Box 118/Folder 95). Winslow's attack on factory heating appeared in *American Labor Legislation Review* 2 (June 1912):297–304 (Folder 91). He attacked overheating generally in "The Relation of Indoor Atmospheres to Human Health and Comfort," repr. from *Transactions of the College of Physicians of Philadelphia* 49 :12 (1927).

4. Winslow's talk is the centerpiece of a 75-page illustrated brochure published by the Fund (New York, 1930). This quotation is on 13. Progressive era ambiguities are examined in Paul Boyer, *Urban Masses and Moral Order in America, 1820–1920* (Cambridge, Mass.: Harvard University Press, 1978). Roy Lubove discusses the "new gospel of benevolence" in *The Professional Altruist: The Emergence of Social Work as a Career 1880–1930* (New York: Atheneum, 1977).

5. A typescript of Winslow's Lecture no. 31, "Climate and Season," dated 29 Apr. 1944, is in Winslow, Series IV/Box 110/Folder 197. His daily walk is mentioned in the *Dictionary of American Biography*.

6. Huntington's 3 Jan. 1913 letter is in Winslow, Series III/Box 93/Folder 1579, and Winslow's 11 July 1916 compliment is in Huntington, Series III/Box 36/Folder 885. Winslow reviewed *Civilization* favorably in the March 1917 issue of *The Geographical Review* 2:252 (Huntington, Series V/Box 10/Folder 70).

7. These examples are in Winslow, Series II/Box 36/Folders 77–79 and 93–96.

8. Cooper says World War I caused the six-year publication delay. E. P. Dutton published *Ventilation: The Report of the New York State Commission on Ventilation* in 1923. Dutton published Winslow's *Fresh Air and Ventilation* in 1926. The 30 Aug. letter from Huntington to Winslow is in Winslow, Series I/Box 14/Folder 362. *Civilization and Climate* is cited in the commission report on 171; Winslow's comments on Huntington appear on 168 and 173 of *Fresh Air and Ventilation*.

9. Duffy, 481–82. On the Tuberculosis Association's efforts on behalf of fresh air, see Martin S. Pernick, "Thomas Edison's Tuberculosis Films: Mass Media and Health Propaganda," *Hastings Center Report* 8:21–27 (July 1978).

10. *Journal of the American Society of Heating & Ventilating Engineers* 29:542–43 (Sept. 1923).

11. Cooper, "Manufactured Weather," 133.
12. The article appeared in *American School Board Journal* 70, June 1925 (Winslow, Series III/Box 94/Folder 1603).
13. Examples of his efforts are in Winslow, Series III/Box 92/Folder 1580.
14. West's letter is in Huntington, Series III/Box 53/Folder 1733. West apparently sent dozens of letters to muster a strong anti-Winslow showing.
15. Huntington's 7 Jan. 1926 response to West is in Huntington, Series III/Box 53/Folder 1733.
16. In-text page references are to ASHVE *Transactions* 32:119–61.
17. The draft report is in Winslow, "Contribution No. 4, New York Commission on Ventilation," 30, Series III/Box 93/Folder 1592. Carrier's article is "New Prospects for an Established Industry," *HPAC* 1:29–30 (May 1929).
18. Huntington's name on the guest list is in Winslow, Series IV/Box 108/Folder 131. See also Martin, 174.
19. Winslow's medal is among his papers, Series VII/Box 137/Folder 27.
20. Huntington, Series III/Box 87/Folder 3604. Winslow chaired the New Haven Housing Authority from 1938 to 1955.
21. *Season of Birth: Its Relation to Human Abilities* (New York: J. Wiley, 1938); Chappell, "Huntington and His Critics," 157–59. The quotation from Huntington's 14 Sept. letter is in Martin, 218. Huntington's *Good Housekeeping* essay is "Ought I to Marry?" (New York: Prentice-Hall, 1938), 27–42.
22. Huntington's clipping service came up with dozens of examples, of which the *Boston Herald*'s "Why Cold Weather Babies Are Luckiest" of 5 Feb. 1939 was typical (Series X/Box 4/Folder 20).
23. The Sweeney letter appeared on the *Tribune*'s editorial page (Huntington, Series IV/Box 20/Folder 195).
24. Sydney F. Markham, *Climate and the Energy of Nations* (London: Oxford University Press, 1944). Subsequent references are in the text. Tasker's review is in *HPAC* 19:115–16 (July 1947).
25. Winslow, Series IV/Box 110/Folder 197, lecture no. 31:7.
26. Winslow and L.(ovic) P. Herrington, *Temperature and Human Life* (Princeton: Princeton University Press, 1949).
27. The 26 July 1950 letter is in Winslow, Series II/Box 57/Folder 628.
28. "Winslow's Window Complex," *Aerologist* 2:12 (March 1926), cited in Cooper, *Manufactured Weather,* 131 n. 37.

3. Pleasures and Palaces

1. *The Great Gatsby* (New York: Scribner's, 1925; repr. 1953), chaps. 7 and 8.
2. Margo J. Anderson, *The American Census: A Social History* (New Haven: Yale University Press, 1988), chap. 6.
3. On blizzards, see my "Buried Alive! New York City in the Blizzard of 1888," *New York History* 74:253–76 (July 1993).

4. *Great Gatsby,* 111.
5. Carrier used the slogan "Every Day a *Good* Day" in its 1919 sixty-one-page promotional booklet, "The Story of Manufactured Weather."
6. Molly W. Berger, "The Old High-Tech Hotel," *Invention & Technology* 11:46–52 (Fall 1995).
7. *World of Goods* (New York: Basic Books, 1979), 95. See also Christopher Berry, *The Idea of Luxury* (Cambridge: Cambridge University Press, 1994).
8. Banham, *Architecture of the Well-tempered Environment,* chap. 9.
9. This excerpt from Lady Hardy's 1881 travel memoir appears in Still's *Mirror for Gotham,* 235. Stangland's comment is in *ASHVE Transactions* 3:220 (New York: Published by the Society, 1897).
10. On ventilation ordinances for public halls, see Cooper, *Air-Conditioning America.*
11. Douglas Gomery, *Shared Pleasures: A History of Movie Presentation in the United States* (London: British Film Institute, 1992) and David E. Nye, *Electrifying America: Social Meanings of a New Technology, 1880–1940* (Cambridge, Mass.: MIT Press, 1990).
12. The commissioner's plug is in Gomery, 54.
13. Robert Sklar's *Movie-Made America* (New York: Vintage Books, 1976) describes how the movie industry bridged the mass-class divide in its early years. See also Gomery, chap. 8.
14. Lewis discusses early movie air-conditioning in his 1957 promotional brochure, "The Romance of Air-Conditioning" (Carrier, Reel 10/Folder 62, 16–17). The Rivoli sign is Plate 26 in William Leach, *Land of Desire* (New York: Pantheon Books, 1993). The Rivoli ad is in the 11 July 1926 *New York Times,* sec. 7–3.
15. Lewis's 22 July 1963 memo with his 3 Dec. 1963 notation that it was never sent is in Carrier, Reel 3/Folder 17.
16. "The Fundamentals of Air-Conditioning," *HPAC* 1:362 (Sept. 1929).
17. McCord to Dr. Ray J. Demotte and other physicians, 15 Dec. 1936; "Air-Conditioning," *Journal of the AMA,* 29 March 1941, 1364. See Carey Pratt McCord Papers, 1913–1971, Box 2/Research Files AC–1, Bentley Historical Library of the University of Michigan, Ann Arbor.
18. The 13 March 1939 article, "Selling Seats with Modern Air-Conditioning," is in Carrier, Reel 16/Folder 20.
19. *Architectural Forum* 59:81 (July 1933); Gomery, 91–93.
20. The Nielsen survey is in Carrier, Reel 11/Folder 91. Lewis's undated notes are in Carrier, Reel 8/Folder 13.
21. Gomery's analysis is in *Shared Pleasures,* 75–76. The installation figure was calculated from an Oct. 1937 list in Carrier, Reel 19/Folder 134.
22. Two excellent department store histories are William Leach's *Land of Desire* and Susan Porter Benson's *Counter Cultures* (Urbana: University of Illinois Press, 1986). Older department store histories, although celebratory, are useful. These include John William Ferry, *A History of the Department Store* (New York: Macmillan, 1960); Frank M. Mayfield, *The Department Store Story* (New York:

Fairchild Publications, 1949); Henry Baker Givens, *Rich's of Atlanta* (Atlanta: University of Georgia, 1953).

23. Williams, "The Dream World of Mass Consumption," in Chandra Mukerji and Michael Schudson, ed., *Rethinking Popular Culture* (Berkeley: University of California Press, 1991), 198–235.

24. See esp. Benson's chapter "'An Adamless Eden': Managing Department-Store Customers, 75–123.

25. Leach, 30–31. See also Jean Maddern Pitrone, *Hudson's: Hub of America's Heartland* (West Bloomfield, Mich.: Altwerger and Mandel, 1991). In 2001, the Target Corporation retired the 120-year-old Hudson name in favor of Marshall Field, its wholly owned Chicago-based group.

26. Leach, chap. 10, "Sell Them Their Dreams."

27. Rich's "great white" nickname is in Baker, 108; Leach, 76.

28. This verse is from a 1928 Jordan Marsh house publication in Benson, 244. It is unclear whether its basement, opened in 1911, was air-conditioned.

29. Donovan, *The Saleslady* (University of Chicago Press, 1929). These quotations are on 29 and 55.

30. The inventory ordeal is related in chap. 7.

31. Eric Partridge assigns a version of this saying to the twentieth century in the supplement to his *Dictionary of Slang and Unconventional English* (London: Routledge & Kegan Paul, 1967), 1182. On advertising, see Roland Marchand, *Advertising the American Dream: Making Way for Modernity* (Berkeley: University of California Press, 1985).

32. Leach, 62ff.

33. Edward A. Filene, *Speaking of Change* (Washington: National Home Library Foundation, 1939), xxii; Mayfield, 116–17.

34. Carrier, Reel 15/Folder 54.

35. The correspondence is in Carrier, Reel 15/Folder 53.

36. The details are from a reprint of "Air Cooled Dining Cars Now," *Transportation* 7, Feb. 1931, in Carrier, Reel 13/Folder 67.

37. Lewis tells this story in his "Romance of Air-Conditioning," 17 (Carrier, Reel 13/Folders 15 and 18).

38. This quotation appears in an undated historical essay prepared by the Association of American Railroads in the late thirties (Carrier, Reel 13/Folder 48).

39. Lewis's letter to his father's sister is in Carrier, Reel 9/Folder 15.

40. A page from the M-K-T Employees' Magazine is in Carrier, Reel 13/Folder 67.

41. This list and statistics are in the American Railroads Association essay.

42. *Official Proceedings of the Western Railway Club* 43 (Jan. 1931). Test's comments are on 29–30 (Carrier, Reel 10/Folder 26).

43. "Air-Conditioning of Passenger Cars Established in Two Years" and "Passengers Unanimous in Approving Air-Conditioned Service" in *Railway Age* 93:390–97. The quotations are on 397 and 395 (Carrier, Reel 13/Folder 67).

4. Cooling the Body Politic

1. Vidal, "At Home in Washington, D.C." in *United States: Essays 1952–1992* (New York: Random House, 1993), 1060.
2. Carrier, Reel 16/Folder 52 contains the complete text of U.S. Congress, House of Representatives, Committee on Appropriations, *Legislative Establishment Appropriation Bill, 1929: Hearing before subcommittee of House Committee on Appropriations,* 70th Cong., 1st sess., 24 Feb. 1928, 128–176. Taylor's comment is on 137. Subsequent references are in the text.
3. Panelists were paid ten dollars a day for expenses and also reimbursed for travel. Joining Winslow were long-time associate Dwight D. Kimball, a New York engineer; the vice-president of American Blower Corporation; a University of Illinois mechanical engineering professor, three New York and Boston consulting engineers, and a Bureau of Mines researcher.
4. U.S. Congress, House, Debate on Legislative Appropriation Bill, H.R. 12875, 70th Cong., 1st sess. *Congressional Record* (13 Apr. 1928), vol. 69, pt. 6:6415–6451. The necrology is on 6421–24 and the quotation on 6420.
5. U.S. Congress, House, Rep. Murphy of Ohio speaking on the Ventilation of the House, 70th Cong., 2d sess. *Congressional Record* (4 Dec. 1928), vol. 70, pt. 1:26–27.
6. U.S. Congress, House, Rep. Rankin of Mississippi speaking on the Ventilation of House Chamber, 71st Cong., 1st sess. *Congressional Record* (28 May 1929), vol. 71, pt. 3:2087.
7. Raymond J. Potter, "Royal Samuel Copeland, 1868–1938: A Physician in Politics" (Ph.D. diss., Western Reserve University, 1967); Royal Samuel Copeland Papers, 1892–1938, Bentley Historical Library of the University of Michigan, Ann Arbor.
8. Copeland Papers, Box 26/Folder: Speeches & Writings, Misc. Jan.–Aug. 1928.
9. An incomplete reprint of Calver's seventeen-page report, "Ventilation Problem of the Halls of the Senate and House of Representatives," from *U.S. Naval Medical Bulletin* 28:1 is in Carrier, Reel 16/Folder 53. These quotations are on 16–17. His findings were also discussed in *HPAC* 2:87–88 (Jan. 1930).
10. The 18 June 1938 *Herald* clipping, and dozens of obituaries and memorial tributes, are in Copeland Papers, Box 35, Scrapbooks.
11. ASHVE's president is quoted in *HPAC* 2:260 (March 1930). Carrier's monthly promotional booklet *The Weather Vein* 9 (Sep. 1929) devoted all 42 pages to the Capitol installation. This statement is on 41 (Warshaw, Air-Conditioning, Box 1/Folder 16).
12. Herrick's article, "It Waxes Warm Down in Washington But Not for Members of Congress," appeared on 18 June in the *Chicago Tribune,* 8–2.
13. Seale's *The President's House* (Washington, D.C.: White House Historical Association, 1986) details White House living conditions. The Navy's cooling

efforts are also mentioned in Charles E. Rosenberg, *The Trial of the Assassin Guiteau* (Chicago: University of Chicago Press, 1968).

14. Kate Scott Brooks's article, "Summering at Capitol Becomes Accepted Vogue," appeared in the *Free Press* on 25 July 1926, 4:4. Blaine Harden, "Swelter," *Washington Post Magazine,* 25 July 1982, 8+ colorfully summarizes Washington's worst summers.

15. Quoted from a contemporary *Washington Post* article in Harden's "Swelter."

16. *Tribune,* "Locate the Capital at Benton Harbor or New Buffalo," 12. The Carrier memo is in Carrier, Reel 17/Folder 10.

17. Lewis's recollection is in a 22 July 1957 memo in Carrier, Reel 17/Folder 10.

18. Rosenman, *Working with Roosevelt* (New York: Harper, 1952), 204.

19. Nesbitt, *White House Diary* (Garden City, N.Y.: Doubleday, 1948).

20. Seale, 1050.

21. *The Haldeman Diaries: Inside the Nixon White House* (New York: Putnam's, 1994), 334. Other such incidents appear on 121 and 205–6.

22. *HPAC* 6:332–35.

23. *HPAC* 7:23 (Aug. 1935).

24. *Refrigerating Engineering* 37:375–78 (June 1939).

25. Mike Causey, "No More Misery Index," *Washington Post,* 16 June 1994, D2. The usage information is in Martha M. Hamilton, "D.C. Without A.C.? Life Here Would Be Positively B.C.," *Washington Post,* 16 June 1994, A1+.

26. Bernstein, *Loyalties: A Son's Memoir* (New York: Touchstone, 1989), 95, 97.

27. "Sweet Summer Nights on the Sleeping Porch," *New York Times* 22 June 2000 <http://www.nytimes.com/library/home/062200porches-home.html> (22 June 2000).

5. Always Fair Weather

1. The role of science, engineering, and design in the thirties is discussed in Jeffrey L. Meikle, *Twentieth Century Limited* (Philadelphia: Temple University Press, 1979); Cecelia Tichi, *Shifting Gears* (Chapel Hill: University of North Carolina Press, 1987); David E. Nye, *Electrifying America* (Cambridge: MIT Press, 1990). On world's fairs, see Rydell, *World of Fairs: The Century-of-Progress Expositions.* His definition of the fairs as "theaters of power" appears on 11. Also, Burton Benedict, *The Anthropology of World's Fairs* (Berkeley: Robert H. Lowie Museum of Anthropology/Scolar Press, 1983); John G. Cawelti, "America on Display: The World's Fairs of 1876, 1893, 1933," in Frederic C. Jaher, ed., *The Age of Industrialism in America* (New York: The Free Press, 1968), 317–63; Paul Greenhalgh, *Ephemeral Vistas* (Manchester: Manchester University Press, 1988); Stanley Appelbaum, comp., *The New York World's Fair 1939/1940* (New York: Dover, 1977); and Helen A. Harrison, et al., *Dawn of a New Day: The New York World's Fair, 1939–40* (New York: Queens Museum/New York University Press, 1980). On period advertising, see Marchand, *Advertising the American Dream.*

2. Some noteworthy examinations of American utopian thinking are Joseph J. Corn, ed., *Imagining Tomorrow: History, Technology, and the American Future* (Cambridge, Mass.: MIT Press, 1986) and a body of work by Howard P. Segal, including "The Technology of Utopias," his essay in Corn, 119–36; *Future Imperfect* (Amherst: University of Massachusetts Press, 1994); and, coedited with Everett Mendelsohn, *Technology, Pessimism and Postmodernism* (Dordrecht, Netherlands: Kluwer Academic Publishers, 1994).

3. Bellamy, *Looking Backward, 2000–1887* (New York: Ticknor, 1887; repr. Modern Library, 1951), 121. Segal (in Corn, 128) is quoting from *The Milltillionaire,* privately printed in Boston in 1895 by Albert W. Howard, a pseudonym for Auburré Hovarré.

4. Tichi, 116.

5. The full manuscript is in Leon Stover, *The Prophetic Soul: A Reading of H. G. Wells's Things to Come* (Jefferson, N.C.: McFarland, 1987). Quoted passages appear on 159 and 270. The 92-minute film was screened on 26 Feb. 1996 at Ann Arbor's Michigan Theater.

6. *The Aerologist* 11:7, Carrier, Reel 12/Folder 34. *HPAC* absorbed this journal in 1937.

7. Carrier, "New Prospects for an Established Industry," *HPAC* 1:29–30.

8. Carrier's popularization efforts included a Jan. 1931 broadcast, "Our Artificial Climate," on Pittsburgh's KDKA-Radio; "He Dries Air with Water and Cools It with Steam," in *The American Magazine,* Feb. 1933, 37+; and a profile in the Sept. 1939 issue of *Future, The Magazine for Young Men* (Carrier, Reel 1, Folder: Air-Conditioning Bits of Early History).

9. Carrier, Box 3/Folder 25.

10. Cawelti, 355.

11. Rydell, 98–99.

12. *Official Guide: Book of the Fair* (Chicago: A Century of Progress, 1933), 23. Other guidebooks consulted were *Official Book of the Fair Giving Pre-Exposition Information, 1932–1933* (Chicago: A Century of Progress, 1933), and *Official Guide Book of the World's Fair of 1934* (Chicago: A Century of Progress International Exposition, 1934). Kahn, Wright, and Fuller are quoted in *The Architectural Forum* 59:25–27 (July 1933).

13. Meikle discusses passenger rail decline. The air-conditioned auto was pictured in *Popular Science,* Nov. 1933, 30.

14. *Science and Health with Key to the Scriptures*, 374:27 and 184:21; on-line edition <http://www.ScienceandHealth.com> (29 March 2001). Eddy's habits are detailed in Gillian Gill, *Mary Baker Eddy,* Radcliffe Biography Series (Reading, Mass.: Perseus Books, 1998).

15. Rydell, 136–37.

16. "The First Step in Cooling a Building" was the *Tribune*'s lead editorial on 17 July 1933.

17. Benedict, 5.

18. The *Tribune* ran daily articles and "Notes of a Century of Progress" from which these examples and incidents are culled.

19. "Short Circuit Cuts Off Fair's Light and Power," *Tribune,* 18 Oct. 1933, 1.

20. Meikle writes that 1930 was the first year refrigerator production surpassed ice-box production. The "semi-luxury" tag was applied to refrigerators and autos in the 8 June 1933 *Tribune.*

21. The term "middle landscape" is Leo Marx's in *The Machine in the Garden* (New York: Oxford University Press, 1964).

22. Louise Bargelt's feature, one of a series on CPE houses, appeared in the 11 June 1933 *Tribune,* 6:5. Details of the careers of brothers George Fred and William Keck are in Narcisco C. Menocal, *Keck & Keck, Architects* (Madison: Elvehjem Museum of Art/University of Wisconsin Press, 1980). *Architectural Forum* 59 devoted most of its July 1933 issue to the CPE.

23. The quotations are in "The Lay Critics Speak" in *Architectural Forum*'s CPE issue, 28.

24. The quotation is in a 1933 pamphlet reprinted in H. Ward Jandl, et al., *Yesterday's Houses of Tomorrow: Innovative American Homes 1850 to 1950* (Washington: National Trust for Historic Preservation Press, 1991), 131.

25. The quotation is in Menocal, 15. A photo of the Dymaxion car at the Crystal House appears in Jandl, 89.

26. Stran Steel's "Homes for Modern Living," Yale Series I.

27. Florida House material is in Yale Series I/Box 14/Florida folder. On the CPE houses' rebirth, see Robert Sharoff, "A Possible Future for Houses of Tomorrow," *New York Times,* 31 Dec. 2000, 40. Status and plans for the Florida House were discussed in an 18 Jan. 2001 e-mail to the author from Todd Zeiger, director, Northern Regional Office, Historic Landmarks Foundation of Indiana, and a 5 Feb. 2001 phone interview with William Beatty.

28. Both brochures are in Yale Series I.

29. *HPAC* 10, Oct. 1938.

30. The 16 Nov. 1937 press release is in NYPL, Press Releases, Box 1013/Folder 210. Teague's comment is in Meikle, 189.

31. Meikle, chap. 9. This quotation is on 192.

32. Futurama is described by Edgar, the young protagonist of E. L. Doctorow's *World's Fair* (New York: Ballantine Books, 1985), 323–27.

33. This and following Democracity quotations are in "Your World of Tomorrow," a brochure putatively authored by Fair President Grover A. Whalen. (Yale Series II/Box 59/General Motors folder).

34. "5400 Tons of Air-Conditioning for New York World's Fair," *Heating & Ventilating* 36:27–29. Ingels's review is "The Refrigerating Engineer's Visit to the New York World's Fair," *Refrigerating Engineering* 38:14 (July 1939).

35. The 6 Sept. 1938 memo is in NYPL, Box 399/Air-Conditioning, Heating, and Ventilating.

36. *Refrigerating Engineering* 38:7, 29–30 (July 1939).

37. This was reported in the 19 May 1965 *New York Times*.
38. Hazen's 23 June 1939 report to Town of Tomorrow consulting architect Otto Teegen is in NYPL, Box 841/Town of Tomorrow/Publicity and Promotion Folder. His results also appeared in *Architectural Forum* 71:63–72+ (July 1939).
39. Fair and Nash-Kelvinator publicity literature is in NYPL, Box 836/Town of Tomorrow/Nash Motors.
40. GE's exhibit material is in NYPL, Box 835/Town of Tomorrow/General Electric Folder. The "Happy Mother-in-Law" appears in a June 1940 handout for exhibit visitors. Servel information is in Box 835/American Gas Association Folder.
41. Details of the American Family promotion are in NYPL, Box 367/American Family Participation Folder.
42. These details come from *Heating & Ventilating* 36:28 (May 1939), and Westinghouse's illustrated brochure, "Conditioned Air for the World's Fair," in the Orth collection.
43. On Florida, before and after air-conditioning, see Mark Derr's *Some Kind of Paradise: A Chronicle of Man and the Land in Florida* (New York: William Morrow, 1989).
44. Ingels made this claim in her draft biography of Willis Carrier (Carrier, Reel 17, Folder 146).
45. Doctorow, 39.
46. The cartoon appeared on 3 Nov. 1938 (NYPL/Box 1048/Cartoons).
47. This official fair guidebook is in the Orth Collection.
48. Benedict and Rydell discuss exotic primitivism at world's fairs. The photo is in NYPL, Box 1423/Carrier Corporation Exhibit.
49. Yale Series II/Chrysler Folder; *Refrigerating Engineering* 38:29 (July 1939); Meikle, 199.
50. *Refrigerating Engineering* 38:7–8.
51. Kuznick, "Losing the World of Tomorrow: The Battle over the Presentation of Science at the 1939 New York World's Fair," *American Quarterly* 46:341–73 (Sept. 1994). Burnham, *How Superstition Won and Science Lost* (New Brunswick, N.J.: Rutgers University Press, 1987).
52. The 25 May 1929 ad is in Carrier, Reel 1/Folder: Advertising, 1929.
53. NYPL, Box 835/Town of Tomorrow/American Gas Association.
54. NYPL, Box 1017/Folder 1659; *Business Week* 4 Nov. 1939, 22.
55. Lyle's 2 Sep. 1939 letter is in NYPL, Box 1048/Building-Carrier.

6. No Place Like Home

1. The 1946 home ownership percentage is in Elaine Tyler May, *Homeward Bound: American Families in the Cold War Era* (New York: Basic Books, 1988). Other especially useful discussions of housing are Rybczynski, *Home* (New York: Penguin Books, 1986); Gwendolyn Wright, *Building the Dream, A Social History of Housing in America* (New York: Pantheon Books, 1981), and Kenneth T. Jackson,

Crabgrass Frontier: The Suburbanization of the United States (New York: Oxford University Press, 1985).

2. The 1889 introduction of electric fans is discussed in Giedion's *Mechanization Takes Command*, 558. Lewis discusses the Gates Mansion in a 24 May 1955 memo to Roy Lansing of Carrier's Chicago office (Carrier, Reel 7/Folder 51).

3. The Junior League of Minneapolis's illustrated brochure from the thirties, "The Gates Mansion: A History and A Description" (Minneapolis: Thayer & Smith, n.d.) is in the collection of the Minnesota Historical Society.

4. Steinmetz was GE's chief consulting engineer when he wrote "You Will Think This a Dream" for *Ladies Home Journal*, Sept. 1915, 12. On the bungalow, see Wright, chap. 9.

5. Ingels's 17 June 1929 resignation letter to Winslow is in Carrier, Series III/Box 93/Folder 1588. Jan. 1930's "Carrier Courier" announced her return (Reel 4/Folder 82). A partial list of her activities between 1930 and 1952 appears in Reel 8/Folder 64. Details of her career appear in "The History of Ventilation and Temperature Control," *ASHRAE Journal*, Oct. 1999. <http://www.confex2.com/ashraejournal/features/archives/oct99-feature3b.htm>(17 Nov. 2000).

6. The 10 May 1932 memo is in Carrier, Reel 14/Folder 105. Harlow and other celebrity clients are recalled in Lewis's 16 Sept. 1959 memo (Reel 14/Folder 115).

7. A. R. Stevenson Jr., et al., "Application of Refrigeration to Heating and Cooling of Homes," *General Electric Review* 35:145–53 (March 1932).

8. Estimates of Airtemp's and Servel's prewar sales appear in a confidential 1947–1948 Carrier Corporation research study.

9. Carrier, Reel 6/Folder 32:6.

10. Demas, *Eleven Stories High: Growing Up in Stuyvesant Town, 1948–1968* (Albany: State University of New York Press, 2000), 177–79. Also, Alan S. Oser, "The Upscaling of Stuyvesant Town," *New York Times,* 28 January 2001, 11–1+. Jon Giman, MetLife housing manager, e-mail to author, 17 Jan. 2001.

11. Carrier, Reel 8 contains two overlapping versions of this study. The July 1948 "Residential Research Program Report to Management" (Folders 35–37) is structured as an oral presentation. Folders 38–41 contain a longer and more formal report dated Sept. 1948 and entitled "The Residential Air-Conditioning Market." The shorter version is identified herein as July 1948 and the longer as Sept. 1948 as needed for clarity.

12. July 1948, sec. 4.4, "The Cooling Market."

13. Robert S. and Helen M. Lynd, *Middletown: A Study in Modern American Culture* (New York: Harcourt Brace Jovanovich, repr. 1990), 53–54.

14. Sept. 1948, Appendix 8.2, 139–43; July 1948, sec. 2.22.

15. These concerns are in July 1948, sec. 3.23, and Sept. 1948, 60.

16. Sept. 1948, 13–15.

17. Sept. 1948, sec. 2.1, 5.

18. *HB* history is in Frank Luther Mott, *A History of American Magazines* (Cambridge, Mass.: Belknap Press, 1968), 5:154–64, and Theodore Peterson, *Maga-*

zines in the Twentieth Century, 2d ed. (Urbana: University of Illinois Press, 1964), 217. The magazine's circulation was 200,000 when Hearst made Elizabeth Gordon editor in 1941 and exceeded 900,000 in 1964 when she retired.

19. *HB* 91, 130–70+. The panelists are introduced on 144. A technical companion series ran from Sept. 1949 through 1952 in the *Bulletin of the American Institute of Architects. HB* continued to run monthly articles under the general rubric of climate control through 1953.

20. Fitch, an architect and ardent preservationist, died on 10 April 2000. His views on air-conditioning appear in Patricia Leigh Brown, "Design Notebook: The Hum Heard Across America," *New York Times,* 27 May 1999, B1+.

21. See Martin S. Pernick, *The Black Stork* (New York: Oxford University Press, 1996), 62–63.

22. The boom peaked in 1955 when there were 1,309,500 starts. See Barbara M. Kelly, *Expanding the American Dream: Building and Rebuilding Levittown* (Albany: State University of New York Press, 1993), 219 n. 3.

23. These comments are in the Sept. 1951 and Nov. 1951 issues of *AIA Bulletin.*

24. *House & Home,* June 1952, 82–111. In-text references are to this special section. *House & Home* ceased publication in 1977.

25. "Merchant-Builder Survey," 97.

26. "Merchant-Builder Survey," 111.

27. Emphasis in original; Sept. 1948 study, 13.

28. "What Do Builders Want?," 102–3.

29. *HB* 97. The Carrier ad is on 5 in the August issue and the GE ad, referring to "proud owners" across the nation, on 109.

30. *HB* 95. Jackie Craven outlines the Farnsworth House controversy at <http://architecture.about.com/arts/ architecture/library . . . farnsworth> (2 Feb. 2001).

    Wolfe weighs in with *From Bauhaus to Our House* (New York: Farrar Straus Giroux, 1981), 71. Gordon's obituary by Julie Iovine is "Elizabeth Gordon, 94, Dies; Was *House Beautiful* Editor," *New York Times,* national ed., 17 Sep. 2000, 57.

31. Wright's kitchen article appeared in the Feb. 1954 issue; the Mueller booklet is in Warshaw, Box 2/Folder 13. He used the "nature" phrase to describe the 1953 Pace Setter House located in the exclusive suburb of Bronxville, New York, and featured in the Nov. 1952 issue.

32. By 1952, according to *House & Home,* June 1952, 102, twenty thousand "volume homebuilders" across the nation were responsible for 83 percent of new housing construction. "Ticky-tacky" was the term Malvina Reynolds used in her catchy 1962 song, "Little Boxes," allegedly to describe Levittown, Pennsylvania.

33. See Rosalyn Baxandall and Elizabeth Ewen, *Picture Windows: How the Suburbs Happened* (New York: Basic Books, 2000). Also, Charlie Zehran, "The Dream Builder," <http://www.lihistory.com> (11 May 2001). This is an on-line version of a *Newsday* series that ran from Sept. 1997 to June 1998.

34. The quotation appears in Kelly, 153. "Cape Cod bungalows," Kelly's term, conjures up every American home-building trait despised by *HB*.
35. At this time, the APHA was recommending a minimum 1,000 sq. ft. for a family of three. Housing writers said 1,200 sq. ft. were needed for true comfort. See Mary Davis Gillies, *McCall's Book of Modern Houses* (New York: Simon & Schuster, 1951).
36. Virginia Scott Jenkins says builders used grass to speed the transformation of new subdivisions into places that looked more like traditional suburbs (*The Lawn: A History of an American Obsession* [Washington: Smithsonian Institution Press, 1994], 97).
37. Kelly, 130.
38. The ads from Winter 1955 are in Ayer, Box 93/Folder 1.
39. Ayer, Box 95/Folder 2.
40. "Air-Conditioned House Prize Winners," *House & Home,* June 1953, 154–59. This article correctly identified Dr. Gilbreth as an industrial engineer.
41. "A Chill on Air-Conditioning," *Business Week,* 6 Nov. 1954, 29.
42. A reprint of this second *House & Home* special section "What's New in Air-Conditioning?" is in Warshaw, Box 4/Folders 16 and 21. "You can live with a sunny indoor garden" is on 6–7; the terrace piece is on 10–11.
43. *HB*'s readiness to use the *House & Home* survey, with attribution, is further evidence of its new enthusiasm for air-conditioning. *House & Home*'s "Sales Arguments for Air-Conditioning" appeared in the March 1954 special section, 14–18. *HB*'s shorter piece is in May 1954, 198+. All quotations are from the *HB* article.
44. Although *HB* at least mentioned the price of the houses, *House & Home* failed to give any data that might help readers interpret the survey remarks.
45. "Operating Costs Are Lower Than You Think," 2–5. Average monthly bills for some other cities were higher. They included $25.42 in San Antonio, Texas, $18.70 in Tampa, Florida, and $17.75 in Columbus, Ohio.
46. Carrier, Reel 19/Folder 38, 1955 *Annual Report,* 9. The contract was not publicized until 1956.
47. The ad appeared in March 1956 issues of *Practical Builder* and *House & Home* (Ayer, Box 96/Folder 3).
48. Whyte's article, "The Web of Word of Mouth," appeared in *Fortune,* Nov. 1954, 140–43+. This quotation is on 140.
49. Whyte, 142.
50. Marchand, *Advertising the American Dream.*
51. The appointment was announced in Carrier's 1945 annual report (Carrier, Reel 19/Folder 26). Ayer held the account until 1985, five years after Carrier's acquisition by United Technologies (Beth Draper, Ayer records manager, phone interview with author, 24 Feb. 1994).
52. The posh couple was featured in the 16 Aug. 1947 *Saturday Evening Post* and 29 Sep. 1947 *Time.* The cartoon was published in the 12 July *Saturday Evening Post* and 4 Aug. *Time.* Both proofs are in Ayer, Box 93/Folder 1.

53. Ayer, Box 94/Folder 2.
54. Ayer, Box 95/Folder 4.
55. Warshaw, Box 1/Folder 31.
56. Warshaw, Box 2/Folder 5.
57. The ad proofs are in Ayer, Box 97/Folder 1 and Box 96/Folder 3.
58. Warshaw, Box 3/Folder 18.
59. *House & Home,* March 1954, 14–18.
60. Warshaw, Box 2/Folder 23 and Box 2/Folder 18.
61. "Fourteen Questions to Cut Air-Conditioning Costs," 19–21.
62. United States Housing and Home Finance Agency, *Women's Congress on Housing,* Washington, D.C., Oct. 1956.
63. Susan Strasser, *Never Done: A History of American Housework* (New York: Pantheon, 1982), chap. 13.
64. This "brown/white" categorization is considered in Christine E. Bose, et al., "Household Technology and the Social Construction of Housework," in Marcel C. LaFollette and Jeffrey K. Stine, ed., *Technology and Choice* (Chicago: University of Chicago Press, 1991), 261–90.
65. Ayer, Box 98/Folder 1.
66. The June ad is in Ayer, Box 98/Folder 3; the September ad, which appeared in *House & Home,* is in Ayer, Box 98/Folder 2.
67. The ad proof is in Ayer, Box 94/Folder 1. Langewiesche's piece is "Climate Control on the Congo," *HB,* Apr. 1951, 126–28+.
68. "Climate Control Around the World," *HB,* Apr. 1952, 154+.
69. John H. Johnson published his first issue of *Ebony* in Chicago in November 1945, saying he would accept no ads until *Ebony* achieved 100,000 circulation. The first ads appeared in the May 1946 issue.
70. Ray Duncan, "Paul Williams Tells: How to Build a Home for $5,000," 42–47. A briefer feature on Williams had appeared in the Feb. 1946 *Ebony.*
71. Levittown racial policies are in Baxandall, 176 ff.
72. Air-conditioning was defined as the "cooling of air by refrigerating apparatus." U.S. Dept. of Commerce, Bureau of the Census. *1960 Census of Housing,* 1:1, United States Summary (Washington: GPO, 1961), xxxix.
73. The 1960 Census lumped all nonwhites into a single category and counted non-white households only in the thirty states where there were 25,000 or more such households. This data is from the *1960 Census of Housing,* table 26, 1:221.

7. The Air-Conditioned Nightmare

1. Miller, *The Air-Conditioned Nightmare* (New York: New Directions, 1945). The quotation is on 229. Mary V. Dearborn describes the circumstances under which the book was written in *The Happiest Man Alive: A Biography of Henry Miller* (New York: Simon & Schuster, 1991).
2. Miller, *The Nightmare Notebook,* a new facsimile of a Henry Miller manuscript,

"Notebook of America Tour," which is the property of the Department of Special Collections, Research Library, University of California, Los Angeles, no. 140 of 700 (New York: New Directions, 1975).

3. Miller's reaction to his first glimpse of the U.S. coastline at Boston is in *Nightmare,* 11. The description of Miller's California house is in Dearborn, 290, and Miller's comment on his lifestyle is in *My Life and Times* (Chicago: Playboy Press), 11.

4. Horowitz, *The Morality of Spending: Attitudes toward the Consumer Society in America, 1875–1940* (Baltimore: Johns Hopkins Press, 1985).

5. Berry, *The Idea of Luxury.*

6. Horowitz, *Morality,* 86.

7. Kasson, *Civilizing the Machine: Technology and Republican Values in America, 1776–1900* (New York: Penguin Books, 1976). This quotation is on 40. See also Marx, *Machine in the Garden.*

8. Lears, *No Place of Grace.*

9. New York: League of Industrial Democracy, 1931, 48–49, 55.

10. *HPAC* 3:683–84 (Aug. 1931). Unlike the technocrats of the thirties, Mees did not suggest that engineers could run things better than politicians. See Edwin T. Layton Jr., *The Revolt of the Engineers* (Cleveland: Case Western Reserve University Press, 1971), 229.

11. New York: Harcourt, Brace, 1934; the quotation is on 313 and subsequent references are in the text.

12. Catton's syndicated daily column ran in the Albany (Georgia) *Herald,* 8 Jan. 1930. The clipping is in Huntington, Series X/Box 4/Folder 18.

13. Huntington, Series V/Box 49/Folder 362. The quotation comes from an unpublished 1939 typescript, "Ozone, Health, & Progress."

14. At the ASHVE meeting in Pittsburgh on 8 June 1943, Lewis's copanelist was Pierce Lab director C.-E. A. Winslow (Carrier, Reel 10/Folder 53).

15. The speech draft is in Carrier, Reel 10/Folder 42. It is unclear whether Lewis or anyone else ever delivered it.

16. "Romance" quotations appear on 12 (Carrier, Reel 10/Folder 62).

17. Horowitz, *Morality,* 164.

18. Potter, *People of Plenty: Economic Abundance and the American Character* (Chicago: University of Chicago Press, 1954), 197.

19. "Promoting the Growth of Air-Conditioning," *HPAC* 26:82–85.

20. Miller, *Nightmare Notebook,* n.p.;Wright (New York: Bramhall House, 1954), 175–78. The Johnson building's innovations are described in Victor Walters, "Building Designed by Frank Lloyd Wright Features Floor Heating, Air-Conditioning," *HPAC* 11:661–63 (Nov. 1939).

21. *The Affluent Society,* college ed. (Boston: Houghton Mifflin, 1960). The most recent paperback edition was published in 1998.

22. Edwin L. Dale Jr., *Times Book Review,* 1 June 1958.

23. "Where Our Leaders Come From," partly ghost-written by Packard, appeared in

American Magazine, June 1946, 38+. The correspondence is in Huntington, Series IX/Box 96/Folder 4056.

24. *The Wastemakers* (New York: David McKay, 1960). Many used the term "jeremiad" to characterize Packard's attacks on his countrymen's wasteful habits, most recently Daniel Horowitz in *Vance Packard & American Social Criticism* (Chapel Hill: University of North Carolina Press, 1994). The quotation appears on 103.

25. This quotation is on 10. Sinclair's blurb appeared in a full-page ad in the *Times Book Review,* 2 Oct. 1960, 15.

26. Horowitz, *Vance Packard,* 123.

27. *Vance Packard,* 177.

28. Stearns, *American Cool: Constructing a Twentieth-Century Emotional Style* (New York: New York University Press, 1994), 1.

29. Millstein's piece appeared on 22 May 1955, 14+.

30. "What Does Non-Violence Mean?," *Midstream* 9:33–44 (Dec. 1963). This quotation is on 39. Jones took his new name in 1970.

31. Stearns, 305.

32. Teri Olcott, "The History of Air-Conditioning–Vintage Cars–05/08/98" <http://vintagecars.about.com> (10 Jan. 2001).

33. "Service Stations Offer 'Free Conditioned Air,'" *HPAC* 25:91 (Aug. 1953). Arsenault's observation is in "The End of the Long Hot Summer," *Journal of Southern History* 50:614 n. 87 (Nov. 1984).

34. *Consumer Reports*, May 1954, 215.

35. "Car Air-Conditioning: Is This Your Year?," *Popular Science,* July 1963, 82–85.

36. These figures include North American–made passenger vehicles and light trucks. They are from annual statistics compiled by the former American Automobile Manufacturers Association and Ward's Automotive Yearbooks (Lisa E. Smith, Ward's Communications, e-mail to author, 16 May 2001) .

37. David L. Lewis and Laurence Goldstein, eds., *The Automobile and American Culture* (Ann Arbor: University of Michigan Press, 1983).

38. Guillory, "*Star Wars* Style and American Automobiles," in Lewis and Goldstein, 383–93.

39. Allison Lowrie of Arnold Worldwide kindly provided a tape.

40. This publicity feature appeared in *Inside Carrier* 7:2+ (Aug. 1956; Warshaw, Box 1/Folder 16).

41. "Baseball's 'Hottest' Team 'Cooled Off'," *Refrigerating Engineering* 54:62–63 (1956).

42. *ASHRAE Journal* 8:89 (Jan. 1966).

43. Sala, e-mail to author, 13 Sep. 2000, and Patrick M. Campbell, Carrier Dome manager, e-mail to author, 30 Oct. 2000.

44. Carrier veteran Laube was later a consultant to Singer's Remington Climate Control Division. His article is in *ASHRAE Journal* 9:46–48; his book is *How to Have Air-Conditioning and Still Be Comfortable* (Birmingham, Mich.: Business News Publishing, 1971). This quotation is on 98; his "Confucius" comment is on 236.

45. Mumford, *The Pentagon of Power,* vol. 2 of *The Myth of the Machine* (New York: Harcourt Brace Jovanovich, 1967–1970.) The quotation is from the preface; other references are in the text. Mumford died in 1990 at age 94.

8. And the Air-Conditioned Malaise

1. *Consumer Reports* 18. "Room Air Conditioners: A Preview" appeared in May 1953, 181, and the full report in the July issue, 280–89. This quotation is from May.
2. "Central Air-Conditioning," *Consumer Reports,* July 1953, 244–47.
3. "Making Long, Hot Summers Hotter," *Consumer Reports,* July 1973, 444.
4. "Room Air-Conditioners," *Consumer Reports,* July 1974, 516–22; "Room Air-Conditioners," *Consumer Reports,* July 1975, 410–16.
5. Newman and Dawn Day, *The American Energy Consumer* (Cambridge, Mass.: Ballinger, 1975). The quotation is on xxiii, the statistics on 6.
6. Newman, 11–31; the quotations are on 28 and 16.
7. Newman, 20.
8. Writings on energy use and abuse were so plentiful by 1982 that University of Kentucky professors Ernest J. and Ann-Marie Yanarella compiled a 347-page guide, *Energy and the Social Sciences: A Bibliographic Guide to the Literature* (Boulder: Westview Press, 1982).
9. Joel Darmstadter, et al., *How Industrial Societies Use Energy* (Baltimore: Johns Hopkins Press, 1977), 66.
10. *The Beer Can by the Highway: Essays on What's 'American' about America* (Garden City, N.Y.: Doubleday, 1961), 217–42.
11. Carl S. Tobie, Edison Institute data specialist, e-mail to author, 21 July 1994.
12. Sale (New York: Random House), 55. Other articles that link energy waste to the South's and the West's consumption of air-conditioning include Wade Greene, "Air-Conditioning," *New York Times Magazine,* 14 July 1974, 12+; Frank Trippett, "The Great American Cooling Machine," *Time,* 13 Aug. 1979, 114; Robert J. Samuelson, "The Chilling of America," *Newsweek,* 10 June 1991, 42. Amy Martin offers a more pro–Sun Belt view in "Why We Need Air-Conditioning," *Garbage* 4:22–28 (July/Aug. 1992).
13. Carter's 18 April 1977 exhortation was the lead story in the 19 April *New York Times.*
14. Broder's analysis appears on the front page of the 16 July 1979 *Washington Post.* The transcript of Carter's speech is on A10 of the same day's *New York Times.* The "malaise" characterization showed up in the *Post*'s 19 July Joseph Kraft column; Caddell's role was mentioned in a 22 July *Times* article. It was at least a factor in Carter's failure to win a second term.
15. Melvin Laird, et al., *Energy Policy: A New War Between the States?* (Washington, D.C.: American Enterprise Institute, 1976), 11. Boren, later a United States senator, took part in the AEI roundtable held in Washington on 2 Oct. 1975.

16. Kevin Horrigan, "Big Brother Tells Us How to Be Cool," *St. Louis Post-Dispatch,* 11 July 1980, 2D.

17. Some examples of disaster scenarios widely disseminated during the seventies include Ernst F. Schumacher, *Small Is Beautiful: A Study of Economics as if People Mattered* (London: Blond & Briggs, 1973) and Barry Commoner's advocacy of solar energy as an antidote to the consumption of fossil fuels.

18. Andover, Mass.: Brick House Publishing, 1981. The Coates quotation is in the general introduction, 1. Bender's essay is "Sharing Smaller Pies," 89–109. This quotation is on 95.

19. EEI, *Economic Growth in the Future: The Growth Debate in National and Global Perspective* (New York: McGraw-Hill, 1976), 100.

20. Newman, 55–57.

21. Houghten and Yaglou, "Determination of the Comfort Zone," *ASHVE Journal* 29:515–36 (Sept. 1923). The photograph is on 515 and quotations are on 518, 529, and 535.

22. The 1966 definition is discussed in A. P. Gagge, et al., "Comfort and Thermal Sensations and Associated Physiological Responses at Various Ambient Temperatures," *Environmental Research* 1:1–20 (June 1967). ASHRAE, formed by a merger in 1959, is the successor organization to ASHVE and is headquartered in Atlanta. Heschong, *Thermal Delight in Architecture* (Cambridge, Mass.: MIT Press, 1979); Rohles, "Temperature or Temperament: A Psychologist Looks at Thermal Comfort," *ASHRAE Transactions* 86:541–51 (pt. 1, 1980).

23. Olivieri, "Energy Conservation and Comfort: Are They Compatible?," *ASHRAE Journal* 21:52–56 (Aug. 1979); emphasis in original on 52.

24. The first issue of *Journal of Environmental Psychology* appeared in 1981.

25. Howell and Stramler, "The Contribution of Psychological Variables to the Prediction of Thermal Comfort Judgments in Real World Settings," *ASHRAE Transactions* 87:609–21 (pt. 1, 1981).

26. *Energy and Buildings* 18:171–268 (1992). Prin's article "On Condis and Coolth" appears on 251–58; Blumstein's quote is on 259.

27. Introduction by Louis Joughin, American Century Series (New York: Hill and Wang, 1957), 21.

28. Stories on City and Koch hospitals appeared in *Post-Dispatch* issues of July 8, 10, 12, and 16, 1980. This letter to the editor appeared on 2C on 22 July.

29. In Kansas and Texas, also severely affected by the July heat wave, household air-conditioning percentages were 78.4 and 83.2 respectively (table 149, U.S. Summary, Detailed Housing Characteristics, 1–142).

30. "Power to cool shouldn't be taken lightly," *Star,* 20 July 1980, 1G+.

31. This is an estimate based on "St. Louis a Leading City in Using Air-Conditioning," *HPAC* 24:144–47 (Jan. 1952).

32. Diane Stafford, "Heat blahs in office make boss hot, too," *Star,* 10 July 1980, 1+.

33. Gregory S. Reeves and Barbara Whitaker, "Heat wave leaves questions about social ills in city," *Star,* 25 July 1980, 1A+.

34. The *Kansas City Star* and *Times* were read from July 1 through mid-September, 1980 as was every July issue of the *St. Louis Post-Dispatch*.

35. Robert J. Pessek, "For those without 'air,' relief has no spelling," *Star*, 1A.

36. Bill Turque, "Locked doors hide heat's gruesome crimes," *Star*, 1A+.

37. 24 July 1980, *Star*, 11A.

38. Yumi Kamada and Kathleen Fisher, "Some elderly shiver through heat," *Star*, 13 July 1980, 8A.

39. "Heat wave leaves questions about social ills in city," *Star*, 25 July 1980, A1+.

40. Bill Turque, "Heat deaths adding to examiner's burden," *Star*, 27 July 1980, 1A. R. T. Watson, et al., ed., *The Regional Impacts of Climate Change: An Assessment of Vulnerability* (New York: Cambridge University Press, 1998). <http://www.epa.gov//oppeoee1/globalwarming> (18 May, 2001).

41. Paul Vitello, "Hospital goes without air-conditioning," *Times*, 11 July 1980, 1+. The hospital's name strongly suggests that it served a primarily black clientele and neighborhood.

42. Robert L. Joiner, "Life in St. Louis Is No Breezeway for Those without Air-Conditioning," *Post-Dispatch*, 11 July 1980, 1B.

43. Complaints about bus air-conditioning were first reported in the *Post-Dispatch* on 1 July 1980, 1C, with follow-up stories on July 10 and 11. An explanation of why bus air-conditioning was so unsatisfactory ran on 20 July, 7A.

44. Davis's letter appeared in the *Star* on 6 Aug. 1980, 18A.

45. Jeffrey R. Coplon's feature "Prisoners of the heat wave" appeared on 14 July 1980 in the *Times* on the tenth consecutive day that the temperature exceeded 100 degrees. An article on the plight of outdoor amusements appeared in the *Star* on July 18.

46. "Important Notice Regarding Montgomery Ward Advertisement in Today's Paper," *Times*, 3 July 1980, D15; James E. Adams, "Cooling Industry Work Is Too Hot to Handle," *Post-Dispatch*, 15 July 1980, 1C.

47. Joseph H. McCarty Jr., "Electric bills and equipment show strain," *Star*, 9 July 1980, 1A+.

48. Sally Bixby Defty, "UE Boosts Forecast on Electricity Use," *Post-Dispatch*, 20 July 1980, 1B; Robert Engelman, "New law may pay cooling bills for poor, elderly," *Times*, 5 July 1980, B1. Utilities in Kansas City and St. Louis gave some residential customers until Oct. 15 in Kansas City and Nov. 1 in St. Louis to pay off their summer bills.

49. Teasdale's manipulation of the heat issue was extensively covered in the Kansas City press. Mark Schlinkmann, "Weather puts its stamp on politics," *Times*, 23 July 1980, 1A. Teasdale's complaint about Mount Saint Helens is in "Teasdale steals campaign show," *Times*, 1 Aug. 1980, B7.

50. "Panels Hear Conway Appeal for Heat Aid," *Post-Dispatch*, 25 July 1980, 1A+.

51. 96th Cong., 2d sess., *Congressional Record* (24 July 1980), vol. 26, pt. 15, 19605–606.

52. Bill Prater, "Leaders give cold shoulder to high-priced plans for utility aid," *Times,* 30 Aug. 1980, B17.

53. The articles cited are Charles M. Madigan, et al., "The Heat Wave's Victims: Joined in Death," 26 Nov. 1995, 1+; Royko, "Killer heat wave or a media event?," 18 July 1995, 3; Ryan, "Coping was key to surviving scorching summer of '55," 2-1.

54. Rosa Maria Santana, "Renters Gain Right to Air-Conditioning," *Chicago Tribune* (Metro Lake ed., 10 Aug. 1995).

55. David E. Sanger, "Energy Plan Urges New Drilling, Conservation and Nuclear Power Review" <http://www.nytimes.com/2001/05/17/politics> (17 May 2001).

56 Lisa N. Singhania, "Some Like It Very Hot in Houston, Where Muggy Air Has Many Fans," *WSJ,* 30 Aug. 1994, B1.

57. Heschong, *Thermal Delight.*

58. Barbara Holland, "The Place Called Summer," May/June 1993.

59. Quoted in Patricia Leigh Brown, "Design Notebook: The Hum Heard Across America," 27 May 1999, B1+.

Conclusion

1. *American Genesis* (New York: Viking, 1989), 2.

2. *The Americans: The Democratic Experience* (New York: Vintage Books, 1973), 358.

3. Dubos, *Man Adapting,* enlarged ed. (New Haven: Yale University Press, 1980), 271.

Illustration Credits

1 and 2. N. W. Ayer Advertising Agency Records, 1889–1972, Smithsonian Institution, Archives Center, National Museum of American History. Courtesy of Carrier Corporation, A Member of the United Technologies Corporation Family.

3. A plate from E. Idell Zeisloft's 1899 *The New Metropolis* depicts a teeming "Hot Summer Night on the East Side," © Collection of the New-York Historical Society.

4. © Bettmann/CORBIS.

5 and 6. Yale Picture Collection, Manuscripts and Archives, Yale University Library.

7. Maps adapted from the World Meteorological Organization's *Climatic Atlas of North and Central America,* Geneva, 1979.

8. John Vachon, FSA-OWI Photograph Collection, Library of Congress, LC-USF33-001965-M3.

9. N. W. Ayer Advertising Agency Records, 1889–1972, Smithsonian Institution, Archives Center, National Museum of American History. Courtesy of Carrier Corporation, A Member of the United Technologies Corporation Family.

10. © Smithsonian Institution.

11. Courtesy Fridaire, Yale Century of Progress—New York World's Fair Collection, Manuscript and Archives, Yale University Library.

12. Warshaw Collection of Business Americana, © Smithsonian Institution.

13. Marjorie Collins, FSA-OWI Photograph Collection, Library of Congress, LC-030034-100576-D.

14. Marion Post Wolcott, FSA-OWI Photograph Collection, Library of Congress, LC-USF33-030043-M5.

15. © Flip Schulke/CORBIS.

16. Schenectady Museum Archives.

17. Todd Zeiger, Historic Landmarks Foundation of Indiana.

18. New York World's Fair (1939–1940) Records, 1935–1945, Town of Tomorrow, Manuscripts and Archives Division, New York Public Library.

19. Edward J. Orth Memorial Archives of the World's Fair, 1939–1940, © Smithsonian Institution.

20. New York World's Fair (1939–1940) Records, 1935–1945, World-Telegram Cartoon "Frigidistic," Manuscripts and Archives Division, New York Public Library.

Index